Race and Education

Policy and Politics in Britain

INTRODUCING SOCIAL POLICY SERIES
Series Editor: David Gladstone

Published titles

Comparative Social Policy: Theory and Research
Patricia Kennett

Education in a Post-Welfare Society
Sally Tomlinson

Risk, Social Policy and Welfare
Hazel Kemshall

Perspectives on Welfare
Alan Deacon

Reconceptualizing Social Policy: Sociological Perspectives on Contemporary Social Policy
Amanda Coffey

Social Security and Welfare: Concepts and Comparisons
Robert Walker

Drugs: Policy and Politics
Rhidian Hughes, Rachel Lart and Paul Higate (eds)

Revisiting the Welfare State
Robert M. Page

Race and Education: Policy and Politics in Britain
Sally Tomlinson

Race and Education

Policy and Politics in Britain

Sally Tomlinson

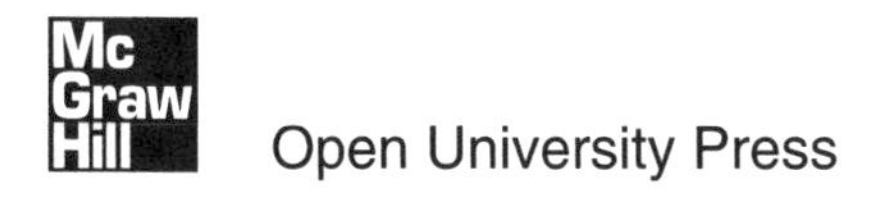

Open University Press
McGraw-Hill Education
McGraw-Hill House
Shoppenhangers Road
Maidenhead
Berkshire
England
SL6 2QL

email: enquiries@openup.co.uk
world wide web: www.openup.co.uk

and Two Penn Plaza, New York, NY 10121-2289, USA

First published 2008

A catalogue record of this book is available from the British Library

ISBN13: 978 0 335 22307 7 (pb) 978 0 335 22308 4 (hb)
ISBN10: 0 335 22307 9 (pb) 0 335 22308 7 (hb)

Library of Congress Cataloging-in-Publication Data
CIP data has been applied for

Typeset by RefineCatch Ltd, Bungay, Suffolk
Printed in the UK by Bell and Bain Ltd, Glasgow

The McGraw·Hill Companies

Contents

Series editor's foreword

Welcome to the ninth volume in the Introducing Social Policy series. The series itself is designed to provide a range of well informed texts on a variety of topics that fall within the ambit of social policy studies.

Although primarily designed with undergraduate social policy students in mind, it is hoped that the series–and individual titles within it–will have a wider appeal to students in other social science disciplines and to those engaged on professional and post-qualifying courses in health care and social welfare.

The aim throughout the planning of the series has been to produce a series of texts that both reflect and contribute to contemporary thinking and scholarship, and which present their discussion in a readable and easily accessible format.

Sally Tomlinson's earlier book in this series–Education in a post-welfare society (first edition 2001, second edition 2005)–was published to widespread acclaim. I was especially glad, therefore, when she offered to produce a companion volume on the highly contentious subject of Race and Education between the 1960s and 2007.

This has been a critical period in Britain's recent history, as the country has moved from the final vestiges of Empire to become a multi-cultural and multi-ethnic society; a transition which has brought with it considerable changes to cultural values and the delivery of public services. It is also the transition through which Sally Tomlinson has lived and worked and about which she has written and researched extensively. She brings to this volume her very considerable academic reputation in the area of Race and Education as well as her personal engagement with the issues which are the subject of this book. It is her scholarly reliance on evidence and discussion together with the clear statement of her personal commitment and values which makes this such an enthralling and authoritative study.

It is a supremely well-informed narrative and chronology of change. But it is also a highly critical assessment of the varied policies by which successive British governments have attempted to incorporate racial and ethnic minorities and to offer them a fair and equal education, whilst at the same time educating the majority to live in an ethnically diverse society. After five decades, that remains the challenge for politicians, policy makers and those involved in the practicalities of education and training. This is a book for them, as well as for those teaching and learning about the controversial and highly topical subject of Race and Education.

David Gladstone, University of Bristol

Acknowledgements

This book owes much to discussion on race, ethnicity and education over many years with friends and colleagues, especially my long-time friend and mentor John Rex.

Thanks to: Tahir Abbas, Chris Bagley, Stephen Ball, Len Barton, Bernard Coard, Alma Craft, Maurice Craft, David Gillborn, Heidi Mirza, Gillian Klein, David Milner, Audrey Osler, Bhikhu Parekh, David Pegg, Fazal Rizvi, Tony Sewell, Christine Sleeter, Brian Tomlinson, Gajendra Verma, Carole Vincent, Geoffry Walford, to the late Barry Troyna and Madan Jha, and to my series editor David Gladstone.

Thanks also to the many teachers, minority parents, students, community workers and others whom I have met over the years and who were committed to creating a better education for all in our multicultural society.

List of abbreviations

A level	Advanced level
ALTARF	All London Teachers Against Racism and Fascism
AMMA	Assistant Masters and Mistresses Association
APU	Assessment of Performance Unit
ARTEN	Anti-Racist Teacher Education Network
ATEPO	Association for Teachers of English to Pupils from Overseas
BME	Black and Minority Ethnic
BNP	British National Party
CARD	Campaign Against Racial Discrimination
CATE	Council for the Accreditation of Teacher Education
CDP	Continuing Professional Development
CEHR	Commission for Equality and Human Rights
CIAC	Commonwealth Immigrants Advisory Council
CIC	Commission on Integration and Cohesion
CNAA	Council for National Academic Awards
CRC	Community Relations Commission
CRE	Commission for Racial Equality
CSE	Certificate of Secondary Education
DCSF	Department for Children, Schools and Families
DES	Department of Education and Science
DfE	Department for Education
DfEE	Department for Education and Employment
DfES	Department for Education and Skills
DIUS	Department for Innovation, Universities and Skills
EAL	English as an Additional Language
EAZ	Education Action Zone
EBD	Emotional and Behavioural Difficulties
EDU	Educational Disadvantage Unit

EMAG	Ethnic Minority Achievement Grant
EMTAG	Ethnic Minority and Travellers Achievement Grant
EPA	Educational Priority Area
ESG	Education Support Grant
ESN	Educationally Subnormal
ESOL	English for Speakers of Other Languages
FE	Further Education
FSM	Free School Meals
GCSE	General Certificate of Secondary Education
GNP	Gross National Product
GNVQ	General National Vocational Qualification
GTC	General Teaching Council
HEFC	Higher Education Funding Council
HMI	Her Majesty's Inspectorate
ILEA	Inner London Education Authority
KS	Key Stage
LAPP	Lower Attaining Pupils Project
LEA	Local Education Authority
LSC	Learning and Skills Council
MC/ARE	Multicultural/Antiracist Education
ME/MRE	Multiracial Education
MSC	Manpower Services Commission
NAME	National Antiracist Movement in Education
NAME	National Association for Multiracial Education
NAS	National Association of Schoolmasters
NC	National Curriculum
NCC	National Curriculum Council
NCVQ	National Council for Vocational Qualifications
NFER	National Foundation for Educational Research
NNTARN	Nursery Nurse Tutors Anti-racist Network
NUT	National Union of Teachers
NVQ	National Vocational Qualification
O level	Ordinary level
OECD	Organisation for Economic Cooperation and Development
OFFA	Office of Fair Access
Ofsted	Office for Standards in Education
ONS	Office for National Statistics
OPCS	Office for Population Census and Statistics
PFI	Private Finance Initiative
PISA	Programme for International Student Assessment
PLASC	Pupil Level Annual School Census
PRU	Pupil Referral unit
PSHE	Personal Social and Health Education
PSI	Policy Studies Institute

QCA	Qualifications and Curriculum Authority
ROTA	Race on the Agenda Trust
SACRE	Standing Advisory Committees on Religious Education
SCAA	School Curriculum and Assessment Authority
SEAC	School Examination and Assessment Council
SEN	Special Educational Needs
TEC	Training and Enterprise Council
TTA	Teacher Training Agency
TTDA	Teacher Training and Development Agency
UCET	University Council for the Education of Teachers
UCU	University and College Lecturers Union
YTS	Youth Training Scheme

Introduction

This book is intended to provide information on educational issues, events and conflicts from the 1960s to 2007, as Britain's education systems[1] attempted, with varying degrees of success, to incorporate racial and ethnic minorities, and to educate the majority to live in an ethnically diverse society. Those regarded as minorities over this period were largely the children and grandchildren of immigrants from former colonial countries who arrived in response to a demand for labour after the Second World War. These immigrants settled in inner cities and in northern towns where work was available and by the 2000s most of them were British citizens. By the 1990s significant numbers of children of refugees, asylum seekers and economic migrants, especially from other European countries, were also entering the education system. By the 2000s there was some recognition that, while compared to other European countries, Britain was relatively successful in accommodating to racial, cultural and religious diversity, the education system had lacked political support and policies which would have enabled all young people to accommodate better to their plural multicultural society (Sen 2006). There was much public ignorance of the reasons for migration, both old and new, not helped by political decisions to encourage labour migration, on the one hand, but support immigration control legislation, on the other. In the 2000s there was still hostility to settled citizens from the former British empire, which merged with antagonisms towards refugees and asylum seekers, and to newer economic migrants, largely from other European Union countries. There was also considerable panic reaction to what was in fact a long-standing issue – global struggles concerning the relationship of Islam to a Christian and secular West – as well as confusion as to the part the education system should play in developing common values in society. This book aims to set educational issues and events within a wider social, political and educational context, taking account of national, and global influences, and changing political beliefs, ideologies and action over the years.

Although there have been some positive legislative and policy developments, particularly the use of civil law and human rights legislation to penalise racial discrimination, the education system over the past 50 years has developed within a socio-political context in which there has been a lack of political will to ensure that all groups were fairly and equitably treated. The climate has been such that politicians of all parties, their advisors and civil servants have to some extent acquiesced in processes of social, political, economic and moral denigration of groups considered to be racially, ethnically or culturally different,[2] and they have seldom provided adequate and positive leadership that would work towards what, by the 2000s, was described as community cohesion. There was much ignorance, on the part of politicians, sections of the media and the general public, of the history and background of immigration and race issues and conflicts. In education, for many years policy makers claimed that issues of race, racism, ethnicity and culture were too sensitive to be discussed overtly. Certainly, local authorities and teachers were caught between the defensiveness of central government and its contradictory policies and their own experiences of teaching minority children, and it was not until the 2000s that conflicts and tensions were discussed more openly. Although from the 1960s some good practice was initiated by teachers, local education authorities and by HMI – the old-style inspectorate – it was not surprising that the system has, over the years, found difficulty in offering racial and ethnic minorities a fair and equal education, and equipping all young people with an understanding of Britain's place in a post-imperial globalised world. From the 1960s several generations of young people have emerged from schools, many still ignorant of the multi-ethnic society and world they live in and many imbued with hostility to other groups. Although some young people of African-Caribbean, Asian and other minorities succeeded in gaining good educational qualifications and credentials, many felt that they had been miseducated and ill-equipped to compete in a global economy. Many also felt that they were not accepted as citizens in the country they were born in. A fragmentation of social welfare programmes via the introduction of market principles, with education becoming a competitive enterprise rather than a preparation for a democratic society, created further problems for minorities. Within this framework this book aims to document both on-going and new educational issues and conflicting socio-political responses concerning education that have emerged and re-emerged over the years covered.

There is a plethora of literature on race, ethnicity and education in Britain, dating back to the 1950s.[3] This covers central and local policy and practice, schooling in multiracial and white areas, differential educational achievements and educational inequalities between groups, language and curriculum issues, teachers and teacher preparation, pre-school, further and higher education, employment prospects, racism within and outside education, pupil perspectives and identity issues, home–school relations, parental and community activism and other areas. Various explanations and meta-theories have been offered to make sense of issues, events and conflicts, from conservative, liberal and Marxist perspectives. More recent theorising uses radical critical approaches to examine postcolonial identities, the politics of gender and race, ideologies of white superiority via critical race theory, and a critical multiculturalism. The literature has also included official policy making and administrative documentation, activist publications, large- and small-scale research studies, reports of conferences and commissions and much journalistic comment and opinion. There is also a growing online literature as younger minorities use the internet to express their own views (Parker and Song 2006). Into the 21st century fierce arguments have continued over multiculturalism, integration and a 'British' identity; over the demographic segregation of minorities in towns and city areas; over resulting segregated schooling; over faith schools; over the continued lower achievements of some groups while others have progressed well, over the possible ethnic penalties young minorities suffer in the labour market; over the reasons for the alienation of some young minorities from education and from the wider society; and more muted debate over whether the school curriculum and pedagogy need updating for a post-imperial globalised Britain. This book is necessarily selective of the abundant literature, but includes references to previous work by the author. Some information on general educational policies, legislation, reports and initiatives is included but more detailed accounts can be found in, for example, Chitty (2004), Lawton (2005), Tomlinson (2005), Barber (2007).

Themes of the book

Around the world the relationships of national majorities and ethnic minorities living in the same territory are matters for intense national and international debate and conflict. The issues are serious. Both historically and at present, individuals and groups are prepared to kill and die for recognition of their ethnic, national or religious identity and to struggle by both peaceful and violent means to obtain their civil rights within majority societies. In post-Second World War Britain the incorporation of groups variously perceived by a white majority to be racially, ethnically or culturally different, in a society slowly coming to terms with the end of Empire and a closer relationship with the rest of Europe, has raised sharp questions about a shared national identity, cultural heritage, multiculturalism and racism in a variety of forms. The functions of an education system in such a situation are crucial, and it has to be said at the outset that, in Britain, the political climate has made it very difficult for educators to help all young people to gain the knowledge, attitudes and skills that are needed in democratic multicultural societies. In the USA and in Britain from the early 1990s there was a declared interest in modernising government and improving the policy-making process by an increased use of evidence. In 2000 the Education Secretary of State asserted that 'social science should be at the heart of policy-making' (Blunkett 2000). But in the area of race, ethnicity and education, policy has seldom been based on evidence, a situation not helped by either political ignorance or the various ideological positions taken up by researchers and activists. There have been acrimonious debates about the role of research versus political or practical activity, about the validity of white researchers investigating the relations between white and non-white, about methodologies used in research, about multicultural and anti-racist education, and about the interconnections between race, social class, gender and disability. Evidence has too often been overtaken by opinion and assertion, with much right-wing comment linking support for a plural multicultural society to left-wing interests in social and racial equality. Funding for large-scale research has been minimal, and close attention seemingly only given to minorities when riots, deaths or overt injustices occurred. Consequently, when the society reached a point where three-quarters of young black men born in the country were reported to be on a police DNA database, despite actually committing less crime than white groups, and some young British-born and educated young Muslims were alienated enough to join violent anti-Western groups and kill their fellow citizens, it seemed timely to ask what the education system had been doing over the years to help create understanding, equity and justice for all groups. One referee for this book commented that the past 50 years constitutes 'a contentious and dangerous area of educational history', which makes it all the more necessary to study what has been and what is currently happening. How to construct and sustain common political and moral values with some measure of trust and understanding among all groups, recognise diversity, and prepare all young people properly for a good economic future, are tasks any education system in a multicultural society and a globalised world should be concerned with.

Narrative themes in the book are concerned with:

- The inequitable incorporation of minorities into a welfare state which, over the years, has been transformed into a post-welfare market state with an overtly competitive education system.
- The lack of positive leadership and public policy discourse on race, ethnicity and education over the decades, with persistent attempts to subsume minority groups under the label of disadvantage, and with moral panics dominating debate. For example, in the 1970s the black, dread-locked Rastafarian male was demonised, and by the 2000s black males were regarded as potentially more responsible for gun and drug crime. In the 2000s the 'Muslim fundamentalist' had become a further demon.

- The differential educational and occupational progress of minority groups within a society that demonstrated enduring racism towards those regarded as different on racial, ethnic or religious grounds, but which some minorities have been better placed to resist. For example, the children of East African Asian, some Indian, and Chinese settlers have, on a group level, progressed better in education than the children of Caribbean, Pakistani and Bangladeshi and mixed race origin, while the progress of travellers and Roma children and more recently arrived refugee children continues to be problematic.
- The attempts by teachers, schools, LEAs, academics, and the old-style inspectorate to develop a more equitable education for all children, and the disappearance from the 1990s of LEA and university courses designed to prepare intended and current educational practitioners.
- The role and impact of minority parents, professionals, academics and community groups and activists in influencing policy and practice.
- The neglect of rethinking the schooling of all young people in a world in which ethnic, racial and religious conflicts were manifestly increasing.

A major theme of the book concerns the inequitable way in which the children and grandchildren of migrants from former colonial countries, and then later migrants, have been incorporated into what was initially an education system biased by social class, but which also became racially biased, exacerbated by a post-1988 market orientation based on 'choice' and competition. The story is partly the incorporation of these children into a class system that consisted of relatively permanent conflict groups, in which some had the power and resources and could deny them to others, and elites could claim superior resources. The English social class system and the use of education as a means of social selection for class position always illustrated this view. Much of what was termed the class struggle in Britain illustrated Max Weber's view that a struggle for status, and a closing of ranks by superior status groups, was as important as market domination (Weber 1968). The upper classes, for example, have seldom contemplated using a state education system for their children, and there is a continually changing terminology to describe the lower classes, by the 2000s the terms yobs and chavs were favourites! But for minorities their story was also one of incorporation into a race system in which, as studies of British imperialism and more recent work by critical race theorists demonstrates, whiteness was taken as an absolutely natural norm (Gillborn 2008). In Britain by the late 19th century, the white Anglo-Saxon 'race' was presented as the world's superior group – biologically, economically, politically, culturally and linguistically. The settlement in the later 20th century of those previously considered 'natural inferiors' (Lloyd 1984) contributed to intense debate as to who belongs within the boundaries of national identity with claims to citizenship rights. A liberal view up to the 1960s was that if minorities were to become part of a national community, they should enjoy the same citizenship rights as the majority. These, following Marshall (1950), comprised civil, social and political rights and were to include freedom of speech and thought, a right to justice, and rights to education, employment and welfare. While Marshall was concerned to demonstrate the acquisition of citizenship rights by the working classes, minority groups have found that their citizenship rights are still not complete. Over the years settled minorities have struggled for inclusion as citizens and also for rights to recognition of cultural and religious identity, claims which have been (and still are) heavily contested. The arrival of newer migrants and the introduction of legislation in the 2000s, which attempted again to define the parameters of nationality and citizenship, by no means settled the question of who was to be included in the British nation and who was to be excluded.

Official policy towards minority settlement has always been fraught with contradictions, especially the encouragement of migrant labour versus legislation to control immigration. As the British Empire disappeared and a Commonwealth of former colonies and protectorates was created, a 1948 British Nationality Act attempted to define who was 'British' and who was a Commonwealth citizen with rights of settlement in the UK. At this time conservative imperial ideologies at least recognised the equal rights of all citizens before the law, liberals believed in equal opportunities, and socialists were still attached to notions of the brotherhood of man. As has been well documented, the English model assumed assimilation, a situation in which migrants relinquish their own cultures and languages to become indistinguishable from the majority – a view still nostalgically presented in some popular and media understanding. But notions of assimilation were always mythological. By the late 1960s a large-scale report of race relations in Britain had concluded that 'the evidence for the existence of discrimination based on colour is overwhelming' (Rose *et al.* 1969). There was minimal evidence then, and later, that the white majority were ever willing to accept non-white citizens as equal. By the 1970s anti-immigrant hostility still dominated the agenda, but the realities of minority settlement led to some public acceptance of economic and social integration and the beginning of an acceptance of Britain as a plural, multicultural society. Educators had certainly begun to accept the view that minorities should acquire equal rights, and retain some measure of cultural diversity but with agreed common values and aims, especially in terms of educational and economic opportunities. It is worth saying and repeating that there has never been any evidence that educators encouraged separatism of groups, or what Sen (2006: 65) called 'plural monoculturalism' where communities live separately. It is also worth noting that while minority groups historically have often been blamed for their failure to 'integrate', minorities in a majority culture need some sense of solidarity, to defend themselves in an often hostile society, and that such solidarity can provide a base from which to lay claim to equal rights. Minority community organisations, especially in education, over the years have pressed for an acknowledgement of the legitimacy of their presence as minorities but also as equal citizens.

From the 1970s to the 1990s more recognition of discrimination and new kinds of racism, and the dominant place skin colour had been accorded in exclusion from 'being British' encouraged anti-racist action by community activists and in some areas of education, and from 1997 a New Labour government was promising a socially just society which would embrace all creeds, races and cultures (Blair 1998). But by the early 2000s cultural and religious antagonisms provided a basis for attacks on multiculturalism and race equality, and a return to myths of assimilation, sometimes disguised as strategies for 'community cohesion'. Such cohesion was manifestly hindered by competition for scarce resources of housing, good schools and jobs, as much as by old imperial attitudes and newer anxieties over Islam. However, as Kymlicka (2004) has pointed out, governments around the world are realising now that antagonism to minorities is not necessarily shared by employers and proponents of a new capitalism. Employers and business work in the interests of profit and capital accumulation. If this means employing any ethnic group, including taking cheaper European labour or even turning a blind eye to illegal labour, a business case for diversity takes precedence over denial of diversity or anti-immigrant stances. Additionally, many minority members are possibly more interested than many in the majority in acquiring globally marketable skills, assisted by the ability to function in several languages and develop international businesses. It may not be too cynical to say that recognising the reality of a plural multicultural society is part of a project to bring about justice and equality, and is also good business in a globalised world.[4]

Plan and personal: Chapters 1–3

The book's chapters are mainly divided by the decades from 1960 to 2007, as political, legislative and educational events can be differentiated this way. The chapters cover ideology and politics, general educational policy and educational issues, and practices relating to race and ethnicity, with an initial list of dates and events. The terminology of each chapter reflects the language used at the time. As I have been involved over the years in many of the events described, I have noted here what my involvement was in each decade. Chapter 1 covers the period 1960–1970, when political ideologies converged to support the notion that immigrants would assimilate at the lower levels of a capitalist economy, taking the jobs white workers were reluctant to do. Contradictory anti-immigrant policies and hostile views were prevalent, particularly inflamed by the Conservative politician Enoch Powell, then MP for Wolverhampton and a member of the Shadow Cabinet.

In 1968 Powell made several inflammatory speeches, in February referring to the lonely white child in the class full of immigrants, and in November describing 'grinning piccaninnies' taunting old ladies. Migrant families responded with both anger and bemusement to this, particularly as, when Minister of Health in 1962, Powell had invited women from the Caribbean to come and work in local hospitals. However, during this decade civil legislation against racial discrimination was passed, and educational policies to incorporate immigrant children were in progress. These focused on English second language teaching, remedial and compensatory education to improve achievement, the first collection of statistics and provision of special funding under Section 11 of a 1966 Local Government Act, the beginning of some relevant teacher training, and less positively, the over-placement of black boys in what were then known as schools for the educationally subnormal. The decade was important in that it was during this period that the settlement of minorities where labour was needed, discriminatory housing policies and white flight from these areas contributed to the ethnic segregation which caused political anxiety in the 2000s. During the later 1960s I was teaching in a primary school in Wolverhampton, my class almost entirely composed of children immigrant from the Caribbean and the Indian sub-continent. After Powell's speeches in 1968 a group of mothers met me in the street to ask 'Who is this man, telling us to go home, when he invited us here to work (in the local hospital)?', and I was made aware of racial injustice in a country already benefiting from migrant labour. At that time I had no special training to teach immigrant children or knowledge of their backgrounds, but I was instructed by my kind liberal headteacher to 'treat them all as the other children'.

Chapter 2 covers the decade 1970–1980, a period when any conservative humanism, idealistic liberalism or labour socialism collapsed under anti-immigrant agitation. A leading Labour politician wrote the 'fear of immigration is the most powerful undertow today . . . we had to out-trump the Tories by doing what they would have done' (Crossman 1975: 299). Out-trumping meant further immigration control measures, and a reluctant acceptance of increased hostility in all social classes to those now described as New Commonwealth immigrants and their children. There was particular antagonism in the white working class among whom immigrants primarily settled, but neither were the middle classes keen to welcome immigrants into their suburbs. Unions worried that immigrant labour would lower wages, but it was often Asian workers who led strikes for higher wages. The consequences of the end of Empire and the creation of a multicultural society became more obvious, yet Powell continued to argue in Parliament that British citizenship should exclude West Indians and Asians. Urban Aid programmes in the 1970s were discovering the poor state of infrastructure and employment in inner cities, but rather than work on the causes of inequalities there was a focus on the deficits of the families living there, and no counter to the scapegoating of immigrant families blamed for the decline. In 1972 Keith Joseph, then Minister for Health and Social Security, set up research to discover how a 'cycle of deprivation' was transmitted in families. Education policies during this period subsumed minorities under the generic label of disadvantage, adopting what US scholar Kirp (1979) described as inexplicit policy concerning race, despite three Parliamentary Select Committee reports documenting specific employment and educational problems for racial minorities. Black parents and community organisations were insistent that educational qualifications were necessary for their children to find good employment and worried about their school achievements, and by the end of the decade a Committee of Enquiry into the education of children of West Indian origin had been set up (DES 1981a), becoming after 1981 an enquiry into the education of all ethnic minority young people (DES 1985a). Black youth became more race-conscious and there were clashes with the police and with the racist National Front Party, a neo-Nazi organisation which eventually turned into the British National Party.

The chapter also notes the increasing acceptance of a cultural pluralism in which issues concerning the retention of minority languages via mother-tongue teaching and bilingualism assumed importance. Teachers, local education authorities and some politicians demonstrated serious concern that 'the curriculum appropriate to our imperial past' (DES 1977) was no longer appropriate and a literature on multicultural and anti-racist education began to appear. At the beginning of the decade I moved into teacher education in the West Midlands, setting up the first course in my college on 'the education of immigrant children' and in 1974 moved on to work with Professor John Rex at Warwick University, carrying out a four-year study of race and community relations in Handsworth, Birmingham (Rex and Tomlinson 1979). During work on this study I variously encountered both liberal and racist decision makers, both deeply concerned and solely self-interested community leaders and activists, many deeply caring and distressed parents and some young people already disillusioned with their schooling and employment prospects. I was jostled by the fascist National Front while observing their marches, and came under police scrutiny for interviewing black groups with links to the African National Congress. On publication of the study, gentlemen of all ethnicities began arriving on my doorstep, having been told that my house was a brothel! I also carried out a study for my own PhD examining the over-placement of black children in special education (Tomlinson 1981).

Chapter 3 documents the period 1980–1990, the Conservatives under Margaret Thatcher having gained power in 1979. Market ideologies in society and in education took over and economic, social and racial divisions became more obvious. The decade was marked by ideological and policy contradictions and also by familiar continuities. Post-industrial market economies needed higher level technical and professional skills, with less demand for unskilled migrant labour, and immigration control and debate over a British nationality remained an issue. While a white working class complained that 'they' were taking 'our' jobs, young second generation minorities demonstrated that they were not satisfied with an underclass position in jobs the white youth would not take. In 1981 there was serious rioting in several areas of Britain, notably Brixton in London, Toxteth in Liverpool, and Handsworth in Birmingham, confirming Mrs Thatcher's view that alien cultures were swamping Britain and there was an 'enemy within' British cities (Gilroy 1987). Education policy was dominated by interest in the free market, competition, and control of public spending, allied to conservative interests in preserving tradition, hierarchy and authority.

During the decade almost every aspect of education was subject to scrutiny, criticism and centralising legislation, a process continued by Conservative and New Labour governments in the 1990s. Early years, school structures, funding mechanisms, local authority influence, inspection, ancillary services, teacher training and higher education were all criticised and the 1988 Education Reform Act consolidated notions of parental 'choice' of school, competition between schools, centralised control of funding and the curriculum, and diminished local authority influence. This latter was partly a reaction to Conservative dislike of local authority action in the area of race and education. By the end of the decade almost two-thirds of LEAs, notably the Inner London Education Authority (ILEA), had produced multicultural, anti-racist or equal opportunity policies and set up curriculum projects. The ILEA was abolished by the 1988 Act. But a major contradiction which emerged during the decade was that while there was intense right-wing hostility to any practice labelled multicultural or anti-racist, which was denounced as left-of-centre egalitarianism, political subversion, and a threat to British values (Palmer 1986), the 1980s was a period of advance in both the education of minorities and for the majority of young people for the society in which they now lived. A large literature and practice emerged, much written and initiated by teachers. The Swann report (DES 1985a) encouraged a more realistic 'Education for All' and this decade appears as the highpoint of advance in education for a multicultural, non-racist society. If there had been at this point some central political leadership in taking seriously how education could contribute to a harmonious cohesive society, it is possible that some of the antagonisms evident by the 2000s could have been avoided. As it was, even the teaching of 'peace studies' was denounced as a dangerous activity by Keith Joseph, then Minister of Education. During this period I was working at Lancaster University in the north of England, teaching a course on race and education, and taking students to visit schools with predominantly Asian intakes, in towns where riots occurred in 2001. I carried out, with colleagues, the first large-scale, six-year study of pupils passing through 20 multiracial secondary schools in four areas of the country (Smith and Tomlinson 1989), and studied all-white schools which had received Education Support Grants to improve education for a multi-ethnic society (Tomlinson 1990). I also spent time serving on a committee for the degree-awarding body, the Council for National Academic Awards (CNAA), which was concerned to bring multicultural perspectives into higher education (a report produced about this was censored), and on a National Curriculum Council committee set up at the request of the Secretary of State for Education, Kenneth Baker, to report on bringing multicultural, anti-racist and global perspectives into the national curriculum. This report never appeared (Tomlinson 1993).

Plan and personal: Chapters 4–6

Chapter 4 covers the period 1990–1997, John Major having replaced Margaret Thatcher as Prime Minister. US scholar Michael Apple suggested that race had become an 'absent presence' (Apple 1999). This government was preoccupied with the immigration of labour migrants from European countries after the 1992 Maastricht Treaty established a European Union, notionally giving all citizens of the Member States (then 15, now 27) the right to live and work in other EU countries. The first Gulf War also brought in refugees from Iraq, and asylum seekers arrived from civil wars in Sri Lanka, Somalia, Sudan, Sierra Leone, Afghanistan and other places, to be joined after the collapse of the old Yugoslavia by Bosnians, Serbs, Croats, Kosovans, Albanians and Roma. Legislation to control migration and asylum seekers was accompanied by media denigration of refugees as scroungers or illegal immigrants, and 'just as the greatest number of refugee students were being admitted to English schools the government changed educational policies in a way which seriously undermined their educational opportunities' (Rutter 2003: 73). The 1991 Census was the first to include an 'ethnic question' asking for a subjective identification by country of origin, colour or cultural affiliation, and the extent of ethnic segregation in Britain became clearer. However, the life trajectories of different minority groups, documented in a fourth PSI study, was now becoming more obvious and 'the differences between minorities have become as important and significant to life-chances as similarities' (Modood *et al.* 1997: 8). This report concluded that the more overt expressions of religion in Muslim communities had to be explained by 'the social location of Muslims in Britain and the reactive and defensive position Islam has had to adopt' (ibid.: 9). Additionally, a black feminist literature was demonstrating gender differences in issues of race and social class, and inequalities in educational achievements by race, class and gender (Mirza 1997a, Gaine and George 1999). In education the government ignored documented racial tensions in schools, reports on the school exclusion of black boys, and the murder of

18-year-old black student Stephen Lawrence by white racists, refusing an enquiry into the murder. There was also a refusal to consider changes or additions to the National Curriculum to reflect a multi-ethnic society, a further reduction in Section 11 funding – still the only designated funding for minority education – and a disappearance of university and local authority courses designed to promote understanding of the issues, for both initial and in-service teachers. There was a centralisation of teacher training via a Teacher Training Agency with no special brief for training teachers for a multi-ethnic society and a new schools inspectorate, which again did not require special training in race issues for the now largely privatised inspectorate. The effects of comprehensive schooling, with more young people prepared and entered for public examinations over the past decade meant that success in public examinations improved in all groups and numbers entering higher education rose, but a growing gap between the school achievements of pupils of African-Caribbean, Pakistani and Bangladeshi origin became more obvious (Gillborn and Gipps 1996). The chapter covers the working out of the 1988 Education Act and its effect on minorities, noting that blame for low attainment now focused not only on individuals, families and cultural groups, but also on 'failing schools', demonised by the media as responsible for a variety of social problems (Tomlinson 1997, O'Connor *et al.* 1999). During the 1990s, I was Professor of Educational Policy, and served as a Pro-Warden (Vice-Principal) of Goldsmiths College, London University. At this time Goldsmiths was the College with the highest number of black and other minority students and most teachers trained there took jobs in London. In the early 1990s, after researching Bangladeshi parents' views of education in Tower Hamlets, London, I worked with the Tower Hamlets Law Centre to produce a report on the large number of Bangladeshi children who had been without any school place over the past ten years (a subsequent court case removed responsibility from the local authority and the DES). I also went to court in 1995 as a witness in a Judicial Review, when a government-appointed 'Education Association' recommended the quick closure of Hackney Downs Boys School in Hackney, London, a school with over 70 per cent black and second language speaking pupils, and a large number of special needs pupils, but demonised in the media as a failing school (O'Connor *et al.* 1999). A City Academy was eventually built on the site of Hackney Downs School at a cost of £25 million to the taxpayer, which became a popular venue for school visits from Prime Minister Blair.

Chapter 5 covers the period 1997–2003, the first and half the second period in office of the New Labour government. The government came to power affirming a commitment to social justice and to education as a means of creating a social just society. Prime Minister Blair asserted that 'nations that succeed will be tolerant, respectful of diversity' (Blair 1999a), and race once more became a 'present presence' in policy thinking. Within a year the new government had attempted to grapple with some long-standing grievances and inequalities, setting up a Social Exclusion Unit with an initial brief to enquire into school truancy and exclusions, particularly relating to black boys, as well as making a decision to offer Muslim and other faiths schools state funding similar to that offered to existing Anglican, Catholic, Methodist and Jewish schools, recognising in their first White Paper inequalities in school achievement between different minority groups (DfEE 1997), replacing the Section 11 grant with an Ethnic Minority Achievement Grant (EMAG) and setting up an inquiry into the murder of Stephen Lawrence (Macpherson 1999). Two important results from this inquiry were the subsequent additional equalities legislation via a Race Relations (Amendment) Act in 2000 and a wider airing of the notion of institutional racism in public services. The new Prime Minister declared that education was to be a priority for his government and a flurry of Acts, White papers, reports and initiatives continued to overwhelm schools. However, there was an acceptance of the Conservative faith in choice and competition between schools with education developing further as a market commodity driven by supposed consumer demand, more private incursions into education and more support for faith schools. There was increased competition between schools via league tables, support for specialist schools and the new form of semi-privatised schools, known as Academies – the 'independent state schools' first suggested by Mrs Thatcher at the 1987 Conservative Party conference.

There was a continuation of parental 'choice' of school, now causing huge problems as parents realised that schools were largely doing the 'choosing', more white flight from high minority schools and a resulting increase in social and ethnic segregation, with failing schools continuing to be demonised. The assumption behind policy was that the key to a successful economy in global economic conditions was to be education and individual investment in human capital. School standards were to be driven up to achieve this. The subordination of education to the economy and the scapegoating of schools and teachers who failed to deliver high quality products underpinned much education policy and legislation during the first period of office, and market policies continued to create a hierarchy between more or less desirable schools, the less desirable being more likely to be attended by minorities, second language speakers and those with special educational needs.

In the 2001 Census some 8 per cent of the population identified themselves as ethnic minority, and as a religious question had been included, over one and a half million people identified themselves as Muslim. Census analysts suggested that the cities of Leicester and Birmingham would become majority-minority from 2010. Shortly after New Labour was elected for a second time there were race riots in English northern towns, notably Bradford, Blackburn, Oldham and Burnley, and government began to take seriously issues of segregation and separation, although with little historical understanding. A Ministerial Group on Public Order and Community Cohesion was set up and a Community Cohesion Review Team, chaired by Ted Cantle, asked to report on the disorders, including the views of local people and communities. The Cantle Report (2001) strongly influenced government views of polarised communities living 'parallel lives' and resulting strategies to promote community cohesion. Citizenship education was made compulsory from September 2002 but there was still no serious attempt to develop a curriculum to educate all young people to live in a multicultural society. Despite a Human Rights Act signed up to in 1998, government policy towards settled minorities and new migrants became more punitive after the attack on the World Trade Center in New York in September 2001, and the invasion of Afghanistan in 2001 and Iraq in April 2003. There was increased confusion between the presence of settled minorities who were citizens (often still struggling for their citizenship rights), the arrival of asylum seekers, and economic migration from European countries. An Asylum and Immigration Act in 2002 increased border controls and required future citizens to pass an English language and citizenship test, and there was confused xenophobic reaction to workers from EU countries, the 'Polish plumber' being a stereotypical welcome migrant, the 'Albanian gangster' an unwelcome one. From 1998 to 2000 I served on a Commission on the Future of Multi-ethnic Britain, chaired by Lord Bhikhu Parekh. This Commission was intended to repeat, in a more modest way, the Rose *et al.* study of *Colour and Citizenship* (1969). Despite the august membership of this Commission (several Lords, professors, a Master of a Cambridge College, a Deputy Police Chief, and others) and a large amount of information collected, our report was received with much hostility by the media, politicians and the general public as attacking 'Britishness' and became a 'politically untouchable document' (McLaughlin and Neal 2004). Jim Rose, who had followed the progress of the Commission's work with interest, died before its completion. One recommendation from the report – that there should be a single Equalities Commission – became law in 2006. Few of the 21 educational recommendations were implemented, apart from the suggestion that better statistical information on minority pupils be collected. The introduction of the Pupil Level Annual School Census (PLASC) in 2002 made this possible. After 2000 I retired from Goldsmiths and became a Senior Research Fellow in the Department of Education, University of Oxford, and later Chair of Trustees of the African Educational Trust, a charity running literacy and numeracy courses in areas of conflict in Africa.

Chapter 6 takes the story from 2003 to June 2007, when Prime Minister Blair gave way to Prime Minister Brown, leaving as the disastrous consequences of wars in Afghanistan and Iraq became more obvious, and the relationship between Muslims and non-Muslims in Britain had become more antagonistic. The chapter points out the increasing contradictions between competitive education policies and a rhetoric of community cohesion. Into the 2000s the New Labour government became embroiled in contradictions as to how government, social institutions and society in general should treat minority citizens, migrants of all kinds, and especially the Muslim population. There were naïve attempts to blame an undefined 'multiculturalism' for the existence of areas of the country geographically segregated by ethnicity, which, as previous chapters have shown, was largely due to earlier settlement for employment, discriminatory housing policies and white flight, and in June 2005 the Conservative Party fought an unpleasant anti-immigrant election campaign. As documented in Chapter 4, some young Muslims were drawn into radical Islamist groups by the later 1980s. The suicide bombing in London in July 2005 by four young Muslims born and educated in Britain signalled further antagonism to Muslims, and a search for 'community cohesion' began with the setting up of interfaith groups and a Commission on Community Cohesion and Integration. There was some belated recognition that there were radicalised young Muslims, educated in British schools, who were influenced by global extremist movements. Criticisms of 'multiculturalism' (particularly as symbolised by dress) increased, with Jack Straw, former Home Secretary and Foreign Secretary, criticising the wearing of the niquab (full-face veil) and a teaching assistant in Dewsbury, Yorkshire, was suspended for refusing to remove this. The emergence of the veil, either the hijab (headscarf) or niquab as a political issue was relatively new in Britain although it had been a contentious issue in other countries for decades. The debate on dress fed into debates on integration, identity, the human rights of women, and public and private roles of religion. It also prompted an increase in self-defence classes by Muslim women, calling themselves 'ninjabis', concerned to protect themselves from verbal and physical abuse from both white and Muslim men. For some women the hijab in the 2000s had become as assertive as the Afro hairstyle of the 1970s was to young black men. In August 2006 Blair claimed that immigration and terrorism were the two major public concerns, thus helping to escalate public hostility to anyone assumed to be an 'immigrant'.

Conflicts, particularly over economic chances, between black and Asian youth were demonstrated by riots in Lozells, Birmingham in October 2005, unemployment in this and other inner-city areas being high. Despite professed anxieties about young Muslims, no representative from the DfES attended the launch of a large-scale Nuffield sponsored inquiry into the education of 14–19-years-olds, which showed yet again that young men of Pakistani and Bangladeshi origin were least likely to obtain good qualifications (Nuffield Report 2006). In addition, black parents and community groups had been galvanised again into protest about the education of their children, triggered in November 2005 by the publication of a book reprinting Bernard Coard's 1971 work, with other contributions, which pointed out yet again *How Schools Fail Black Children* (Richardson 2005). These parents were not conciliated by a DfES response that black achievement at GCSE A–C level had increased to 36 per cent, given that white achievement had increased to 52 per cent. The chapter covers the legislation which gave schools, including faith schools, yet more autonomy with the ability to form 'Trusts' and become independent of local authorities, but also required all schools to become 'inclusive', with a reliance on citizenship education as an answer to lack of community cohesion. Although Blair had begun his premiership with assertions that education would be his passion, by the time of his leaving education policy appeared to be dictated by two unelected men, Andrew Adonis, a former advisor made a Lord and an Education Minister by Blair, and Cyril Taylor, head of what had become the Academies and Specialist Schools Trust. The new Prime Minister Gordon Brown, taking over in June 2007, immediately signalled more change by splitting the DfES into two Departments, one for Children, Schools and Families (Secretary of State Ed Balls) and one for Innovation, Universities and Skills (Secretary of State John Denham), the word 'education' disappearing from government departmental descriptions. At Oxford I continued to examine doctorates and at the present time have examined over 110 PhDs, many of them the published research reported in the following chapters.

The conclusions to the book attempt to draw together the political and educational context in which minority young people have been absorbed into a majority society, which has demonstrated much enduring hostility to those perceived as different on racial, ethnic, cultural, religious grounds, and unwelcome as refugees, asylum seekers or economic migrants. Some negative continuities from the 1960s were very evident; the failure to adapt to the presence of minorities and offer all young people an equal education in terms of resources, funding and properly prepared teachers; the acceptance of white flight from areas of high minority settlement and a subsequent blaming of the minority communities themselves for lack of integration; the minimal and grudging adoption of measures to increase the achievement levels of all minority groups; and a failure to rethink the curriculum to inform and prepare all young people for their multicultural society and a globalised world characterised by racial and religious conflicts. Continuities which disadvantaged both white working-class children and minorities were also evident in the general education policies which increased social and racial selection and separation of children by 'choice' and also by faith. By the 21st century in Britain education had become a competitive enterprise between parents and students competing for the 'best' schools and higher education institutions, with an increase in social and ethnic segregation in schools and localities. Education could not be said to be supporting declared aims of creating social cohesion and mutual tolerance and understanding. Old issues of reconciling unity with diversity took on new dimensions as beliefs in Western secular enlightenment clashed with religious fundamentalisms of all kinds.

But the history of the period covered here demonstrates that there has always been groups and individuals working in local authorities, in schools, in the teaching profession, in teacher unions, in the inspectorate, plus parents and community groups, academics and others, who have been committed to finding ways of creating an education system that would prepare all young people to live independent and fulfilling lives in a plural, multicultural society. By the early 21st century it was becoming obvious that education in Britain needed to become clearer as to its principles, purpose and content if it was to be relevant to the kind of society that now made up 'Britain'. The book concludes with some tentative suggestions. A major principle should be that an education system in a plural, multicultural society is shaped by a public service culture in which majorities and minorities agree on common values reflected in a common curriculum, but with sufficient scope for community values and viewpoints. This would need a repudiation of much of the competitiveness in the current set-up, as a system driven solely by market forces, competition, institutional or group self-interest cannot be fair or guarantee social and racial justice. An equally important principle should be that education has a duty and key role in clarifying and tackling the basis and manifestations of inequality, racism, and discrimination in its own practices and institutions and in the wider society. The major purpose of education in a plural, multicultural society must remain that of providing all young people with the means to live independent and inter-dependent lives, economically, socially and politically, in a globalised world. Exhortations to achieve well and obtain qualifications are only of use if there are political and economic policies aimed at securing a productive life for all members of the society.

Notes

1. Most of the educational policy documented in this book refers to England and Wales, although in 1999, after a devolution of government, Wales took control of its own education system. Scotland largely controlled a separate system after the 1945 Education (Scotland) Act and from 1999 the Scottish Parliament controlled its system, as does Northern Ireland.
2. There is a plethora of literature defining and discussing race, racism, ethnicity, culture and multiculturalism. For a small selection see Barry (2001), Pilkington (2003), Bhavani *et al.* (2005). This book does not deliberately add to this literature but the reader is referred to Rex (1986: 17): 'Racial and ethnic groups are groups to whom common behavioural characteristics are imputed, rather than groups which have such characteristics . . . racial groups are groups thought to have a genetic or other deterministic base, ethnic groups are thought of as those whose behaviour might change.' The reader is reminded again that the terminology used in each chapter reflects that used during the particular decade in question.
3. Early reviews of the race and education literature can be found in Tomlinson

(1977, 1983a), Verma and Bagley (1979), Taylor (1981), Taylor and Hegarty (1985).

4. As part of an international strategy on managing global migration, in 2007 the government promoted Britain as a migration destination for business and skilled migrants. The Immigration Minister was reported as wanting to explore the potential of Britain's Indian and Chinese communities to expand trade links (Travis 2007).

Assimilation aspirations (1960–1970)

> A Rubicon was crossed in the spring of 1968. This was when the British government decided, on ground of expediency rather than principle, that it could no longer accept responsibility for certain of its citizens because of the colour of their skin.
>
> (Rose *et al.* 1969: 11)[1]

The fabled ship *Empire Windrush* arrived in England in June 1948, carrying 492 skilled workers from Jamaica. While the ship was still at sea a British government that had encouraged the post-war immigration of some 200,000 Polish and other European displaced persons, panicked at the potential arrival of a few hundred 'coloured' workers. The Privy Council sent a memo to the Foreign Office requesting that 'no special effort be made to help these people . . . otherwise it might encourage a further influx' (Winder 2004: 340). Who knows, as Winder pointed out, what might have happened had the government provided anything resembling the political leadership that had been forthcoming for white workers? The situation for black and Asian migrant workers and their children and the attitudes of a white majority might have been considerably different over the next five decades, and an education system able to prepare all young people for a globalised world might have begun to develop.

This chapter begins with a brief documentation of political action on race and immigration and its ideological basis during the 1960s, without which it is not possible to understand educational policies directed towards minority children, and the schooling they have received over the years. In particular a study of the history of the last five decades aids understanding of the way in which the settlement of minorities in areas where their labour was needed, accompanied by discriminatory housing policies and white flight and then by the creation of education markets, contributed to ethnic segregation in schooling, which by the 2000s had become a focus for intense political anxiety. This chapter outlines general education policies, and the main policies adopted in respect of immigrant children, particularly those relating to English language acquisition, funding, statistical collection, curriculum issues, teachers and teacher training, achievement, special education and ESN placement. During the decade the contradictions between anti-immigrant agitation and legislation, and the early 1960s view that immigrant workers and their children, described in one book as *Dark Strangers* (Patterson 1963), needed to be assimilated into an undefined British way of life became more obvious. By the later 1960s notions of assimilation gave way to discussion of integration and cultural pluralism (Rose *et al.* 1969: 24). The decade of the 1960s was important in that it set the tone for future debate on the integration and acquisition of full citizenship rights, and the entitlement to equal education, of what by the 2000s were some five million minority group members. The chapter illustrates the relationship between the British class system, which is actually a system of status classification as well as an economic one, and the class structure of Empire, which had embodied beliefs in a caste-like barrier between citizens of the 'mother country' and subjects of the Empire. Whatever class conflicts went on in Britain, all social classes to some extent united in hostility to the permanent arrival of former colonial subjects. Reactions ranged from overt semi-fascist attempts to remove the arrivals, to a half-hearted liberal and business welcome via assimilation and integration, to mixed reactions from socialist movements fighting for the working class, but confused when this class began to incorporate an unwelcome colonial underclass which had no intention of staying in that position. The language of the decade in both official documents and academic work referred to immigrants, a coloured population, second language speakers, West Indian, Asian and white, and legislation used the terminology of race relations and racial discrimination.

Chronology of Acts and issues

1944 Education Act establishes secondary education for all to age 15 and a tripartite selective system of grammar, secondary modern and technical schools. General Certificate of Education O and A levels established in 1951.

1948 British Nationality Act distinguishes between citizens of independent Commonwealth countries (mainly white) and those in colonies and dependent territories. *Empire Windrush* brings 492 workers from Jamaica.

1958 Race riots in Nottingham and Notting Hill. West Indians attacked by white groups.

1959 Conservatives elected for third time since 1951.

1960–61 Proposed immigration restrictions lead to beat-the-ban immigration from the Indian sub-continent. Birmingham Education Department sets up the first Department for teaching English as a second language. Birmingham Immigration Control Association and Southall Residents Association set up and oppose immigration of 'New Commonwealth' (non-white) citizens.

1962 Conservative Immigration Control Act. Commonwealth Immigrants Advisory Council set up to advise the Home Secretary.

1962 Certificate of Secondary Education (CSE) established. Association for Teachers of English to Pupils from Overseas (ATEPO) set up.

1963 Newsom Report on *Half our Future*. Robbins Report on *Higher Education*.

1963 HM inspectors produce 'English for Immigrants' and set up short courses for English as a second language. Edge Hill College, Lancashire introduces first teacher training course for teaching immigrant children. Protest by white parents in Southall, London, against a school with 60 per cent immigrant children. Education Minister Edward Boyle rejects the idea of segregated education.

1964 Voucher system restricts immigration. (October) Labour elected. Conservative wins Smethwick, West Midlands, using the slogan 'If you want a nigger neighbour, vote Labour'. Campaign Against Racial Discrimination set up (CARD) and a Commonwealth Immigrants Advisory Council recommends the school dispersal of immigrant children.

1964 Ministry of Education becomes Department for Education and Science (DES).

1965 The DES recommends in Circular 7/65 that no school have more than 30 per cent immigrant children. Several LEAs adopt dispersal by bussing. The North London West Indian Association worries about children referred to ESN (educationally subnormal) schools. The first Race Relations Act passed in October, education not mentioned. A Race Relations Board and a National Committee for Commonwealth Immigrants set up (Chaired by Archbishop of Canterbury).

1965 Circular 10/65 requests all schools to reorganise on comprehensive principles. Home office produces a White Paper, *Immigration from the Commonwealth.*

1966 Labour re-elected, Smethwick regained and the new MP declares 'we have buried the race issue'. Home Secretary Roy Jenkins envisages a society based on cultural diversity, mutual tolerance and equal opportunity.

1966 Local Government Act, via Section 11, in which the Home Office provided a 50 per cent rate support grant for staff in high immigrant areas. DES arranges for first collection of statistics of New Commonwealth children. Leeds project to develop English teaching materials set up. Census shows 'coloured population' of UK as being 924,000, mainly from India, Pakistan, Jamaica, and other Caribbean countries.

1967 Enoch Powell suggests that coloured immigrants, especially from Kenya, be kept out of England. Plowden report on *Children and their Primary Schools* includes a chapter on immigrant children.

1968 Home Secretary James Callaghan introduces a Commonwealth Immigration Act (passed in a week). Those who are patrials with a father or grandfather born in UK have priority. Powell proposes a Ministry of Repatriation and on 20 April makes an anti-immigration speech, pro-Powell marches take place in London and other towns. Black Peoples Alliance set up at a conference in Leamington Spa.

1968 (November) Second Race Relations Act passed. Education not mentioned. Parliamentary Select Committee on Race Relations and Immigration set up. Prime Minister Wilson sets up an Urban Aid fund which includes help for New Commonwealth children.

1969 House of Commons Select Committee on Race Relations and Immigration report on *The Problems of Coloured School Leavers*. North London West Indian Association lodges a complaint of racial discrimination over ESN schooling. Arthur Jensen publishes 'How much can we boost IQ and scholastic ability' in the *Harvard Educational Review*. Rose *et al.* publish *Colour and Citizenship: a report on British Race Relations*.

1970 Bernard Coard galvanises black parents with a speech and subsequent publication on *How the West Indian Child is made ESN in the British School System*.

Politics and ideology

The British Nationality Act, passed in 1948, notionally gave all imperial subjects the right of free entry into Britain, although it distinguished between citizens of the white Commonwealth countries and those of the UK and Colonies. The extensive territories of the British Empire (see Appendix) and legends of imperial triumphs still formed the basis for nostalgia and notions of an unproblematic British heritage. It was unsurprising that over 30 years later a 12-year-old white girl told researcher Rob Jeffcoate that 'once we owned the whole world and now we've only got a little piece. There are too many coloureds in our country' (Jeffcoate 1979: 99). The arrival of the ship *Empire Windrush* carrying migrant workers from Jamaica has been well documented (Fryer 1984, Phillips and Phillips 1999), with the Ministry of Labour already describing the small numbers on board as an 'influx'. Post-Second World War migrant labour had been encouraged by government and employers, and numbers of European 'displaced persons' were accepted for work and settlement, but during the 1950s anti-immigrant agitation and hostility on the basis of skin colour was very evident. Leary Constantine, famous West Indian cricketer and later a life-peer, was one of the first to bring a legal challenge of colour discrimination. He then documented the extent of racial hostility and discrimination in his book *Colour Bar* (Constantine 1954). Racial beliefs deriving from 19th-century imperial expansion and Social Darwinism helped create a popular consciousness in all social classes that the white British had economic, moral and intellectual superiority over arrivals from colonial countries. However, during this decade liberal beliefs in equality before the law were mostly sustained, with white youths being jailed for attacks on black people in Notting Hill in 1958.

Ideological self-images of a Britain characterised by paternalistic tolerance and fair play for those regarded as racially different came under strain in the 1960s as the numbers of migrants from the Caribbean and Asian subcontinent increased. Contradictions between a need for unskilled and semi-skilled labour, and the incorporation of new arrivals and their children, versus antagonism to 'coloured immigrants' and immigration control legislation characterised the period. There were also contradictions between a recognition that migrants settled in towns and cities where there were jobs, and the reluctance to house them. After a period of intense political hostility to immigration, the Conservative government introduced an Act in 1962 which limited Commonwealth immigration by the issue of vouchers. This was opposed by Labour leader of the opposition, Hugh Gaitskell, who pointed out that economic conditions were already regulating migration (Peach 1968). In 1964 the Conservatives won a parliamentary seat in the West Midlands with the candidate running a racist anti-immigrant campaign that included the slogan 'If you want a nigger neighbour, vote Labour'. Although the new Labour Prime Minister, Harold Wilson, asserted that this MP would be a 'parliamentary leper' because of his views, a voucher system to control immigration was endorsed by the Labour government in 1965 and a 1968 Act was implemented that was designed to limit the entry of Kenyan Asians by distinguishing those 'patrials' with a father or grandfather born in the UK, and the rest. This was the Act that led Rose and his colleagues (1969) to comment that skin colour was a deciding factor in government repudiation of its non-white citizens.

Although the Labour government maintained a liberal stance on racial discrimination, passing a Race Relations Act in 1965 which set up a Race Relations Board and a National Committee for Commonwealth Immigrants, and a further Act in 1968 which turned the latter into a Community Relations Commission, the 'Liberal Hour was passing' as Nicholas Deakin, an associate in the Rose study, put it. Enoch Powell, a member of the Conservative shadow cabinet became an important and charismatic figure, articulating a populist xenophobia and racism which would eventually be taken over not just by extreme right-wing parties but later would be incorporated into some mainstream party thinking. In the 1960s Britain, or more precisely England, was searching for a new post-imperial identity and Powell's 'tribal nationalism and outright racism' (Rich 1986: 207) provided a basis for this. Although Lord Elton, in 1965, had used images from imperial Rome to declare that an empire in decadence 'imported subject races to discharge its menial tasks' (Elton 1965: 19) it was Powell who, in his speeches in 1968, conjured up the prospect of an English River Tiber foaming with blood as civil unrest occurred due to immigration. After a speech on 20 April 1968, dockers in London marched in support of Powell's views, something of an irony in that dockers' jobs were usually taken by family members or by word of mouth and there were very few black dock workers. Although Powell was sacked from the shadow cabinet by Conservative leader Edward Heath, his long-term legacy was an encouragement of a narrow 'white' nationalism, and suspicion of immigrant communities, especially when they claimed citizenship rights and welfare benefits on a par with other citizens. Richard Crossman, Minister for Housing in 1965, agonised over the Labour Party 'becoming illiberal' (Crossman 1975: 299) but took the Powellite view that immigrants placed a strain on social housing and other social institutions, a view for which there was no actual evidence but which helped push the Labour Party in the direction of popularist anti-immigrant views. There was little political connection between discriminatory housing policies which helped create 'immigrant communities' and the consequence that local schools would naturally incorporate their children. It was ironic that over 35 years later it took riots for a Ministerial Working Group to notice that some schools were segregated by ethnic group (Ministerial Working Group on Public Order and Community Cohesion 2001).

The end process of migrations may be assimilation into a majority society. This was a major aim in the USA from the 1920s, although with distinct ambivalence about black assimilation. Early 1960s Britain was characterised by the liberal assumption that assimilation of immigrants into an undefined 'British way of life' was possible, despite hostile views that immigrants constituted a social problem, and numbers must be limited. A 1965 White Paper on *Immigration from the Commonwealth* encapsulated the contradictions evident in 'control of the entry of immigrants so that it does not outrun Britain's capacity to absorb them' (Home Office 1965: 2), with a Labour spokesman articulating 'the melancholy view that only immigrants most likely to be assimilated into our national life should be permitted to stay in Britain' (Patterson 1963: 109). There was no recognition that the national life was in fact made up of a complex class system with a plurality of values. In particular, there was no official recognition that while white workers were happy to see black workers take jobs they did not want, there was disquiet that these workers should live among them, or that the middle classes had little intention of welcoming black and Asian neighbours into their suburbs. By the later 1960s the realities of colour and cultural difference had penetrated official thinking and a language of integration and pluralism had superseded assimilation. A large-scale study of race relations in Britain in the 1960s (Rose *et al.* 1969) defined integration and cultural pluralism together as

> a process whereby a minority group, while retaining its own culture and religion, adapts itself to and is accepted as a permanent member of the majority society. Its members enjoy full political, civil and social rights and perform their obligations to society as equal citizens but may remain members of separate communities, preserving their own language within the home.
>
> (1969: 24)

Roy Jenkins, Labour Home Secretary for six months in 1966, declared in a much quoted speech that the objective of policy was 'Equal opportunity accompanied by cultural diversity in an atmosphere of mutual tolerance' (Jenkins 1966), although evidence of white tolerance of black immigrants or black people born in Britain, was hard to detect. Shortly after this speech Chris Mullard, born and brought up in Hampshire, and later an education academic received a letter telling him 'Get out of our country, black rubbish, You can never, never be English' (Mullard 1973: 17). Race relations policy by the mid-1960s was undoubtedly influenced by the civil rights movement and riots in cities in the USA. Bleich (2003), in a study of race politics in

Britain, considered that at this time potentially troubling race issues needed action to avoid images of cities in flames. Overall, assimilation aspirations did not last long within official policy making. By the later 1960s educational policy documents were using a language of adjustment, integration and equal opportunity.

Education policy in the 1960s

The post-Second World War education system in the UK was regarded as central to the creation of a welfare state intended to redistribute resources more fairly and encourage economic growth. From the 1940s to the 1970s, education policy was largely based on a liberal democratic consensus that governments should regulate and resource education to achieve more social justice and provide equal opportunity. Before the 1944 Education Act nearly 90 per cent of young people left school at 14, only 10 per cent achieved passes in public examinations and 5 per cent went into higher education. This Act emerged out of a consensus between a coalition government, the churches and the education service, and introduced secondary education to age 15, but with a separation of children at age 11 into grammar, secondary modern and technical schools, the latter strand remaining undeveloped. It soon became apparent that the Act benefited middle-class children, with some 80 per cent of mainly working-class children attending secondary modern schools, the middle classes dominating grammar schools with some concessions to the 'bright' working-class child, and the rich and influential sending their children into private education (Lawton 2005, Tomlinson 2002a).

The notion that children could be separated at 11 on the basis of measured intelligence or ability was soon challenged by research (Heim 1954) but the enduring belief that different social or racial groups could be designated as more or less intelligent cast a long and pernicious shadow into the 21st century. Even the liberal report by Lady Plowden and her colleagues in 1967 referred to the difficulty of deciding whether an immigrant child 'lacks intelligence or is suffering from culture shock or simply from inability to communicate' (Plowden Report 1967: 70). However, both the Newsom Report (1963) on the education of 13–16-year-olds and the Robbins Report on higher education (1963) rejected deterministic theories of intelligence. Newsom noted that 'intellectual talent is not a fixed quantity but a variable that can be modified by social policy and educational approaches' (Newsom Report 1963: para. 15), and in a foreword the Conservative Minister of Education, Edward Boyle, wrote that all children should have an equal opportunity to 'develop intelligence'. Research from the 1950s also demonstrated that social class had a major influence on educational achievement and that school segregation and school practices of streaming and setting disadvantaged the children of manual, working-class parentage (Floud *et al.*

1956, Mays 1962). Despite this, many teachers found it hard to divest themselves of what later came to be known as low expectations of working-class and immigrant children. Until the early 1960s there were no public examinations in the secondary modern schools and it was not until 1962 that a Certificate of Secondary Education (CSE) was offered alongside the O level exam. While offering all children a secondary education up to 15 (16 in 1973), the 1944 Act did not promote equality of opportunity for working-class children to receive a balanced and well-resourced education, and the inner-city schools which a majority of immigrant children entered in the early 1960s were poorly resourced schools never intended to offer public examinations or high levels of education.

Nevertheless the 1960s was a remarkably optimistic decade in education. Disquiet over selection at 11+ led to a broad political consensus that comprehensive schools be established and higher education expanded, and a government circular in 1965 requested all local authorities to submit plans for reorganisation. A majority did this but with no specific requirement, some authorities procrastinated so that into the 2000s some 15 retained full selection and 21 partial selection at age 11. Anthony Crosland, Education Minister in 1965, was vocally liberal in his view that selection for secondary education should end and all political parties recognised that educating more young people to higher levels was an economic necessity. For many teachers, pupils and parents, the 1960s was a time of positive innovation, with a Schools Council for the Curriculum and Examination, established in 1964, working on curriculum change, requirements that in future all teachers should be educated to degree level, and the Plowden Report recommending a more child-centred approach to education and the creation of Educational Priority Areas with extra funding in disadvantaged city areas (Plowden Report 1967). Despite shortcomings, it was also a period when many schools began to give some consideration as to how to educate racial minorities in a system designed to give white elites priority. In some ways the 1960s could be regarded as the 'Liberal Hour' of education, when, as with immigration, different political reactions and leadership with less pandering either to elite pressure groups or to popular prejudice, could have set Britain on a path to a more equitable society. But optimism based on beliefs that a democratic society should educate all its young people rather than selected elites, was always under attack from a right wing dedicated to retaining a traditional, hierarchical education system. Both during the decade and subsequently, the 1960s were portrayed as a period of liberal anarchism when traditions were destroyed and educational standards lowered. Headteachers of grammar schools and their associations were at the forefront of campaigns to retain selection, and the national media began to demonise comprehensive schools as 'blackboard jungles', a term redolent with the primitive savagery depicted in 19th-century imperial literature (Tomlinson 1989). The demon of lowered standards was depicted in fearsome detail in a series of unfortunately named 'Black Papers' published by right-wing academics and political advisors between 1969 and 1977 (Cox and Boyson 1977), which resurrected deterministic theories of intelligence and eugenic views of the poor. Poverty and low educational performance were explained in terms of working-class innate incapacity and feckless behaviour. While Black Paper writers blamed the poor for their situation, liberal policies advocated compensatory education and remedial education to prevent cycles of disadvantage and cultures of poverty recurring. There was little discussion, in educational circles, of the macroeconomic conditions that create poverty and disadvantage or of political failures over redistributive social justice.

Educational responses to minority group children

Educational responses to immigrant and minority group children were, during the 1960s, linked closely to political views of the relationship of minorities to the majority society (Kirp 1979, Tomlinson 1983a). But Britain was not alone in its contradictory response to migration and the incorporation of migrant children. Post-war movement of racial and ethnic groups around the world had led to world-wide debate about the merit of assimilation versus pluralistic co-existence, particularly in the area of education. The idea that a nation-state should consist of one majority culture, with minorities abandoning their original cultures in order to become effective citizens was originally espoused by both liberals and traditionalists, and education was regarded as a major vehicle to bring this about. The second report of the government's Commonwealth Immigrants Advisory Council encapsulated this view in 1964, asserting that:

> A national system of education must aim at producing citizens who can take their place in society properly equipped to exercise rights and perform duties the same as those of other citizens . . . a national system cannot be expected to perpetuate the values of immigrant groups.
>
> (CIAC 1964)

But assimilation ideologies were challenged as ethnic revitalisation and civil rights protest movements emerged world wide during the 1960s (Bhatnager 1981, Banks and Lynch 1986). Within these movements racial discrimination and racism were recognised as major factors in perpetuating educational inequalities. In Britain, a first generation of settlers had strong incentives to move towards absorption into a society that appeared to offer social and economic mobility for their children, but soon realised that physical and cultural difference meant a denial of equal educational opportunities, at best through ignorance and naïvety on the part of educationalists and at worst through overt and covert discrimination. Black and Asian protest movements against injustice in employment and education developed during the 1960s, particularly after a visit to England by Martin Luther

King, Jr in 1964. A North London West Indian Parents Association was particularly active in voicing concerns over the education of black children, and in 1968 was one of 50 organisations forming a Black Peoples Alliance (Sivanandan 1982).

There was initially no central policy or planning to meet the needs of immigrant children in the British school systems. The DES later defended this on the grounds that 'neither the scale of future immigration not patterns of settlement could be seen with any assurance until the early 1960s' (DES 1971b: 14). The major central response was to voice concern that the concentration of immigrant children in some schools would be detrimental to indigenous children and hinder English language acquisition. The absorption of immigrant children in the 1960s was spurred on by the realisation that more families had arrived in an attempt to 'beat the ban' on migration imposed by the 1962 Immigration Control Act and that concentration in inner-city areas with a deprived working class could create social and educational problems. A major issue was that, although mainly created by housing policies at the time, 'coloured' settlement, particularly in inner-city areas, would increase as white families moved out. Rex and Moore, studying housing in Birmingham in the 1960s, noted that 'the visitor to Birmingham in the early 1960s could not but be struck by the way racial problems dominated public discussion' (Rex and Moore 1967: 19), including one suggestion from a local councillor that immigrants should be licensed in order to guarantee their good behaviour! The 1965 White Paper on immigration did refer to 'excessive and undesirable concentrations of Commonwealth immigrants' which should be broken up (ibid.: 18) and the Birmingham Association of Schoolmasters lamented that racial enclaves were here to stay, leading to concentrations of immigrant children in some schools.

At this time the English education system was largely decentralised, with some 146 local education authorities responsible for all educational administration and planning, distribution of funds, school organisation and staffing. The potential for different authorities to respond in different ways to the arrival of immigrant children was obvious. However, central government assumed that dispersing immigrant children out of their local areas was desirable, given that by 1963 white parents in Southall, London had already protested to the Minister of Education about the large number of immigrant children in two primary schools. The Minister of Education had made a personal visit to Southall and later reported to the House of Commons that some schools were 'irretrievably immigrant' and that a limit of 30 per cent of such children would be desirable in the future (Hansard 685, November 1963). The second report of the Commonwealth Immigrants Advisory Council (CIAC) in February 1964 recommended the dispersal of the children on the grounds that their presence affected the rate of progress of other children and also prevented their assimilation into 'normal' British school life.

> We are satisfied from evidence that we have received that educational problems are created by a rapid influx of a large number of immigrant children . . . the presence of a high proportion of immigrant children in one class . . . hampers the progress of the whole class. . . . If a school has more than a certain percentage of immigrant children among its pupils the whole character and ethos of the school is altered, immigrant pupils will not get as good an introduction to British life as in a normal school.
> (CIAC 1964, para. 25)

In 1965 the DES produced Circular 7/65 on *The Education of Immigrants*, which included a section entitled 'Spreading the Children'. This recommended no more than one-third immigrant children in a class or school and that dispersal between schools should be adopted by local authorities. The proposals in the Circular were incorporated into the 1965 government White Paper (Home Office 1965) and dispersal became an official policy recommendation. Few LEAs took up the suggestion of dispersal by bussing, most complaining about transport costs, and by 1970 only 11 authorities bussed children (Townsend 1971). Although five authorities with numbers of immigrant children – Bradford, Ealing, Hounslow, Huddersfield and West Bromwich – bussed children, the ILEA and Birmingham, who had the largest number, rejected bussing. The policy attracted considerable criticism until it was finally ruled to be illegal in 1975 after a court case involving the Race Relations Boards versus Ealing LEA (Kogan 1975). American scholars Kirp (1979) and Killian (1979) both pointed out that while in the USA bussing was hailed as a victory for justice and a defeat for racism, in Britain the eventual ruling that it was discriminatory was hailed as a victory over racism. The difference between the countries was that bussing in England was only one-way, there was no suggestion that white children be bussed. Kirp was also of the opinion that bussing failed because it was an explicit policy, whereas British race and schooling policy, as with other social policies, preferred to be largely inexplicit, eventually subsuming immigrant problems under those of general disadvantage, The stress on dispersal meant that the public were not informed of positive work being done in local authorities and in schools with large numbers of immigrant children. Spring Grove School in Huddersfield, which had introduced intensive English teaching, was documented as very successful (Burgin and Edson 1967) and in 1960 Birmingham LEA set up a department for teaching English which pioneered peripatetic teaching. Dispersal policies and fear of immigrant concentration set the scene for the future stigmatisation of schools with large numbers of immigrant and minority children, leading one black journalist to ask later 'Who's afraid of ghetto schools?' (*Race Today*, January 1975), given that all-white schools were never regarded as white ghettoes.

Policy responses in the early 1960s were hampered by lack of information on actual numbers of immigrant children. From 1966 the DES decided to require schools to provide statistical information on children born outside the British Isles with parents born abroad, and children born in the UK whose parents had come within the previous ten years, mixed-race immigrant children being excluded. The thinking behind this was that after ten years the children would not require any special treatment. The first statistics showed that in 1966 1.8 per cent of the school population were immigrant (131,043). This figure rose by January 1970 to 3.3 per cent (263,710). There were wide variations between authorities, in 1969 the outer London boroughs of Brent and Haringey having 26 per cent and 28 per cent immigrant children on roll, and inner London boroughs Islington and Hackney 24 per cent and 26 per cent. Half of LEAs had no immigrant children in their schools and only 9,907 out of over 28,000 schools took in immigrant children in that year. By 1972 the DES had decided that the figures were inaccurate and of little help in distributing funding, and collection of statistics was discontinued from that year. More accurate numbers on minority pupils in schools and their achievements was not collected until 2002 with the introduction of a collection of information on pupil level attainment data (PLASC) alongside information on social class and ethnicity.

One specific government policy to emerge in the mid-1960s was that of grants made by the Home Office (not the DES) to local authorities via Section 11 of a 1966 Local Government Act for any special provision as a 'consequence of the presence within their area of substantial numbers of immigrants from the Commonwealth whose language and customs differ from those of the community' (Local Government Act 1966: S 11). Dorn and Hibbert (1987: 59) later characterised Section 11 funding as a bizarre saga exhibiting the characteristics of a TV soap opera. They related the funding to the Labour government's realisation of the depth of anti-immigrant feeling in the country, and the need for quicker assimilation of immigrants. Member of Parliament Roy (later Lord) Hattersley expressed the view that the language and customs of immigrants were both a cause of their disadvantage and an obstacle to assimilation. He hoped that when Section 11 money was distributed the Secretary of State would bear in mind that as well as providing English classes it would 'remind parents of their new obligations in Britain . . . it is essential to teach these children basic British customs, basic British habits, and if one likes, basic British prejudices . . . if they are to live happily and successfully in an integrated way in this community' (Hansard col. 1336, 1966). The notion of teaching British prejudice was certainly bizarre, given the demonstrable prejudice against immigrants. Grant aid to LEAs was at a 50 per cent level in 1967, £1.4 million that year, raised in 1968 to a 75 per cent level, and was originally intended to support extra staff in education and social services. Fifteen years later the funding was £46 million between authorities and was still the only money directed exclusively at alleviating what was by then described as racial disadvantage (Home Affairs Committee 1981).[2]

HMI and English for immigrants

Although with hindsight it is easy to disparage the often naïve and patronising response of educationalists in the 1960s towards the incorporation of immigrant children into schools, historical credit should be given in particular to members of Her Majesty's Inspectorate (HMI), highly regarded at this period as independent of the Ministry of Education, and offering Ministers considered advice backed by evidence.[3] Taking the view that 'The most urgent single challenge facing the schools concerned is that of teaching English to immigrant children' (DES 1971a: 9), in 1963 HMI produced a pamphlet on English teaching methods and encouraged the projects set up by the Schools Council to produce materials for teaching non-English speakers. Organised by June Derrick, the Leeds University project on *English for the Children of Immigrants* (Derrick 1967) produced *Scope* materials for use in schools with children of mainly Asian origin. A further project at Birmingham University developed materials for teaching English to West Indian children, accompanied by much argument over the use of Creoles, dialect and *Black British English* (Sutcliffe 1982). Indeed, one writer considered that by the end of the 1960s 'Language is used effectively by members of certain West Indian sub-cultures as a particularly effective way of resisting assimilation . . . it becomes an aggressive assertion of racial and class identities' (Hebdige 1976: 46). HMI encouraged specialist language teachers who came together to form an Association for Teachers of English to Pupils from Overseas (ATEPO), organised five conferences in LEAs between 1966 and 1968, encouraged initial teacher training courses and welcomed the setting up of the Educational Priority Areas (EPAs) that the Plowden Report had suggested. Some 156 areas in 51 LEAs were designated as priority areas and HMI concluded that 'many immigrant children living in areas of deprivation will benefit' (DES 1971b: 13). HMI also welcomed the Urban Aid programme, set up by the Labour government in 1968, partly as a response to Enoch Powell's inflammatory speeches. Initially over £20 million was made available to local authorities on the basis of overcrowded housing and the presence of over 6 per cent immigrant children on school rolls. Capital projects included reception centres and language centres for immigrant children. HMI encouraged the setting up of a committee to examine the needs of young immigrants, which produced a report on *Immigrants and the Youth Service* (Hunt 1967), and in 1969 carried out their own survey on the assessment of pupils from overseas (DES 1971a). By the early 1970s HMI was able to draw together information on policies and practices during the 1960s in two publications, *The Education of Immigrants* (DES 1971b) and *The Continuing Needs of Immigrants* (DES 1971c). These documented general DES policy, the response of schools, local authorities and voluntary groups, special education, teacher training, further education and the youth service and careers guidance, and later the response to what by 1971 were referred to as second-phase immigrant pupils – those needing further English language teaching. Section 11 funding was not mentioned, as it came via the Home Office.

Most importantly, at the end of the 1960s, HMI encouraged the Education Department to fund research into the education of immigrant children. The results of these projects, carried out at the Slough-based National Foundation for Educational Research (NFER), provided the most comprehensive information on how LEAs had organised during the decade to meet the needs of what were eventually referred to as multiracial schools, what was happening in the schools, and how the schools were viewed by teachers and pupils. Commissioned in 1969, the NFER researchers sent out questionnaires to all 146 LEAs, receiving full returns from 71 and partial returns from 16 who had all made arrangements for receiving immigrant children in their schools (Townsend 1971). In a second phase 200 primary and secondary schools were surveyed (Townsend and Brittan 1972). NFER was also commissioned by the Schools Council from 1972 to carry out a study of curriculum development in multiracial schools (Townsend and Brittan 1973). Apart from HMI, the National Union of Teachers, National Association of Schoolmasters and the National Association of Head Teachers all gave support and advice, on the assumption that without information schools could not incorporate immigrant children equitably. The Townsend surveys provided information on LEA arrangements for reception, placement, English language teaching, assessment and selection, teacher preparation, finance and home–school relations, reporting that 'in some cases arrangements are deliberately played down because of the possibility of drawing attention to the immigrant community in areas of particular sensitivity or diverting resources from the general demand' (ibid.: 109). Claims that any resources offered to immigrants or minorities meant less funding for the majority have been a continuous theme since the 1960s.

The schools survey reported that, by the turn of the decade, multiracial schools regarded teaching English to non-English-speaking children as a major task, plus a need to improve assessment techniques, home–school contacts, and teacher preparation. Indeed 'the outstanding feature . . . is the lack of preparation of teachers for such an important task as teaching in multiracial schools' (Townsend and Brittan 1972: 138). Incomprehension and ignorance of other languages and cultures and parental expectations on the part of teachers, and similar incomprehension by parents of the school system were noted. Conflicts over, for example, West Indian assumptions that physical punishment was a necessity, and Indian and Pakistani desire for different treatment for girls were documented. Although in a small study in Sparkbrook, Birmingham pre-1967, Jenny Williams had reported that the schools she visited saw themselves as 'a socializing, anglicising, integrating agency' teaching Christian values (Williams in Rex and Moore 1967: 237), schools in the larger NFER survey reported liberal attitudes towards religion, with arrangements made for the withdrawal of non-Christian children from religious education and the morning 'act of worship' (both requirements under the 1944 Education Act). Also, if requested, special arrangements were being made for Muslim children to have visits from an Imam, prayer meetings and mosque attendance. While some reported comments from teachers contributed to stereotyping of children, with references to the warmth and ebullience of the West Indian character, plus their sporting prowess, and the gentleness of Indian and Pakistani girls, HMI were of the opinion that 'a great deal of dedicated and successful work with immigrant pupils was being carried out by an increasing number of teachers in schools and colleges' (DES 1971a: 118). As with much of the early research on education and immigration, the voice of parents was absent, and the researchers did not appear to be aware of the community associations and publications articulating parental concerns.

Testing, achievement and ESN

Children of New Commonwealth parentage had barely arrived in the British School system(s) before researchers began to conduct psychometric studies purporting to measure their ability, achievements, potential or 'intelligence' using standardised (on white populations) verbal and non-verbal tests, and standardised group tests of attainment in reading and mathematics. One of the first reviews of the research literature was by Goldman and Taylor (1966). Further reviews of testing, assessment and attainment research carried out during the 1960s and 1970s can be found in Verma and Bagley (1979), Tomlinson (1980, 1983a), Taylor (1981), Taylor and Hegarty (1985).[4] Most of the studies from the early 1960s set out to compare the ability or performance of immigrant children with individual or groups of white, mainly urban and working-class, indigenous children. Assumptions that the experiences of the children were roughly similar and fair comparisons could be made were dubious in the extreme. Given that a debate on the racial politics, educational value and morality of IQ and other forms of psychometric testing had been in progress both in the USA and Europe for some decades, and test results had been used consistently in the USA to denigrate immigrant and black groups, much of the 1960s research can be regarded as politically naïve and damaging to the education of immigrant children in Britain.

Research carried out in the early 1960s by a Canadian Professor, Phillip Vernon, comparing English boys in England with boys in Jamaica, helped legitimate comparisons which initially were usually between simple categories of white, West Indian and Asian, although some early studies differentiated immigrant background. Vernon's later studies in England were particularly noted by HMI in their education surveys, including a 1967 study of immigrant pupils in London schools from which he concluded that the mean IQ of children who had been in the country for six years or more was higher than those who had had less than two years schooling, a score of IQ 91 against 76 (Vernon 1968). HMI also recorded instances of children with no 'speech' assessed with low IQs, which amazingly increased as the children learned English. Some of the early testing studies certainly demonstrated John Rex's comment that 'psychometrics is the least sensitive and brashest of the empirical human studies' (Rex 1972: 168).[5] More sensitive research was initiated from 1966 by the Inner London Education Authority's Research and Statistics group. This group described immigrant children as West Indian, Pakistani, Indian, Greek and Turkish Cypriot and others (Little *et al.* 1968), noted the improvement of immigrant children's performance with length of schooling in Britain and white flight of able children from immigrant neighbourhoods. Research directed by A.H. Halsey in four EPA areas in the later 1960s and early 1970s, while documenting the lower school performance of immigrant children, did suggest that school processes might contribute to lower performance (Payne 1974).

The explanations put forward over the years to explain any lower educational performance of minority children have certainly run the gamut of probabilities. Lack of English, dialect interference, migration shock, low socio-economic status, family (dis)organisation, cultural difference, female dominance, male dominance, male absence, identity problems, low self-esteem, child-minding, low teacher expectations, school processes, stereotyping and racial hostility were some of the explanations purporting to explain what was variously described as educational retardation or under-achievement. Certainly, minority parents over the years have often borne the brunt of explanations for their children's performance couched in terms of their own economic or cultural or intellectual deficiencies, family structures, languages spoken, or lack of involvement with schools. From the 1960s it was also apparent that explanations offered for any lower educational performance of pupils of Asian origin were far more limited than those offered to explain the performance of West Indian children and were not sought in the areas of children's innate capacities. The early research 'may have unwittingly colluded in ensuring that Asian pupils were offered a fairer deal in education than pupils of West Indian origin' (Tomlinson 1983a: 59).

The debate on the 'heritability' of intelligence and the nature–nurture debates took on crucial significance for racial minorities with the 1969 publication of Jensen's article in the American Harvard Educational Review asking 'How can we boost IQ and scholastic ability?' (Jensen 1969), which concluded that compensatory education for black children might be misplaced given their lower mental capacities. Eysenck, a London University Professor, and a former student of Jensen, managed to conclude that 'American negroes' and the Irish have lower IQs, but this is due to 'crimes committed against their ancestors' (Eysenck 1971: 142). The importance of the IQ debate and 1960s studies was that they did to some extent 'bolster the belief that coloured children are intellectually inferior' (Bagley 1968: 44), and so did influence teacher beliefs concerning the innate intellectual capacities of immigrant children. The media publicity given to the writings of Jensen and Eysenck, and a consequent resurgence of genetic explanations for the lower educational performance of black children in particular, contributed to the concerns of West Indian parents in the 1960s.

From the point of view of the parents during the 1960s, the issue of the overplacement of black children in schools for the 'educationally subnormal' (ESN) became the dominant educational issue. It had symbolic significance in that it symbolised the apparent underachievement of their children in the English school system, and contributed to anxieties among first generation immigrant parents that their children might subsequently be allocated to inferior status and employment. The category of educationally subnormal was one of 11 statutory 'categories of handicap' defined in 1945,[6] encompassing children previously described as defective, retarded or backward, children being assessed by psychological, medical and educational personnel and referred to special schools. The categories of handicap were not abolished until the 1981 Education (Special Education) Act, when the concept of Special Educational Need (SEN), as suggested by the Warnock Committee, became a general descriptive category (DES 1978). From the 1950s ESN schools had become places where children with learning and behaviour problems too difficult for mainstream schools to deal with were quickly consigned. By 1965 the North London West Indian Association was expressing concern at the disproportionate numbers of West Indian children placed in ESN schools relative to the proportion in the total school population.

These numbers were first noted in an ILEA inspection report in 1966. That year the percentage of immigrant (mainly West Indian) children in the authority's special schools was 23.3 per cent compared to 13 per cent in all the primary and secondary schools. By September 1967 this had risen to 28.4 per cent, when a survey of 22 special schools was carried out by the inspectorate (ILEA 1968). The headteachers felt that a misplacement was four times more likely in the case of immigrant children and that this was largely due to problems with assessment. They also thought children were referred to them more for behavioural than educational reasons, and that although the 'IQ' of the West Indian children was about the same as that of non-immigrants, the West Indians were more likely to be 'noisy and hyperactive' (ILEA 1968: 3). The headteachers 'recognized the importance of easy and friendly contacts between schools and immigrant parents' and reported that West Indian parents were least likely among all groups to show a lack of interest in their children's education. In their 1971 report HMI noted that 'very little has been written about the problems involved in the special education of immigrants' (DES 1971b: 64) and few authorities collected statistics, although one special school in an unnamed authority recorded 49 per cent of mainly West Indian children in the school compared to

28 per cent in all schools. HMI rejected low IQ as an explanation but referred instead to behaviour problems, 'pidgin English' and cultural deprivation as reasons for slow learning.

In 1969 the North London West Indian Association met with the Chair of Haringey LEA and in January 1970 lodged a complaint of racial discrimination against the authority with the Race Relations Board. The Board found no evidence of an unlawful act, but criticised the use of IQ tests. West Indian parental anxieties appeared crystallised when Bernard Coard gave a speech in 1970 to the Caribbean Education and Community Workers Association, later publishing the paper as *How the West Indian Child is made ESN in the British School System* (Coard 1971). Coard criticised IQ tests, low teacher expectations and pointed to the negative self-image black children acquire in a hostile white society.[7] By the end of the 1960s black parents were certainly aware that the school system appeared unable to teach their children to levels they expected, had developed a number of protest groups and a number of supplementary schools were already in operation. These tended to be named after leaders of recently independent countries – the Kwame Nkrumah supplementary school – or black US civil rights fighters – the Marcus Garvey school and the Malcom X Montessori school.

Teachers and curriculum

Teachers are crucial agents in any society that is attempting successfully to incorporate immigrant and minority group children into the education system and offer them equal opportunity to learn. In a society in which the majority are hostile to minorities, teachers also have a key role in educating the majority towards knowledge, understanding and acceptance of minorities as equal citizens. However, it became clear during the 1960s that teachers, in both state and private schools, had no clear conception of the importance of their role in a multi-ethnic society. This was not surprising, given that most had themselves been educated via an ethnocentric curriculum in which maps on classroom walls displayed over a quarter of the world (in pink) as part of the British Empire. As historians of curriculum have noted, values comprising elements of nationalism and racial arrogance, combined with beliefs in superior moral and Christian benevolence towards imperial subjects, persisted into the late 20th century (MacKenzie 1986, Tomlinson 1989). While a majority of teachers may have been well meaning and liberal, evidence accumulated that teachers lacked knowledge of minority children and their backgrounds, and their attitudes to and expectations of the children were influenced by their racial beliefs and also their lower expectations of children from manual working classes. The publication in the USA of *Pygmalion in the Classroom* (Rosenthal and Jacobson 1968) indicated the complex relationship between teacher expectations and pupil reactions in terms of academic performance and behaviour, and research was soon demonstrating that teachers in Britain had lower expectations of black pupils and often exhibited negative patterns in teaching them. Coard (1971) suggested that teachers in the 1960s seriously underestimated the abilities of all black children, with the children responding by building up resentment and emotional blocks to learning.

Evidence suggested that initially most teachers were committed to notions of assimilation, but were aware that race, as defined by skin colour, constituted something of a barrier. They perceived the needs of minority pupils as mainly linguistic, and the teaching of English to non-English speaking children as the major task (Townsend and Brittan 1972). But there was also growing awareness during the decade that in the absence of policy direction, apart from actions which implied that immigrant children constituted a problem for schools, teachers had been left to respond to the development of education for a multiracial society on their own. Nandy (1971) pointed out that while 'assimilationist fervour' declined during the 1960s, there were four separate problems facing teachers at the time. First, the teaching of English; second, helping immigrant children adjust to a new society; third, understanding what it was like to belong to a minority group marked out by colour, religion or culture; and fourth, what were the educational needs of a multiracial society, in which white and non-white would live together. The first collection of essays by practising teachers in the 1960s, *The Multiracial School* (1971) edited by McNeal and Rogers (Julia McNeal being former Labour leader Hugh Gaitskell's daughter), indicated that without much help from central government some teachers were taking seriously issues of organisation, curriculum and resources, and were also aware that white English children needed an education to combat 'the indifference and hostility which exists between different national and racial groups' (McNeal and Rogers 1971: 15). There was also an awareness that hostility could exist between minority groups and 'conscious efforts had to be made if children were not to group themselves along ethnic lines' (ibid.: 34). Teacher attitudes and expectations, and their willingness and ability to make changes, depended largely on the preparation they received during their training. Evidence suggested that preparation for what was a momentous change in the school population was (and has never been) regarded as an urgent priority. By the mid-1960s a few Colleges of Education were beginning to offer optional courses for the teaching of immigrant children, Maurice Craft at Edge Hill College being a pioneer in such courses and later with courses in 'training the trainers' (Craft 1981, 1986, 1996). Initially, training courses presumed that only teachers of immigrant or minority children would need any special training, and it was not until the later 1960s that there was some recognition at government level that 'all teachers be equipped to prepare children for their life in a multicultural society' (Select Committee on Race Relations and Immigration 1969, para. 214). A rhetoric that more immigrant teachers be employed was not matched by any collection of numbers, and while the Ministry of Labour was issuing vouchers to teachers trained abroad, many LEAs would not employ them. An NUT survey in 1967 reported that immigrant teachers faced racial discrimination in their employment (National Union of Teachers 1967).

Curriculum change for what at the end of the 1960s was variously being described as a multiracial, multicultural or multi-ethnic society was minimal during the 1960s, perhaps best summed up by the headteacher who responded to Townsend and Brittan that 'I do not consider it the responsibility of an English state school to cater for the cultures and customs of a foreign nature' (Townsend and Brittan 1973: 13). But there was a growing awareness of tension between those who believed that an unproblematic British heritage and set of values should be reflected in the school curriculum, and those who believed it was time to reconsider a curriculum largely inherited from an imperial past. History and geography textbooks began to be recognised as presenting Europeans as devoted to the civilising and well-being of subordinate races, with one text still used in the 1960s stressing that 'under the guidance of Europeans, Africa is steadily being opened up . . . Europeans have brought civilization to the peoples of Africa' (Stembridge 1956: 347). Popular literature and cinema also legitimised notions of a superior white race. Tarzan stories (Burroughs 1919), later presented on film, television and in comics, provided a good example of the presentation of Anglo-Saxon superiority over 'savage natives in the jungle'. The early 20th-century public school curriculum, incorporating imperial patriotic pride, racial superiority and militarism, filtered down into the state education system. Studies of working-class youth noted that an ideology of imperialism made a direct appeal to boys for whom existing cultural traditions included fighting, gang warfare, and sexist assertions of masculinity (Willis 1977, Humphries 1981). The cultural values filtering down from the upper to the lower classes, still incorporated in the 1960s curriculum, encouraged beliefs in the economic, political and racial superiority of white Europeans, and goes some way towards explaining the xenophobia and racism which has continued to be part of the British heritage.

Summary

This chapter has illustrated the contradiction between policies designed to encourage immigrant labour to undertake low skill jobs and immigration control policies designed to limit entry of those defined as racially different. In a country reluctantly coming to terms with losing an Empire, and schooled within a curriculum that still emphasised imperial notions of the superiority of the 'white races', attempts to assimilate the children of former colonial immigrants were unlikely to be successful. The hostility towards immigrant children entering schools, with assertions that their presence lowered standards, can partly be explained by the status threat to those white working-class people who already felt threatened by industrial and social change. It must also be explained by the lack of political leadership in combating the sheer unpleasantness of the nationalistic, racist anti-immigrant lobby which marked the decade. Although there was legislation against overt racial discrimination, the stage was set for future decades when Crossman's 'fear of immigration' would dominate political debate. While the education system was changing in a more egalitarian direction during the 1960s, and there were considerable efforts made by HMI, some LEAs, schools and teachers to incorporate immigrant children fairly, the belief that their presence constituted a problem, and the lingering pseudo-scientific beliefs in the intellectual inferiority of black children also marked the decade. The high expectations of parents that migration would improve the education and employment prospects for their children quickly became perceived as unlikely, and parents began to take action via supplementary schooling and legislation. Positive efforts were made to teach English to non-English speakers, but children of Asian origin did appear to benefit more from their positive treatment of language problems than pupils of West Indian origin, and the spectre of teachers' lower expectations of black and working-class children entered educational debate. Although by the end of the 1960s there was some recognition that integration of minorities without assimilation might be possible, the increased hostility to racial minorities during the 1970s, and the reactions of the minorities themselves, contributed to the fears of enacting explicit education policies and the subsuming of immigrant children under the label of disadvantage.

Notes

1. The Institute of Race Relations was an organisation founded in 1958 to facilitate the 'study of relations between the races everywhere'. With grants from the Nuffield Foundation and elsewhere a number of studies were commissioned, carried out and published during the 1960s and early 1970s. The Rose *et al.* (1969) survey was the largest publication. From 1971 conflict in the Institute and a 'revolution' of the staff led to funds being withdrawn and the Institute becoming a smaller Marxist-oriented organisation headed by A. Sivanandan. The Institute's Journal *Race* became *Race and Class*, its first editor being Darcus Howe, later a TV producer and documentary maker. In 2006 the Institute's excellent library collection was moved to Warwick University.
2. Section 11 of the 1966 Local Government Act was for many years the only specific race-related educational policy, designed to offer help to local authorities with increasing numbers of 'immigrants from the Commonwealth whose language or customs differ from those of the community'. The grant was the focus of a series of reviews and changes over the decades, the Home Affairs Committee in 1981 recommending that the grant be expanded to include all ethnic minorities, including Greek and Vietnamese children. In 1994 it became part of a Single

Regeneration Budget for deprived areas, and in 1999 became the Ethnic Minority Achievement Grant (EMAG).

3. In particular, HMI John Singh, Joe Mundy and Eric Bolton worked to persuade the DES to produce policies that would benefit immigrant children.
4. In 1980 I read and overviewed almost all the studies on immigrant and minority testing, assessment and performance over 20 years. This was published in Tomlinson (1980). My assumed uncritical acceptance of the vocabulary of underachievement was criticised by Troyna (1984) and Figueroa (1992).
5. In replying to criticism that there was no research offering evidence against work which proposed the intellectual inferiority of black people, John Rex (1972) noted that the only convincing evidence would be to subject a group of white Americans and Europeans to slavery for 200 years in West Africa, downgrade white culture and language, deny them education, and then after limited emancipation compare their educational performance on tests standardised in West African countries. No funding has been forthcoming for this study!
6. The categories were reduced to ten and in 1970 the educationally subnormal category was subdivided into ESN (severe) and ESN (mild or moderate).
7. Coard, originally a teacher in a special school, returned to his home island of Grenada as Minister of Education. He was implicated in a political coup and after the invasion of the island by the USA he spent 19 years in prison. He continued to teach other prisoners and write about education. His 1971 paper and other contributions were reprinted in a 2005 book (Richardson 2005).

Post-imperial anxieties (1970–1980)

> The possibility has to be faced that there is at work in this country, the familiar cycle of cumulative disadvantage by which relatively low-paid jobs for first generation immigrants go hand in hand with poor and overcrowded living conditions and a depressed environment. If job opportunities, educational facilities and housing are all poor the next generation will grow up less well equipped to deal with the difficulties facing them . . . It is the Government's duty to prevent these morally unacceptable and socially divisive inequalities from hardening into entrenched patterns. It is inconceivable that Britain in the last quarter of the twentieth century should confess herself unable to secure for a small minority of around a million and a half citizens their full and equal rights.
>
> (Home Office 1975: 3–4)

> If we went on as we are, by the end of the century there would be four million people of the New Commonwealth or Pakistan here. Now that is an awful lot and I think it means that people are rather afraid that this country might be swamped by people with a different culture.
>
> (Margaret Thatcher, interview on Granada Television, 30 January 1978)

By the 1970s, traditions of a paternalistic imperial conservatism, liberal human rights and brotherhood of unionised labour were disappearing and all political parties were in agreement that immigration, either of workers or their families, from the non-white countries of the former British Empire should be limited. Despite some recognition of discrimination and resulting inequalities it was taken for granted that any policies specifically directed at immigrants and their children would be electorally unprofitable. This chapter documents the continuation of an anti-immigrant ideology evident in all political parties, especially the fascist National Front party, the linkage with the notion of an exclusive British identity, and the developing reactions of a younger generation becoming more race conscious. Educational policies during the 1970s are briefly outlined, noting that by the end of the 1970s moves towards non-selective education and curriculum change had become a focus for charges that educational standards were too low and had failed to produce a literate and skilled workforce. A desire to play down any special arrangements or resources for immigrants, noted by Townsend in the late 1960s (Townsend and Brittan 1973: 109), now underpinned an official education policy which subsumed minority issues under the label of disadvantage. Immigrant children were assumed to 'share with indigenous children the disadvantages associated with an impoverished environment' (DES 1974: 2), a position adhered to despite evidence that minorities experienced problems different from and in excess of those experienced by a white majority.

The chapter discusses the subsuming of immigrants within the category of disadvantage, the continuing issue of the lower school achievements of minorities, and an increasing acceptance of pluralistic perspectives in which issues concerning the retention of minority language via mother-tongue teaching and bilingualism assumed importance. It also covers the emergence of a curriculum reform movement which recognised that preparing children for a multiracial society would need changing from one produced in an imperial hey-day, and parental and teacher actions and reactions. In 1979 the Conservatives won power for the next 18 years, and although Margaret Thatcher had voiced populist fears that the nation might be 'swamped' by different cultures, she did reluctantly allow a committee set up to investigate the education of ethnic minority children to continue (DES 1981a). By the end of the decade various committees and commissions had made 228 policy proposals to improve the education of minorities and prepare all pupils for life in a multiracial society (Tomlinson 1986). On a theoretical level, the 1970s and the 1980s further illustrated the Weberian view that most societies incorporate relatively permanent conflict groups concerned with status and power as well as a market position within an economy. Status groups usually include a distinct culture and lifestyle and a hierarchy of perceived worth. Within the British Imperial social structure, created over some three hundred years, all classes in the 'mother country' came to regard themselves as being in a superior status position to colonial workers. In the 1970s white workers felt their status was lowered by the presence of non-white groups, which this imperial legacy had taught them to regard as inferiors. In addition, politicians did little to minimise the resentment on the part of those who felt that immigrant minorities took away scarce resources, and all social groups united to exclude immigrant minorities as potential members of any class (Rex and Tomlinson 1979: 13). The language of the decade still included immigrant, new Commonwealth, West Indian and Asian, but a political terminology of black and minority began to be used (see note 4).

Chronology of Acts and issues

1970 Conservatives elected. Circular 7/70 cancels the expectation that all secondary schools will become comprehensive.

1971 Immigration Act further restricts immigration. Right of abode limited to patrials, others to obtain a work permit and register with the police. UK Immigrants Advisory Service in operation. Home Office sets up Race Relations Research Unit.

1971 Julia McNeal and Margaret Rogers publish *The Multiracial School*, with chapters written by teachers. Eysenck publishes *Race, Education and Intelligence* suggesting that blacks and the Irish have lower IQs than other groups.

1971 DES Survey 10, *Potential and Progress in a Second Culture*, and Survey 13, *The Education of Immigrants*, outline policy objectives. Townsend publishes a survey of LEA responses to *Immigrant Pupils in England*.

1972 DES discontinues the collection of statistics on immigrant pupils. (With 3.3 per cent – 280,000 – recorded as immigrant.) School leaving age raised to 16.

1972 David Lane, Conservative Minister for Race Relations says Britain is an overcrowded island and no more immigrants should come. Expulsion of Ugandan Asians by Idi Amin. Enoch Powell predicts a national catastrophe if more immigrants arrive. 27,000 arrive from Uganda and 21,000 pass through 'camps'. Leicester city council reports that 'Leicester is full' and urges migrants to go elsewhere.

1973 Select Committee on Race Relations and Immigration produces a report on education, making 24 recommendations. Trevor McDonald becomes ITN's first black newsreader. (He retired in 2005.)

1973 West Bromwich by-election. National Front candidate comes third, ahead of the Liberal Party. War in the Asian subcontinent. Pakistan secedes from the Commonwealth. Bangladesh now a separate country.

1974 DES produces *Educational Disadvantage and the Needs of Immigrants*. Centre for Disadvantage set up in Manchester (closed 1980). Community Relations Commission (CRC) produces a pamphlet on the educational needs of minority group children with 12 recommendations. National Association for Multiracial Education set up (NAME).

1974 Second PSI report into *Racial Disadvantage in Britain* (Smith 1977) introduces the concept of indirect discrimination, taken up in 1976 Race Relations Act.

1974 Labour forms a minority government after a General Election. Roy Jenkins (Home Secretary again) announces an amnesty for illegal immigrants.

1975 Black parents and students movement set up in north London. Home Office White Paper on *Racial Discrimination* and Lord Bullock's report on *A Language for Life* published.

1976 Third Race Relations Act. Education is mentioned under sections 17–20, 36 and 71. Commission for Racial Equality (CRE) set up. Working party of Chief Education Officers seek alternative funding to Section 11 grants. Prime Minister Callaghan makes speech at Ruskin College attacking education as failing to prepare a workforce properly.

1976 Gurdip Singh Chaggar stabbed to death at a Southall bus stop. Police say it was not a racial crime. Enoch Powell says 'mugging' is a racial crime. The Archbishop of Canterbury (Coggan) concludes there must be limits to immigration. Shadow Home Secretary William Whitelaw says 'The British Empire has paid its debts' and calls for inner-city programmes to defuse racial tensions. Clashes between black youth and police at the Notting Hill carnival. Repeated at 1977 carnival.

1977 EEC Directive on *The Education of Children of Migrant Workers*.

1977 Select Committee on Race Relations and Immigration reports on *The West Indian Community*, makes eight recommendations on education and a call for an inquiry into the education of West Indian children. A DES Consultative Paper, *Education in Schools*, stresses that 'we are a multiracial and multicultural country'. The Inner London Education Authority produces the first LEA policy on multicultural education. Black Paper 5 (Cox and Boyson) attacks comprehensive education and 'Marxist infiltration' in education.

1977 National Front marches in London and Birmingham. In the Stechford and Ladywood by-elections in Birmingham, Liberals again beaten into third place by the National Front. Strikes by Asian workers at Grunwick Laboratories in London. OPCS census reports 1.77 million 'coloured population' (3.3 per cent of total population).

1978 Home Office replies to the Select Committee report on the *West Indian Community*, paras 17–24 on education. The government accepts the need for an inquiry into black school achievement. The Warnock Committee reports on *Special Educational Needs* – no mention of black parents and their concerns over special education. Viv Anderson becomes first black footballer to play for England.

1979 Rampton Committee set up to inquire into the education of children from ethnic minority groups. Conservatives win the General Election. Mrs Thatcher reluctantly allows the committee to continue.

1979 During confrontations at a National Front rally in Southall, London, an area of Asian settlement, Blair Peach, a teacher, is killed.

1981 Home Affairs Committee reports on *Racial Disadvantage* with 36 recommendations on education.

Politics and ideology

By the 1970s primary immigration from post-imperial countries had effectively been controlled by the employment voucher system. In distinguishing between 'patrials' with a father or grandfather born in Britain and the rest, which more or less separated white and non-white migrants, the 1971 Act went some way to satisfying the anti-immigration lobby. Attention turned towards controlling the admission of dependent wives, children and elderly parents and the 'threat' supposedly posed by a concentration of ethnic minority groups in inner cities. While immigrant minorities had settled in cities where their labour was sought, and discriminatory housing policies and a white flight had largely ensured spatial segregation, the presence of former imperial subjects, from a variety of rural and urban backgrounds, and with a variety of languages, religions and cultural traditions, was openly regarded as a 'racial threat' to a British national identity. Although Conservative leader Edward Heath had asserted in 1970 that 'there was no reason why cultural diversity should not be combined with loyalty to this country' (Heath 1970), both local and national conservative groups gained media attention asserting notions of patriotism and national homogeneity that excluded non-whites. Following Powell's[1] populist appeals for a white racial identity, a group of Conservative MPs in the 'Monday Club', campaigned for black repatriation, and against a 'race industry' working for and supporting race relations acts and commissions. The journal *The Salisbury Review* provided a venue for intellectual discussion of an exclusive racial nationalism. Roger Scruton, conservative philosopher and editor of the journal, offered critical discussion of the nature of multiculturalism (Scruton 1986).

Immigration and antagonism to the settlement of minorities were brought together in a parliamentary debate in July 1976, reported in the *Guardian* newspaper under the headline 'Racism pollutes the Commons' (Barker 1981: 12). Members of Parliament from the two major parties expressed varying degrees of racism against 'alien peoples' and called for control of numbers to allay 'genuine fears' of white constituents. The expulsion of Ugandan Asians by the dictator Idi Amin in 1972 had led to a further entrenchment of negative positions. Immigration was now a synonym for non-white settlement. Also the neo-Nazi National Front party[2] was making electoral gains, particularly in the West Midlands, in 1973 and 1977, with overtly anti-immigrant campaigns. Enoch Powell, although now representing an Ulster Unionist Northern Irish constituency, continued to stir white nationalist sentiment, predicting a national catastrophe if some 27,000 Asians from East Africa, mostly educated people with entrepreneurial skills, were allowed into Britain. On arrival many of these passed through special reception camps, and although Leicester city council announced that 'Leicester was full' and the migrants should go elsewhere, many did settle in the city, and subsequently rejuvenated business there. Powell also drew attention in 1976 to a report by Hawley, a civil servant, which referred to queues of dependants from the Indian subcontinent (divided by 1973 into India, Pakistan and Bangladesh) and possible illegal immigration. Later in the 1970s similar anti-immigrant agitation was stirred up against the entry of Asians deported from Malawi, and Vietnamese 'boat people' – refugees fleeing from wars in the former French Indo-China colonies. Both Conservative and Labour parties responded by producing papers and manifestos outlining further immigration controls and plans for entitlement to British citizenship. There was considerable wrangling over the entry of dependent wives, children and fiancées from the Indian subcontinent and a scandal when it was disclosed that some immigration officers had been subjecting women to a 'virginity test' to establish the credibility of their claims to entry as fiancées. By 1977 the Labour government had produced a Green Paper outlining proposals for a new Nationality Law, and the incoming Conservative government published a White Paper in 1980 setting out three categories of citizenship, with a British Nationality Act passed in 1981. This Act effectively marked the end of any obligations to people in the remnants of the British Empire.

Immigration control movements during the 1970s were linked to an emergent theory of nationalism – part of what Barker (1981) described as a new racism – and to a political pragmatic recognition that minority settlement in already deprived and disadvantaged inner-city areas would antagonise the white working classes. The former was encapsulated in the view that 'Britain is . . . not open to all comers with one foot in their old home and one in the new. It is the national home and birthright of its indigenous peoples' (Sherman 1978) and in Margaret Thatcher's well known 'swamping' speech made on television (30 January 1978) and reported widely in newspapers the following day. But the 1976 House of Commons debate had outlined a political consensus that numbers of immigrants needed controlling to encourage racial harmony and reduce the 'fears and resentments' of an indigenous inner-city population (Hansard 1976: 965).[3] Politicians in all parties did nothing to diminish the scapegoating of black and Asian settlers in city areas as being responsible for a decline in public services, and taking unfair shares of scarce resources, the opposite being nearer the truth as first generation migrants worked in low wage jobs, were denied council housing and took fewer social benefits. While industrial disputes did not become a major focus of racial tensions during the 1970s, Asian workers, especially women, were involved in disputes concerning low pay or lack of promotion to skilled work, notably at Imperial Typewriters in Leicester and Grunwick Laboratories in West London. They were supported by the long-standing Indian Workers Association and other immigrant associations, but the traditional unions were reluctant to consider specific problems of immigrant workers, and nervous of alienating white workers (Rex and Tomlinson 1979: Chapter 4).

However, the early 1970s Heath government and the mid-1970s Labour government did acknowledge that there was considerable racial discrimination against what was still described as the coloured population, living in major conurbations in disadvantaged circumstances, and a 1975 White Paper on *Racial Discrimination* was followed by the 1976 Race Relations Act. The Paper asserted that 'The time has come for a determined effort by Government, by industry and the unions, and by ordinary men and women, to ensure fair and equal treatment for all our people, regardless of their race, colour or national origins' (Home Office 1975: 2). The Act made direct and indirect discrimination unlawful in the areas of employment, training, education, housing, public services and advertising. Incitement to racial hatred had been covered in the 1965 Act and a Public Order Act. It became unlawful for any educational establishment to discriminate and allowed for provision of education to meet the particular needs of pupils from any ethnic or national group. A Commission for Racial Equality (CRE) was set up in place of the Community Relations Commission, with more powers to investigate complaints, the first Chair being former Conservative MP David Lane, whose views on race relations became more liberal during the 1970s, earning him the displeasure of Margaret Thatcher.

A major political issue in the 1970s was that of the actions and reactions of a younger second generation of immigrant descent, partially or wholly schooled in Britain. This was a decade in which a generation literally moved from being 'immigrant' to being 'ethnic minority', aware of the racism and disadvantages their parents faced, and their own possible disadvantages in obtaining equal rights to education and jobs. After the beginnings of an economic recession in 1973 and with increasing youth unemployment, research studies documented the racial disadvantages of both black and Asian young people in youth training schemes, job applications and obtaining employment (Home Affairs Committee 1981, Troyna and Smith 1982). However, although shared disadvantages, particularly to hostile policing, encouraged a younger generation to take on the shared political label of 'black', different trajectories and contrasts between the lifestyles and life chances of those of West Indian origin and those from the Asian subcontinent or other parts of the former empire were becoming clearer, and a second survey of minorities in Britain showed different patterns and responses to racial disadvantage (Smith 1977).[4]

By the 1970s recognition of their racial disadvantages led to assertions of a militant black identity, particularly by some young West Indians, influenced by civil rights and more militant movements in the USA, the Pan-African National Congress and the anti-apartheid African National Congress.[5] Asserting an identity via wearing symbols of the Rastafarian movement became popular and schools worried over allowing pupils to wear dreadlocks or Rasta hats. Some headteachers regarded 'black power' as a threat from which young black children needed protection (Tomlinson 1981: Chapter 3). Relations between the police and young black men deteriorated during the 1970s, police using 'sus' laws (questioning on suspicion of crime) against black males, and the tabloid media stoking up fears of black crime. A report on crime in Handsworth, Birmingham, in 1977 claimed that crime in the area was mainly committed by 'some 200 West Indian youths who have taken on the appearance of the followers of the Rastafarian Faith, by plaiting their hair in locks and wearing green, gold and red woollen hats' (Brown 1977). Gilroy, writing with others from a Marxist perspective, analysed the Rastafarian movement in Britain as 'a sophisticated expression of the critical consciousness which informs the black struggles' (Gilroy 1982),[6] and Rastafarian youth became a demon for the press and public, contributing to right-wing fears that 'the barbarians are at the gates' (Turner 1977). Disturbances at the Notting Hill carnivals in 1976 and 1977 created further media presentation of a threatening black presence, a view which was exploited by the National Front party, who did well in by-elections in the Midlands in 1977. However, the police did not consider the stabbing to death of a young Sikh, Gurdip Singh Chaggar, in Southall in 1976 to be a racial crime, a contrast with later recognition of race hate crime. There was also reluctance to bring any prosecutions when teacher Blair Peach, opposing the National Front at a rally in Southall, died from injuries in an altercation with the police. Towards the end of the decade, what the Home Affairs Committee described as a deteriorating state of race relations in Britain had been illustrated by what the press recorded as race riots, and government publications described as racial disturbances, which took place in 1980 in the St Paul's area of Bristol, and in 1981 in Brixton and Southall in London, Toxteth in Liverpool, in the West Midlands and other towns. These led the Home Affairs Committee to note 'dangers which will grow more serious through inaction. The dangers concern above all those young Asians and West Indians for the most part born in this country caught in the clash between the sometimes grim realities of their situation and their own and their parents expectations' (Home Affairs Committee 1981: vii). Grim realities could have included the existence of a cumulative principle, first described by Gunnar Myrdal (1969), whereby racist hostility and discrimination, once established, leads to conditions which justify the beliefs.

Education policy in the 1970s

Educational policies during the 1970s signalled a retrenchment from the attempted breakout from a selective, class-oriented system to more egalitarian and innovative schooling. Global economic issues put schooling under stress as the effects of a rise in oil prices and a recession affected wage structures and the employment of young people. Supporters of selective education and traditional teaching continued to suggest that non-selective education and progressive curriculum change, barely established by the 1970s, were lowering standards and failing to produce a literate workforce. In the Conservative government elected in 1970 Margaret Thatcher was made Education Secretary, her first action being to cancel Circular 7/65 and issue Circular 10/70, which left LEAs free to continue selective schooling. Her second action was to cancel free school milk! Despite antagonism to comprehensive reorganisation by the end of her tenure, the number of comprehensive schools doubled and over 60 per cent of children attended them. However, the retention of grammar schools meant that only half were genuine comprehensive schools, and grammar schools continued to be presented as the only schools able to preserve high standards. Despite promises of increased levels of education spending on nursery education, higher education and teaching degrees, the recession led to cuts in the education budget from 1973, the year that the school leaving age was raised to 16. This partly took care of youth unemployment, as did a series of Youth Training Schemes, set up under a Manpower Services Commission. The Labour government, elected in 1974, did revert to a more egalitarian agenda with a 1976 Act requiring all schools to become non-selective, integrating children with disabilities as far as possible, and abolishing the 154 direct grant schools, which since 1925 had educated mainly middle-class children with grants from central government. There was mostly cross-party support for the recommendations in the Bullock Report (1975), the report of a committee set up by Mrs Thatcher in 1972, that all schools should have a policy for 'language across the curriculum' and that minority languages should be recognised and supported. Another report on school governance recommended that school governing bodies be given more powers and parents be given more choice of school – measures incorporated into the Conservative 1980 Education Act.

Choice and standards became important ideological and policy concerns. Mrs Thatcher and Keith Joseph, Education Minister in the 1980s, set up a Centre for Policy Studies in 1975 which attacked comprehensive schools and a state monopoly on schooling. Joseph made a speech in Birmingham in 1974 in which he called for a reassertion of 'civilized values', blaming 'the bully boys from the left' who were apparently responsible for a decline in educational standards in schools and universities, and for delinquency, truancy and vandalism and a decline in national pride. He also asserted that 'our human stock is threatened by single mothers of low intelligence', and praised the 'brave woman' Mrs Jill Knight MP who 'speaks up when others speak their minds in private' – a reference to Mrs Knight's anti-immigrant stance (Joseph 1974). Joseph's speech brought an angry response from Max Morris, Past President of the National Union of Teachers, but the development of non-selective schooling was persistently linked to left-wing extremism.

By 1976 an education system which most politicians and employers had regarded as adequate while there were unskilled and semi-skilled jobs to fill, was condemned as inadequate by politicians of all parties. Labour Prime Minister James Callaghan, in a speech at Ruskin College in October 1976, attacked what he called the 'educational establishment' for failing to prepare young people for employment. One result of this prime ministerial intervention was to demoralise teachers, but much publicity was given to business and employers who argued that schools did not serve the needs of industry, and from this time educational policy became more closely linked to notions of industrial regeneration. Callaghan's criticisms of the education service pleased the right wing (Cox and Boyson 1977) but was regarded as something of an own goal by his party.[7] One view of the opposition to a common education and any curriculum change by those on the political right, was that egalitarian policies, by encouraging groups hitherto destined for lower levels of education and lower-status jobs, were undermining the authority of the state (Gamble 1988). Changes in the traditional family and gender roles, a decline in Britain's economic position, demands for citizenship rights and opportunities, especially those made by immigrant minorities, certainly worried many on the political right and some in the old traditional left.

The political left had never developed the democratic egalitarian ideals that were inherent in a common schooling with equalised opportunities and resources. Despite a commitment to comprehensive education there were no coherent plans to educate working-class and immigrant children to higher levels, or for dealing with a private sector that sustained privilege. The role of education in selecting and allocating children from minority groups to occupations and a status in the class society of the 1970s was crucial. Labour, as Lawton later pointed out (Lawton 2005) had always upheld a belief in meritocracy, where merit was intended to remove some deserving children from poor schools, rather than concentrating on improving schools and education for all. The urban schools most migrant and minority children attended during the 1970s were housed in deteriorating buildings, with high teacher turnovers, little access to playing fields or open spaces, and with a low-level curriculum, followed by low-level youth training courses with no guarantee of permanent work. Where there were selective grammar schools, minority children, especially black or Muslim, were less likely to be selected than white working-class children. It was unsurprising that minority parents developed strategies to overcome the poorer education that their children were undeniably offered during this decade, which included complaints to schools, LEAs and government committees, supplementary schooling, supporting selective schooling if there was the possibility that even one child in a family might be selected, buying private schooling and tutoring if affordable, and debating the possibility of segregated schooling.

Educational disadvantage and the needs of immigrants

From 1973 there was sustained pressure on central government to produce national policies and funding to deal with the incorporation and successful education of minority children. The House of Commons Select Committee on Race Relations and Immigration produced 24 policy recommendations in their 1973 report on *Education*. The report criticised the DES who 'had not been well-informed of what is being – or not being – done' both locally, nationally, and by teachers and unions, and 'were frequently struck by the haphazard way in which a critical part of human race relations has been dealt with' (Select Committee on Race Relations and Immigration 1973: 55). Collection of statistical information on numbers of children, imperfect though it was, had been discontinued in 1972 and the DES was dependent on local estimations as to how many children from various groups they were concerned with. The Select Committee, referring to the children as immigrant with ethnic backgrounds, documented arrangements made by Brent, Haringey, Ealing, Leicester, Liverpool and Bolton LEAs, noting that most authorities did not disperse children, were handicapped by lack of knowledge of numbers, concentrated on teaching English and had insufficient arrangements and funding for older students who now wanted further education. There was conflicting evidence given to the Committee from the National Union of Teachers and the National Association of Schoolmasters

(NAS). The former took a more international stance arguing that although it was debatable how far schools should 'transmit the cultural and religious values of any nation or race', the curriculum should have a wider international outlook and 'the future must lie in the concept of an education directed to the needs of a multiracial society and not the specific question of educating children from immigrant families' (ibid.: 21). The NAS, on the other hand, reported that 'many people would take the view that it is incumbent on immigrants to abandon their established cultural attitudes and seek total assimilation into . . . the British way of life', but they did acknowledge the antagonisms towards such assimilation and complained of a 'vicious cycle of mistrust which exists between white and coloured people in our country' (op. cit.: 22–3).

The response of the DES to this report (DES 1974) was optimistic and conciliatory that 'the education service has important contributions to make both to the well-being of immigrant communities . . . and the promotion of harmony between the different ethnic groups of which our society is now composed'. There was also some acknowledgment of a possible preference for minorities retaining some 'social objectives associated with their own culture' (ibid.: 3). But apart from some help for newly arrived immigrant children, the DES preferred to lump together all minority children, whether immigrant or not, with those of the urban disadvantaged, asserting that 'the majority of children are likely to share with the indigenous children of those areas, the educational disadvantages associated with an impoverished environment' (DES 1974: 2). The DES, as with other government departments, was undoubtedly influenced by the policies in the USA stemming from the War On Poverty declared during the Kennedy-Johnson administrations in the 1960s, which by providing improved education, training and employment opportunities, were intended to allow families, both white and black, to escape from what were described as tangles of pathology (Moynihan 1965) and cultures of poverty. In 1972 Keith Joseph, then Minister for Social Security, proposed research into 'cycles of transmitted deprivation' to examine how poverty and disadvantage was reproduced by generation, which included racial disadvantages (Rutter and Madge 1976); however, educational policies at the time were driven by the general political desire to play down specific policies or extra finance for minority children. The DES used the language of disadvantage, deprivation or non-English speaking and 'preferred almost any identifying label to the racial one' (Kirp 1979: 50). Despite the use of the terminology of race in Race Relations legislation and wider official publications, the use of race or racism in educational documentation was largely avoided.

The government response to the Select Committee report on *Education* mainly returned any action or responsibility to local education authorities, schools and teacher trainers, refusing the suggestion that a central educational fund for immigrant children and adults be set up. Section 11 money and the urban fund were quite enough. However, money comes before ideology and three years later the DES did make efforts to acquire funds from the European Economic Community, claiming, in response to a Directive on the children of migrant workers, that the children of British immigrants did indeed have particular needs. The response also indicated a refusal to set up a suggested immigrant advisory unit in the DES, although it was accepted that an Educational Disadvantage Unit for all disadvantaged children be developed, and an Assessment of Performance Unit (APU) to monitor all educational performance be created. These were set up but soon closed down, despite the success of the APU in checking on educational achievements. A Centre for Educational Disadvantage was set up in Manchester in 1974, but was poorly resourced and staffed and closed down in 1980. Otherwise local authorities were exhorted to tackle problems of teaching English, increasing nursery provision, and finding money for further and adult education. Schools were exhorted to improve home–school contacts and make decisions on curriculum change. Although provision varied, most local authorities with large numbers of minority children did make considerable efforts, without additional funding, to take account of the presence of minority children. The Inner London Education Authority produced the first document on multi-ethnic education (ILEA 1977), and by the end of the 1970s some 25 LEAs had appointed multicultural education advisors. The 51 Educational Priority Areas set up in disadvantaged inner cities after the Plowden Committee recommendations continued to obtain funding into the 1970s, although one measure of disadvantage for all the children was the presence of non-English speaking children (Plowden 1967: 59). A Centre for Urban Community Education was set up in Liverpool, directed by Eric Midwinter (Midwinter 1972). Again, the focus was on general disadvantage and deprivation, although Midwinter urged the development of the community school, open to all local communities all day (a notion that reappeared in official government thinking in 2004 with Extended Schools). The mismatch between those focusing on general disadvantage and the realities of racial antagonisms was illustrated by Midwinter's genial account of successful community activities in one local school, while at the same time a white parent was telling the Select Committee that he wanted to be rehoused out of the area to prevent his children going to the school 'to be educated with coons' (Select Committee 1973, vol. 3: 557).

Subsuming the needs of racial minorities under those of the disadvantaged was reiterated as official policy in a 1977 White Paper, *A Policy for the Inner Cities* (Department for the Environment 1977), which identified economic decline, physical decay and adverse social conditions as major problems for inner cities. But in the proliferation of urban programmes in the 1970s race was never absent from political thinking, with Conservative MP Peter Walker asserting during a debate on the Queen's speech in 1976 that 'real explosion, rioting and ghastly conditions in inner cities were nearer than the public want to recognise' (Hansard 1976). The Home Office, however, remained wedded to notions of disadvantage, replying to Chief Education Officers, who were pleading for a national strategy on funding for minorities to replace Section 11 provision, that 'The government's basic analysis is that a great deal of the disadvantage the minorities suffer is shared with the less-well-off members of the indigenous population and their most fundamental needs, jobs, housing, education and the health service, are essentially the same as those of the general population' (Home Office 1978: 1). This official policy was again challenged by the Select Committee who made eight recommendations concerning the education of West Indian children in their 1977 report (Select Committee 1977), and by the Commission for Racial Equality who made a further 19 recommendations (CRE 1978). Little and Willey, reporting a survey of LEA practices (Little and Willey 1981), made 58 policy recommendations for the education of minorities, and the Home Affairs Committee (1981) made 26. Rutter and Madge (1976) pointed out that minority children did suffer specific disadvantages over and above any indigenous disadvantage – notably racial discrimination – and Rex and Tomlinson (1979) noted that the problems of so-called disadvantage were presumed to be intractable, not a category minority children seeking equality needed to be in. The interim report of the Committee of Inquiry into the Education of Children from Ethnic Minority Groups (Rampton Report) provided a summary of 81 recommendations and regretted that 'we have received some evidence about the lack of leadership given by the DES in the field of multicultural education' (DES 1981a). However, this stricture should not have covered HMI, who continued their attempts to advise their colleagues and government that the pluralist society now demanded a broader curriculum and a questioning of the basic values and assumptions held by the majority society:

> It is important for the majority community to realize that minority cultures are an established . . . component of the British scene. The most effective contribution that schools can make is to ensure that the knowledge and information handled is of a kind that removes the ignorance upon which much racial bigotry, prejudice and discrimination are based.
>
> (Bolton 1979)

Achievement anxieties

The educational performance and achievement of minority children and young people assumed crucial importance during the 1970s. There was continued documentation of the lower school achievements of minorities, especially West Indian children, and their parents became anxious and angry that the education system could not provide their children with qualifications and a non-racist curriculum. Policy makers and politicians acknowledged that a younger generation was emerging with few qualifications but with little intention of taking up the low level jobs their parents were in, and these policy makers and politicians were fearful of the racial antagonisms that were very evident during the decade. Researchers continued to use psychometric tools, measuring 'ability, intelligence or potential' using standardised verbal and non-verbal tests, giving tests of attainment, especially in English and maths, and collecting information on test and public examination performance. The researchers increasingly worked on the assumption that what they were measuring was the comparative performance of minority children and urban indigenous children, and that comparisons were therefore fair. Historical, social, economic and political factors affecting the urban education of working-class and immigrant minority children did not figure much in the research.

The Inner London Education Authority's Research and Statistics Group continued to monitor the performance of minority children as compared to indigenous children, a first literacy survey reporting that Inner London children had a reading age six months below their chronological age and immigrant children one year below (Little 1975). The final literacy survey reported West Indian reading scores as very low and explained this by 'adverse environmental circumstances', language problems, poor self-image and low teacher expectations. At the same time Rutter and his colleagues were researching ILEA schools, showing that the greater commitment of black pupils to education – with more staying on at school or in further education – contradicted the social deprivation explanations (Rutter *et al.* 1979). A Black People's Progressive Association in the outer London Borough of Redbridge established a working group to examine the performance of black children in the borough, as not one West Indian pupil had passed an A level in 1977. They concluded that poorer performance was due to 'self-identity and the effects of a hostile white society' plus teacher attitudes, and dialect speech, but again discounted social deprivation arguments (Redbridge 1978). Some research attempted to identify factors associated with the success of black children in achieving school leaving qualifications, with Driver's (1980) study noting West Indian pupil success in some school subjects, and Fuller's (1980) study documenting the strategies black girls used to achieve despite teacher expectations. Explanations for lower black achievements focused heavily on supposed problems of identity, self-concept and self-esteem, and social psychologists urged schools and families to find ways of presenting positive self-images to the children. David Milner's early 1970s study attempting to describe the development of children's racial attitudes came in for much hostile comment in that it showed black children preferring white doll figures, and children of all groups attributing negative characteristics to minority figures. Indeed one six-year-old white child voiced a degree of hostility that 'would not have disgraced the National

Front or the Ku Klux Klan' (Milner 1983: 122). A re-write of the book ten years' later still came in for somewhat unfair criticism that black children were represented as self-hating victims with low self-esteem.[8] Black educationist Maureen Stone criticised the often patronising and ethnocentric efforts to 'compensate black children for not being white' as the reality for most black children at this time was 'a wageless existence or low wages in an unpopular or menial job' (Stone 1981).

The ESN issue continued to simmer. There was a deliberate refusal on the part of the DES to monitor the numbers of West Indian children in ESN schools but they acknowledged, in a letter to all Chief Education Officers in 1973, that West Indian children appeared to be four times over-represented in the schools and Asian children were then under-represented. The letter also stated there was no requirement to collect numbers, only to review the local situation and check on assessment tools. It was also suggested that West Indian children might speak English in a dialect incomprehensible to teachers and that it was permissible to place them quickly in special schooling (Tomlinson 1981). The Committee of Inquiry into *The Education of Handicapped Children and Young People* (DES 1978) barely considered the issue, and by the end of the decade the Rampton Committee looking into the education of West Indian children wrote that 'we were unable to establish whether there are still disproportionate numbers of West Indian children in ESN schools, although it is clear there used to be. That knowledge and the worry that it may be true are matters of deep and understandable concern for West Indian parents' (DES 1981a: 48). This was something of an understatement, as Coard's 1971 polemic had galvanised parents, and articles in the journal *Race Today* pointed out that the issue had become the battleground for a more general controversy over the failure of schools to educate West Indian children properly (Dhondy 1974). Sixteen official bodies gave evidence to the Select Committee for their report on *Education* over the ESN issue and nine for their report on *The West Indian Community* (Select Committee 1977), noting that this was a very bitter area for parents. The issue also became part of a last ditch attempt to suggest innate genetic explanations for any lower performance and attainments of black children. IQ tests were routinely being given in assessment for special education and Eysenck had suggested that in both the USA and Britain black-white differences in IQ were in part genetically caused. He rather spoiled his case by suggesting that the problems of lower intelligence could only be solved by 'the general abolition of the lumpen proletariat, both black and white' (Eysenck 1971: 150). It was also noticeable from the 1970s that black and Irish pupils were heavily over-represented in exclusion units set up to remove those regarded as disruptive or exhibiting behaviour problems from mainstream classrooms. Under various labels – nurture classes, educational guidance centres, disruptive units, or in popular parlance 'sin-bins' – it was quicker to refer children out of the classroom this way than through the more cumbersome special education route. Evidence mounted that teachers did consider black pupils more likely to behave badly in class, and were particularly threatened by assertions of a black cultural identity exemplified by the Rastafari hair and hats.

The performance and achievement of children of Asian origin and their post-school destinations continued to be researched, often via crude comparisons between white/Asian/West Indian, although much work did distinguish different Asian groups, for example, Bhatra Sikhs, Pakistani Punjabi boys and girls, or using religion as a marker (Tomlinson 1983a, Taylor and Hegarty 1985). But Asian educational performance quickly became a stick to beat West Indian children with. Following the publication of the Rampton Report (DES 1981a) a *Times* leader concluded that 'The committee's research shows a striking difference of achievement between children of West Indian and Asian origin, the latter are much closer to white children in their pattern of exam success, yet Asian children also suffer from poverty, overcrowding and discrimination' (*The Times* 18 June 1981). The leader went on to suggest that Asian children overcame their disadvantages because of more positive parental and cultural attitudes, in contrast to West Indian parents. These assumptions affected government policy and media presentation into the 2000s. In fact, research indicated that explanations for Asian achievements in the 1970s being lower than white were far more limited than that offered for West Indians. They centred around second language learning, adjustment problems and cultural and familial difference. Explanations were not sought in suggestions of lower innate capacities or lower self-esteem. Asian children were less likely to be referred for special education or behavioural units and their learning problems were regarded as educational problems, which the school could overcome with remedial and language teaching and home–school liaison. Cultural difference was often regarded as a positive force, the 'stability of the Punjabi family' and strong desires for upward mobility being mentioned. What was not stressed was that schools acknowledged that Asian children did have learning problems and put in place strategies and structured teaching programmes, which meant that they had a fairer deal in education than many West Indian children. It was not surprising that Monica Taylor was able to title her review of Asian educational performance as *The Best of Both World's* (Taylor and Hegarty 1985).

Language and culture

Language and religion, as many anthropologists would claim, are the most significant manifestations of a culture, although they would also point out that culture is not a static 'traditional' entity but a dynamic changing process. Language was where debates on multiculturalism began in the 1960s. Within the assimilation–integration perspective, the arrival of non-English-speaking children posed a major challenge and the focus was on teaching

ESL. By the 1970s the development of ESL teaching took second place to the retention and development of mother-tongue. Worldwide, as population movements became more commonplace, the retention of minority group languages began to be regarded as crucial to the maintenance of a cultural identity, and modernising governments were reminded that forced assimilation usually began by denial of language, the history of the Welsh language being a reminder to the English. The report produced by Lord Bullock's committee was influential in persuading the DES, local authorities and teachers that children should not be required to 'cast off the language and culture of home at the school threshold, nor to live and act as though school and home represent two totally different cultures which have to be kept apart' (Bullock 1975: 286). After 1977 the DES worried about compliance with an EEC Directive on the education of children of migrant workers, which dealt with both tuition in the language of the 'host country' and a requirement in Article 3 that EEC member countries 'take appropriate measures to teach mother tongue and culture of the country of origin'. The Directive certainly worried politicians that there might be a requirement to train teachers of English as a second language, teachers of mother-tongue, bilingual, multicultural, and multilingual education (EEC 1977).

While minority communities had, from the 1960s, provided for language retention through after-school classes at mosque, temple, gudwara and through private tuition, mainstream schools took the view that Britain was monolingual and monocultural and that mother-tongue languages (which by the 1970s were mainly Gujerati, Hindi, Urdu, Punjabi, Bengali, Arabic, Cantonese and Creoles) should not have a place on the curriculum. While bilingualism in a European language was considered a desirable attribute, speaking Asian languages was not (Khan 1978). Tomlinson (1981) recalls visiting an immigrant Indian family where the nine-year-old boy, fluent in three languages and the official translator for his parents, was being assessed for special schooling! In keeping with the lack of any national policy on mother-tongue teaching, different arrangements were made in different LEAs. Some offered school or other LEA premises for after-school teaching, some used Section 11 money to pay bilingual teachers, and by 1981 the Home Affairs Committee could report that 'few issues are generating more argument than that of mother tongue teaching' (Home Affairs Committee 1981: xiv). The DES sponsored two Linguistic Minorities Projects from 1979, the first mapping 55 languages spoken by pupils in London schools, the second documenting languages spoken in a range of local authorities (Linguistic Minorities Project 1983). The use of mother tongue as a transitional medium through which children acquire a majority language was also the subject of DES and School Council sponsored projects, with a study in Bradford concluding that children partly taught in Punjabi in their first year of schooling did better than a group taught only in English (Fitzpatrick and Rees 1980). The Schools Council and ILEA produced materials to incorporate mother tongue into the curriculum in London schools, and the NUT recognised a need for continuity and liaison between home and school for children arriving not speaking English. The NUT gave evidence to the Rampton Committee welcoming advice from the DES, which once again put the onus of provision on local authorities with no national policy or guidance, suggesting that mother-tongue teaching be promoted, and schools 'make it clear by means of posters, notices, stories, library books and pictures that ethnic minority languages are held in equal regard to English' (NUT 1981: 6). While Examination Boards had previously not considered the implications of what was now described as a multicultural curriculum, two Boards began offering Urdu and Gujerati at O and A level public examination levels. Public recognition of their languages was welcomed by minority communities as necessary to retain a cultural and group identity, but debates continued on how far the use of the languages was compatible with full participation and equal opportunity in the wider society. One issue unresearched from the 1970s was that of Muslim women who were not encouraged to leave the home to learn English, an issue which for some persisted into the 2000s.

A focus in the 1970s was on the use of Creoles or dialect speech by children and young people of West Indian origin, and the extent to which this 'interfered' with the acquisition of standard English and affected educational performance. The debate coincided with a general debate on whether the language used by working-class children was less likely to prepare them for an academic education or was simply another code (Bernstein 1973). In the USA Labov (1972) defended use of black English as different but not deficient, and the Bullock Report noted that linguists studying Jamaican and French Creole described them as languages with their own grammar and vocabulary. While eventually the Rampton Committee rejected the use of dialect and Creoles as an explanation for lower school performance, both Bullock and Rampton noted that many teachers held negative attitudes to the speech, regarding it as lazy, sloppy or deficient, and Townsend and Brittan recorded that some schools simply placed the children in remedial classes. While the Schools Council's project in Birmingham had produced materials for writing standard English (Concept 7–9) these were not widely used in schools, and the Community Relations Commission, giving evidence to the Select Committee that for their 1977 report, recorded that 'At the time when Creole dialect did cause problems of communication or comprehension in school the question was ignored. By the time it was identified as an educational issue the majority of West Indian children were no longer speaking it in schools'. However, it was noted again that dialects had become an assertion of identity. Black youth were developing the speech as part of a cultural identity, particularly linked at the time to the popularity of the Rastafari movement and Reggae music. Meanwhile, some conscientious teachers were attempting to recognise and value the languages in the classroom, and capitalise on the literary talents of young people, and an Afro-Caribbean Educational Resource project in London produced materials in dialect. However, some pupils, both black and white, found the efforts to teach dialect highly embarrassing, and generally the debate over dialect speech raised 'unruly passions' (Sutcliffe and Wong 1986). The use of dialect and reggae and soul music were, however, regarded by some activists as important to the development of a black identity and also provided links with young white working-class youth, notably the punks, supporters of 'Rock Against Racism' and with the 1977 Anti-Nazi League, an organisation developed in response to National Front Activities.[9]

While black youth were often demonised by the media and presented as in conflict with the police, there was a strong religious dimension in West Indian community life. In a survey in 1976, 77 per cent of West Indian respondents said they attended Anglican, Baptist, Methodist or Pentecostal church regularly and church pastors were in a position of moral leadership (Rex and Tomlinson 1979: 266). In a small study of black women in British universities, several mentioned the influence of the Pentecostal church, one noting that 'you hear a lot about the influence of Rastafarians but no-one writes about the Pentecostal church influence' (Tomlinson 1983b: 73). For the various Asian communities religious issues did not become an area of open debate and conflict between homes and schools during the 1970s, although some Muslim leaders and educationists were already making requests for voluntary-aided Muslim schools, in line with the settlement under the 1944 Education Act by which Church of England, Roman Catholic and some Jewish schools were granted voluntary-aided or voluntary-controlled status – essentially state-supported religious schools. The British Secular Society, opposed to all faith schools, wrote that 'The policies of some of the Muslim leaders in the north of England could lead to social disaster' (*The Sunday Telegraph* 1975), although they made no similar strictures on Northern Ireland separatist religious policies between Catholic and Protestant. Sikh and Hindu parents, having established gudwaras and temples attended by men and women, which were centres of social and religious life, made no demands for separate schools, but were concerned about the lack of single-sex schools for girls, sex education in schools and school dinners (Ballard and Ballard 1977).[10] Muslim parents stressed their needs in respect of dress for girls, halal diet, single-sex education and religious education, and most Muslim children routinely attended mosque school, for instruction in the Koran and in Arabic and Urdu, after a state-school day. A literature on Islamic education appeared and 'demands made by Islamic organizations became more persistent' (Taylor and Hegarty 1985: 95). A number of Muslim private schools were set up, some supported by community money, others with outside funding, notably from Saudi Arabia.

The Union of Muslim organisations particularly supported single-sex schools and Islamic studies in the curriculum, and the Muslim Education

Trust, a charity set up in 1964, pointed out that Muslims in Britain came not only from India, Pakistan and Bangladesh, but also from Cyprus, Malaysia, Africa and the Middle East. Laying out the educational problems Muslim parents faced in trying to preserve their children's Muslim identity, the Trust was concerned about the 'features of Western cultures – materialistic outlook, free mixing of the sexes, alcoholism and loose morals' corrupting young Muslims (Sawar 1983: 7). A Trust publication laid out a series of demands for schools and LEAs, especially concerning dress, food, no participation in dance, drama, music, swimming or sex lessons, encouraging the training of Muslim teachers, withdrawal from religious education, and allowing religious assemblies with an imam. Although there were some reservations in schools, notably from teachers who found the situation of some girls and women in Islam less than compatible with struggles for women's emancipation in the West, most schools with numbers of Muslim children gradually accommodated to Muslim requirements, many eventually developing school uniforms which included the headscarf (hijab), and making arrangements over religious assembly and education. A National Muslim Educational Council, set up in 1978, developed the case for state-funded Muslim schools further, but the evidence in the 1970s indicated that there was no great demand for Muslim schools, although parents preferred to send their children to voluntary-aided state schools where there was an emphasis on a faith. With a drop in the birth rate and school places empty, voluntary-aided schools were happy to take Muslim children. Although there was little focus on the extent of racism faced by young people, Kitwood and Borrill, in one of the few 1970s studies of young Muslims in Bradford and Manchester, wrote that 'Right from the start of schooling, an Asian child in the north of England has to face being called such names as Paki, Wog, Curry and Chapatti face' (Kitwood and Borrill 1980: 250), and noted that inter-racial conflict was a feature through their school life and into further education.

Curriculum battles

The issue that aroused more unruly passions during the 1970s was that of curriculum change. The introduction of more child-centred, 'progressive' approaches to the curriculum and teaching methods, and the development of comprehensive schooling made the questions 'who gets what knowledge and where' and 'what kinds of knowledge are encapsulated in a curriculum' important. Arguments raged over who has the power to define knowledge and encapsulate it in subject boundaries, and answers to these questions differed according to left and right perspectives. The Schools Council for the Curriculum and Examinations, set up in 1964, found itself challenged by the DES, who wished to take over curriculum responsibilities. This ambition was assisted by Prime Minister Callaghan who in 1976, as noted above, had criticised schools as failing to prepare young people for the world of work. What followed was a closer realignment of the curriculum with the world of work, and a strengthening of bureaucratic control of the curriculum by the DES after the publication of a Green Paper *Education in Schools* (DES 1977). However, the Green Paper did accept the need for curriculum change for a society that was by now routinely referred to as multiracial and multicultural.

> Ours is now a multiracial and multicultural country and one in which traditional social patterns are breaking down . . . the comprehensive school reflects the need to educate our people for a different sort of society . . . the education appropriate to our Imperial past cannot meet the requirements of modern Britain.
>
> (DES 1977: paras 10–11)

No national policies were forthcoming as to what a curriculum for a democratic multicultural society would look like, and official publications continued to stress the 'problems' of children from other cultures. LEAs, schools and teachers were left to formulate their own local changes and innovations. But the CRE (1978) welcomed the government's commitment to education for a multicultural society, urged schools to reject majority cultural elitism and show that minority cultures were valuable. There was no suggestion, as later critics have supposed, that cultural relativism – accepting that all cultural practices, however repellent – be acceptable, and most documentation from the 1970s was preoccupied with reconciling acceptance of cultural diversity with common values. What followed in the 1970s and particularly in the 1980s was an avalanche of literature advocating commitment to and implementation of a multicultural curriculum, and an equally large literature critiquing this literature and supposed practices. Some leftist critics assumed that those advocating teaching about other cultural backgrounds or non-Christian religions were blind to racism, and led an often virulent critique. An All London Teachers Against Racism and Fascism group (ALTARF) argued that raising teachers' levels of consciousness of their own racism should take precedence over curriculum change, and the focus should be on combating white racism. Others on the right attacked 'the multi-ethnic brigade' as divisive, 'teaching children a biased view of history which sees racism as a white monopoly' (Hastie 1981). Mullard (1982) regarded anything labelled multicultural as a prop for assimilation and a means of social control of black students and Stone (1981) assumed, with no evidence, that black students had somehow been diverted into what she described as multiracial education (MRE) rather than into formal subject areas.

What actually happened in schools was virtually unrecorded apart from supposition and anecdote. James and Jeffcoate wrote 'For all the discussion of the multicultural curriculum it has not been easy to find well argued sets of proposals for specific areas of curriculum practice . . . or records of implementation' (1981: xii). Dissatisfaction with the 1960s curriculum had led teachers in schools with minority children to make their own changes and suggestions, but no sooner had a few been converted to the need for change and a few LEAs had appointed multicultural advisors, than critics assumed there was a full-blown movement. Lack of clarification of the concept, national policy guidelines, or teacher preparation, made attack easy. By the end of the 1970s multicultural education 'tends to be an umbrella term to cover a variety of approved or demanded practices in educational establishments . . . mother-tongue teaching, ethnic school dinners, the elimination of ethnocentricity in history and other subjects and racial bias in books, and the inclusion of non-Christian religions' (Philipps-Bell 1981: 21). Specific changes did indeed include recommendation by the teacher unions that 'text books and curriculum materials should not propagate racist ideas' (NUT 1979) and by 1985 Klein was able to document initiatives by teachers, parents, libraries and publishers to challenge racist material and produce new books and resources' (Klein 1985). While some critics eventually came around to the idea of removing or using in an historical context offensive material, a feeling persisted that banning books or other texts was unacceptable censorship, a dilemma which continued into the 2000s. Black studies, emanating from courses developed in the USA as part of the civil rights movement, had a short-lived history in Britain, a course at a London school being viewed with some hostility by some teachers and parents, and a course at a Birmingham school being closed down after a visit by the Director of Education. The inclusion of non-Christian religions in the required religious education period was a matter left to individual local authorities. Birmingham LEA produced a syllabus for teaching about all faiths in 1973, but it was criticised for including humanism and communism as 'faiths' and eventually discontinued, one councillor asserting that the syllabus had been influenced by 'left-wing theologians'. Teachers were understandably nervous of 'teaching race relations' and teachers on the Schools Council were responsible for a veto on the publication of a 'race pack' commissioned by the Council, the publication of results from a Curriculum 5–13 project which criticised teachers for failing to spot young children's racism, and a geography project (*New Society* 16 February 1978, Gill 1982). Anxiety over the racism expressed by very young children led to an early years anti-racist movement. Teachers in all-white schools or those with few minority children were not persuaded that any multicultural curriculum materials were necessary in their schools (Widlake and Bloom 1979).

Parents and teachers

Despite the different backgrounds from which minority parents originated, and by the 1970s there was much literature on this, the majority were schooled in colonial education systems and had their beliefs and expectations shaped by their own experiences in colonial schools. In India, a Western-style education was seen as a means to acquire status and mobility as early as 1844 when government job preference was given to those with an 'English' education. In the Caribbean there was primary education for a plantation workforce, no general secondary education until 1953 and corporal punishment was taken for granted (as it was in English schools until 1987). But whatever their own levels of education, migrant parents assumed that even if they took low-paid work, their children would have educational and job opportunities, and many were deeply shocked and angry at the levels of discrimination both they and their children faced. Teachers, mainly through liberal ignorance rather than racist intent, seldom understood or acknowledged the courage and dignity which parents displayed as they attempted to understand the education system and cope with racial antagonisms. Even well-qualified parents had no guarantee their qualifications would lead to commensurate employment. Smith (1977) found many Asian men working at jobs they were 'over qualified' for. West Indian women were far more likely to be in work than women in any other group, although even in 1971 40 per cent of Indian women worked outside the home.

There was no specific demand for curriculum change from minority parents. What they wanted was equality of opportunity for their children to acquire credentials in basic literacy and in whatever subjects were currently regarded as leading to worthwhile qualifications. But black parents and students also wanted the curriculum to reflect their history and Caribbean backgrounds, and as noted above, Asian, especially Muslim parents, had particular demands for less participation in some school activities, and more regard for their cultural practices. By the 1970s the provision of supplementary education by Asian communities, related to maintenance of language, religion and cultural identity, was well established. For West Indian parents, enough initiatives had been taken by black parents, teachers, community workers and academics for a recognisable black education movement to have emerged (Tomlinson 1984). Participants were united by the belief that schools designed for a white majority were not offering equal learning opportunities to black children. Diverse parent and community groups acted as pressure groups on schools. In London a Haringey group, developing out of a black women's action group lobbied schools and the LEA over low achievement, and their efforts were noted by the Rampton Committee. Wandsworth Community Relations Council worked with West Indian parents to challenge ILEA over numbers of black children suspended from school or placed in behavioural units. Supplementary education, run on Saturdays and after school, expanded and some received local authority or Home Office funding. The schools focused on instruction in accepted curriculum subjects but some 'endeavoured to give a truer and fairer account of historical events' relating to colonialism and development in the Caribbean and Africa. The Harambee School in Birmingham, for example, chose a different black role model to study each week. The perceived failure of state schools to educate black children to expected levels led to suggestions for segregated schooling, with the West Indian Standing Conference suggesting in 1977 that a black school be set up as a pilot project. There was media publicity, including a TV programme, given to the John Loughborough School, a Seventh Day Adventist school in Tottenham, London, attended mainly by black pupils and run along the lines of a traditional English grammar school. Suggestions of segregated schooling horrified education officials, one HMI giving evidence to the Home Affairs Committee noted that 'This would seem to be a form of educational apartheid contrary to all we have been doing to build up a multiracial society' (Home Affairs Committee 1981, evidence p. 443). Nevertheless the movement of white families out of inner cities meant that many schools were de facto segregated schools. Throughout the 1970s many white parents, both working and middle class, remained antagonistic to the idea of their children attending school with minority pupils, feeling that the presence of black pupils stigmatised the schools, and also claiming that time and expense was being spent on these children to the detriment of white children.

The 1970s was a period of exhortation to improve both initial and in-service training of teachers for a multiracial multicultural society, and at the end of the decade Craft noted that 'it is profoundly depressing to find the same kinds of recommendations appearing again and again' (Craft 1981: 2). Although more courses had been developed in University and College Departments of Education, there was no overall guidance as to aims and content of courses, no extra funding, teacher trainers themselves were not 'trained' in understanding the issues and teachers who did not or were not intending to teach in schools with minority children saw no need to attend courses. It was becoming obvious that liberal professional intentions were not enough and that, being left to develop practice on an ad hoc basis, many teachers did hold stereotyped or negative views of minority children and found difficulty in responding to calls for acceptance of cultural pluralism or anti-racist moves. Some teachers were in the vanguard of attempts to improve practice, and a National Association for Multiracial Education (later changed to become a National Antiracist Movement in Education) developed from a small organisation in the early 1970s to an influential group in the 1980s. Teacher unions were also increasingly supportive of training and changed practice, and while initially the DES had been reluctant to accept the qualifications of teachers trained overseas, there was now a focus on recruiting more teachers from minority groups, a supposed solution to the issue of black education that was continually put forward into the 2000s. However, a National Convention of Black Teachers, an umbrella organisation for minority teachers groups, did point out the problems they faced in employment and promotion due to racial discrimination.

By the end of the decade the Rampton Committee was regretting the wide gulf of mistrust and misunderstanding growing between schools and minority parents and expressing surprise that 'parents appear to be losing confidence in what schools are teaching their children' (DES 1981a: 41).

Summary

This chapter has illustrated the continuities from the 1960s of increasingly hostile immigration control policies, supported by all political parties, and now directed at minimising family settlement, and the increasing understanding that the white population, suffering a bad case of post-imperial anxiety, were by and large aghast at the idea that former colonial workers from the Empire had now come to live, work and remain in Britain. After studying the situation of immigrants through the 1970s, Rex and Tomlinson concluded that 'The question of the absorption of immigrant minorities into the working class has been settled against absorption, with the (white) working class rejecting black immigrants and uniting with other indigenous classes against them' (Rex and Tomlinson 1979: 276). Successive governments understood that racial discrimination was a source of resentment and potential conflict, particularly on the part of the young black people, and accordingly passed race relations legislation, and to some extent listened to the various commissions and committees reporting the situation of minorities, and were in turn taken aback by the assertions of a black identity. The 1970s was a decade of violent clashes between white and black, with over 30 racial murders of black and Asian people recorded between 1976 and 1980. But it was always understood that overt action in support of minorities, or providing positive leadership in explaining the realities of the place of post-imperial Britain in the world, was not something any government could do if they wished to be elected. Indeed, Mrs Thatcher's 'swamping' speech was a negative signal that helped her to election victory in 1979. It was not surprising that the DES decided to subsume the problems of immigrant minorities under those of the disadvantaged, and minimise any special help given to minorities. This policy was certainly not successful, as white parents continued to believe that immigrant children took an unfair share of resources and teacher time, and resented their children attending schools with black and Asian children. During the 1970s the education system was moving contentiously towards a common comprehensive schooling, but an economic recession and the disappearance of much manual work had increased the need for qualifications and immigrant parents were doubly concerned that the system was not preparing their children for decent jobs or a future. It was already becoming apparent that Asian minorities were able to assert a more positive cultural identity which was taken more seriously by schools, while the educational problems of West Indian children were reflected back to their supposed individual or family deficiencies. Muslim parents, while still keeping a low profile, were asserting that their religious and cultural practices be respected. While the Labour government did recognise that considerable change in the school curriculum would be necessary to prepare all children for a multicultural, post-imperial world, no national policies were forthcoming as to what sort of a curriculum was right for a democratic multicultural society. It was left to local authorities, schools and teachers to take a lead in trying out new ideas, often naïve and well intentioned, sometimes blind to the extent of racism even young white children felt, and to the anxiety many black parents felt for their children.

Notes

1. Enoch Powell, despite leaving England to become a Northern Irish Unionist MP in 1974, continued to argue that West Indian and Asian migrants could never become British citizens. Barker (1981) took the view that Powell was important both as an architect of a new racism that denied national citizenship to minorities on the ground of cultural difference, and to a theory of the nation as a place where social cohesion was threatened by such difference.
2. The National Front party, developing out of the Nazi-inspired fascist movements of the 1930s, was originally anti-Semitic, but also strongly racist against immigrants and non-white minorities. The party later linked with other fascist movements to become the British National Party (BNP), making electoral gains at a local level, and collaborating with European fascist parties. The author's children, in Birmingham schools during the 1970s, brought home National Front literature given to them at the school gate.
3. Winston Churchill MP, grandson of the famous Winston, spoke in Parliament of the 'deep bitterness of ordinary people who one day were living in Lancashire, and then woke up the next day in New Delhi, Calcutta or Jamaica' (Hansard 1976: 998).
4. Into the 1970s, government publications, including those on education, used a vocabulary of immigrants, racial minorities, racial disadvantage and discrimination. What later became referred to as a politics of identity emerged among younger people of West Indian and Asian origin who adopted the political label of 'black', although this was a disputed label, particularly among older Asians. Academic research had begun to differentiate between South Asian groups, especially in terms of religion – Hindu, Sikh, Muslim. Research into the settlement and education of other groups – Chinese, Greek and Turkish Cypriots settling after the partition of Cyprus in 1974, Italian, Ukrainian and Vietnamese settlers, the situation of gypsy and travellers' children and black youth in Liverpool (Taylor 1988) – led to an increasing adoption of a vocabulary of minority or ethnic minority.
5. Political links made in the 1970s between young blacks in Britain and African liberation movements were undoubtedly disturbing to the authorities. As the cold war against communist countries was ongoing, any links that might be made with revolutionary communist-inspired groups were taken seriously, although it is ironic that the same politicians who spoke against the anti-

apartheid African National Congress, were among those welcoming Nelson Mandela and a liberated black South Africa in 1994.

6. Paul Gilroy worked with a group of young Marxist scholars at the Birmingham Centre for Contemporary Cultural Studies in the 1970s. He and another young scholar, John Solomos, attacked sociologists who purported to study race relations. They both eventually became Professors of Sociology studying race relations. Gilroy's mother Beryl Gilroy, was one of the first black headteachers appointed to a London primary school.
7. Neil Kinnock, Leader of the Labour party 1983–92, reported that he found Callaghan's speech 'dismaying'. 'The great shame was that if he had got in touch with a host of practitioners, he would have found they shared his frustrations and would have had constructive suggestions to make' (personal communication with author, 12 October 1992).
8. Criticism of David Milner's work was not only academic. Activists showed their displeasure by fire-bombing his kitchen.
9. Gilroy (1987) took the view that black and white youth joined together at this time to combat the resurgence of nationalist patriotism and racism, particularly via music, quoting the Stranglers 'I feel like a wog', the Clash 'Police and Thieves' and 'White man in the Hammersmith Palais'. The lead singer of the Sex Pistols was reported as saying that 'punks and niggers are almost the same' (ibid.: 124).
10. Tomlinson attended meetings with Sikh, Hindu and Muslim parents at schools in Lancashire during the period 1979–1982.

Race, riots and markets (1980–1990)

> During the weekend of 10–12 April 1981 the British people watched with horror and incredulity an instant presentation on their television sets of scenes of violence and disorder in their capital city, the like of which had not been seen in this century in Britain. In the centre of Brixton a few hundred young people, most but not all black, attacked the police on the streets with stones, bricks, iron bars and petrol bombs, demonstrating to millions of their fellow citizens the fragile nature of the Queen's peace.
>
> (Scarman 1982: 13)

The 1980s began with a bang as far as race relations were concerned, with rioting, notably by young black men, in inner cities. This was to be a decade in which immigration assumed less importance as a politically exploitable issue, but conflicts surrounding the acceptance of black Britons into a multiracial and multicultural society and their equal participation as citizens became the major contested issue.[1] Although government had now accepted that settled black and Asian minorities suffered racial disadvantage and discrimination, there was still no leadership to inform a hostile white population of the economic reasons and benefits for immigration and settlement, tensions continued between the police and young black males, although the influence of black pressure groups became stronger. Ethnic minority candidates entered local and national elections, four black MPs being elected to Parliament in 1987, and Councillor Ajeeb become the first Muslim Lord Mayor, in the city of Bradford in 1985. Assertion by Muslims during the 1980s made sure that religion was incorporated into debate on race and ethnicity and much of the action centred on Bradford. The altercation in that city between Muslims and headteacher Ray Honeyford in 1984 and the burning of Salman Rushdie's book, *The Satanic Verses*, in January 1989 ensured that issues of religious and cultural identity were to become as contentious as 'race' issues. By the 1980s the old British Empire had been transformed into a Commonwealth of former Colonies and Protectorates. Closer links with Europe were becoming a reality, with Parliament signing up to a Single European Act in 1986 and the Maastricht Treaty of February 1992 transforming a European Economic Community into a European Union (EU) with, at that date, 15 Member States. What eventually became described as globalisation and a global economy was taking shape (Sklair 1995), which was to affect considerably movement and migration of people and their labour and bring about cultural convergences and resistances between countries. In Britain questions of national identity became crucial, and much antagonism to minorities over the decade centred on whether differences of colour, culture and religion were permanently at odds with traditional notions of a British national identity. Meanwhile, under the leadership of Margaret Thatcher, a radical restructuring of public welfare provision in the UK began to take shape, with the introduction of market forces and competition into education, health, housing, social and other public services. The licence given to people to pursue personal and familial profit, with a diminished emphasis on redistribution, equity and social justice, eventually resulted in a considerable increase in social and economic inequalities and enhanced disadvantages for some groups. What became known as the 'new right' – a coalition of neoliberals interested in free markets, competition and control of public spending, allied to Conservative groups interested in preserving 19th-century notions of tradition, hierarchy, authority and social order – were able to influence significantly the direction of education policies. Similarly, the 'new racism', expounded by some politicians, academics and practitioners, further developed Powellite views of who was to be included or excluded within a British national identity and provided a rationale for xenophobia and racism towards minorities.

But despite initial reluctance by central and local government to focus specifically on the education of minorities or on institutional changes to prepare all pupils for a multiracial society, the 1980s was a period of educational advance for minorities. The decade witnessed 'a growing awareness of the political, social, and economic reasons for developing an education system relevant to an ethnically diverse society' (Tomlinson and Craft 1995: 3). This chapter documents policy moves from subsuming minorities under the label of disadvantage, to a focus on the educational needs of a multi-ethnic society and on race equality, achievement and a changed curriculum, with the publication of the Swann Report (DES 1985a) constituting what a former Education Secretary of State described as 'the boldest most comprehensive statement on multicultural education so far produced in Britain' (Williams 1988). The chapter describes some of the positive initiatives by both central and local government, in teacher preparation and school and curriculum development projects, it also overviews the plethora of multicultural anti-racist literature produced, together with the antagonisms between various approaches, and notes the enduring efforts of political and educational nationalists seeking to preserve an imperial notion of a British national identity from 'alien' cultures. It also covers the more confident Muslim assertion of religious identity, and the implications for minorities of the 1988 Education Reform Act. The terminology of the 1980s increasingly used black and Asian, although New Commonwealth and immigrant were still in use and minority groups were increasingly referred to by country of origin or religion.

Chronology of Acts and issues

1980 Conservative Education Act introduces first attempts at a market in schooling by allowing parents to express a 'preference' of school. Comprehensive schooling declared to be no longer national policy.

1980 Riots in Bristol. The National Union of Teachers in Avon links young black frustration to poor schooling and employment prospects (Avon NUT 1980).

1981 (January) Thirteen young black people died in a fire in New Cross, allegedly started by fascists, 15,000 black people marched from New Cross to central London for racial justice. (April) Riots in Brixton, London, Toxteth, Liverpool and elsewhere. Lord Scarman's report linked black economic and social insecurity to poor education.

1981 (June) Rampton interim report on *West Indian Children in our Schools* (DES 1981a) makes 81 recommendations. Sir Anthony Rampton resigns and is replaced by Lord Swann. A Schools Council survey makes 58 recommendations on multi-ethnic education.

1981 British Nationality Act further excludes Commonwealth citizens from entering the UK. (96,000 settled minorities apply for British citizenship in 1982.)

1981 Special Education Act. Categories of Handicap abolished to be replaced by the concept of Special Educational Needs (SEN).

1982 Approximately 20 LEAs have written multicultural education policies. Home Office issues new guidelines for claiming Section 11 funding. Around 40 black supplementary schools known to be in operation. (April–June) Falklands War against Argentina.

1983 Conservatives re-elected. Muslim parents in Bradford request that five Islamic schools become state funded on the lines of Anglican and

Catholic schools. Request refused. Schools Council for the Curriculum and Examinations abolished, replaced by School Curriculum and Development Committee and Schools Examination Council.

1984 Population with New Commonwealth origins recorded as 2.2 million. Third PSI survey found evidence of upward movement of some minorities in Britain but overall their survey 'gives us a depressing picture of the economic lives of people of Asian and West Indian origin in Britain' (Brown 1984: 293).

1984 Ray Honeyford, a white Bradford headteacher, suspended after publishing articles in the *Salisbury Review* attacking multicultural education. Council for the Accreditation of Teacher Education (CATE) set up, and all courses are required to include training for a multicultural society.

1985 Swann Report *Education for All* published, with ten pages of recommendations, stressing that all those involved in education should share in developing a democratic pluralistic society with equal opportunities. ILEA begins collection of examination results by ethnic background. Archbishop of Canterbury's report on *Faith in the City* labelled a Marxist document.

1985 More riots in Toxteth, Liverpool and Handsworth, Birmingham. Riots in Tottenham, London in which a police officer is stabbed to death. A black headteacher advocates separate education for black pupils. NAME becomes the National Antiracist Movement in Education. White Paper on *Better Schools* published (DES 1985b), stressing that pupils are to be given an understanding of the (unspecified) traditions and values of British society.

1986 Parliament ratifies the Single European Act which allows free movement of EC nationals between Member States. Mrs Thatcher later complains she was not told of its significance.

1986 DES offers Education Support Grants to LEAs for projects in white areas (120 projects funded by 1988). Approximately 60 LEAs produce policies on multicultural/anti-racist education, notably the ILEA. O levels replaced by GCSEs. Education Act abolishes corporal punishment in schools. In-service education courses for teaching in a multi-ethnic society among 21 national priority courses.

1986 (September) Ahmed Ullah stabbed to death by white pupil in Burnage School, Manchester. The media blames anti-racist policies.

A book on the event, *Murder in the Playground* (MacDonald *et al.* 1989), also attacked in the press.

1987 Conservatives win a third General Election, four black MPs elected. DES creates a post for 'inner city education and education for a multicultural society' with Baroness Hooper appointed. Twenty-eight white parents in Dewsbury refuse to send their children to a school with 80 per cent Asian children, and educate them in a local pub. Nick Seaton sets up a *Campaign for Real Education*[2] to support 'British culture' and the Christian religion in schools.

1988 Brent development programme for racial equality described by the *Daily Mail* as 'race spies in the classroom'. CRE publishes *Learning in Terror*. St Georges Hospital Medical school admits that their selection procedures discriminate against ethnic minorities and women. Immigration Act removes absolute right of New Commonwealth men and women to bring in marriage partners but EC citizens have freedom of entry.

1988 Education Reform Act. Introduces a National Curriculum, Key Stage assessment, open enrolment and parental rights to 'chose' schools, schools to publish exam results, schools to be delegated own budgets, schools able to opt out of LEA control and become 'grant-maintained', i.e. funded directly from central government. ILEA abolished. Religious education to be of a broadly Christian character. National Curriculum Council (NCC) and School Examination and Assessment Council (SEAC) set up.

1989 Schools in Smallheath, Birmingham and Stratford, London, with largely Muslim intakes, vote to become grant-maintained with own admissions. Chair of Governors at Stratford School (Councillor Mohammed Aslam) fears his school will become 'all-Asian'. Christian fundamentalist groups also demand state-aided schooling. In January the Salman Rushdie book, *The Satanic Verses*, is burnt in Bradford on the decision of the Bradford Council of Mosques. Secretary of State for Education, Kenneth Baker, says he will not allow schools to be taken over by fundamentalist groups.

1989 Labour Party issues *Multicultural Education: Labour's Policy for Schools*.

1989 Secretary of State for Education requests the NCC to take account of the multi-ethnic nature of society. NCC sets up a multicultural working group, their subsequent report being censored. CRE produces a code of practice to eliminate racial discrimination in schools. DES issues a circular on the collection of numbers of ethnic minority teachers. DES guidelines on modern languages in the national curriculum lays out two schedules, European languages in the first, Asian languages in the second.

1990 Education Secretary rules that a white parent in Cleveland has a right to remove her child from a multiracial school, arguing that parental choice legislation overrides race relations legislation. Norman Tebbit MP suggests that Asian loyalty to Britain can be judged by whether they cheer for the English cricket team (*The Times* 1990). He also rejects his own government's agreement to allow 50,000 Hong Kong Chinese to settle in Britain, and claims that people in Britain do not want to live in a multicultural society.

Politics and ideology

In the 1980s grudging political acceptance of the reality that migrants and their children from the New Commonwealth were 'here to stay' moved the ideological debate from exclusion by immigration control to the limits and conditions of inclusion into the nation. As Britain embarked on a transition from imperial status to national status with dwindling influence on world affairs, a crisis of national identity developed. Salman Rushdie took the view that in its post-colonial period there was 'a crisis of the whole culture, of society's sense of itself' (Rushdie 1982). The majority society was attempting to reconstitute an image of itself by defining who was *not* British, with non-white, ex-colonial people being candidates for exclusion. But at the same time, support for free markets and the rights of all citizens to develop as competitive individuals and work for national success in a global economy meant that discrimination against particular groups was bad for business. The free-marketers and proponents of a racist nationalism were occasionally in competition, although they had in common distinctly old 19th-century views of economic and social life. In the 19th century a belief in free markets with no state interference or regulation created such inequalities in wealth, living conditions and access to work that state regulation became necessary, eventually developing in Britain after 1945 into a managed market economy and the Beveridge inspired welfare state. Mrs Thatcher's new right in the 1980s was inspired by the possibility of a return to free markets in both public and private spheres, which, while bringing raised prosperity to some, eventually created similar consequences of inequalities and insecurities. Much of this insecurity was exemplified by the class politics embodied in the miners strike in 1984, their eventual capitulation and mine closures being regarded as a victory for market capitalism over a recalcitrant working class.

But despite job insecurities created during the 1980s there was increased population migration to richer countries (Gray 1998).

Racism in the 1980s incorporated 19th-century beliefs in white racial biological and cultural superiority, with a white majority holding on to Victorian racial beliefs in order to sustain a narrow intolerant view of 'who belongs' within the boundaries of a national identity. This view was certainly encouraged by right-wing politicians and commentators. During the Falklands War against Argentina in 1982 a *Sunday Telegraph* article asserted that 'if the Falkland Islanders were British citizens with black or brown skins, spoke with strange accents or worshipped strange Gods, it is doubtful whether the Royal Navy would be fighting for their liberation' (Worsthorne 1982). After the war Mrs Thatcher claimed that Britain was still the nation that had 'built an Empire and ruled a quarter of the world' and after the incorporation into legislation of free movement of European nationals in 1986, she suggested that a British national identity would be threatened by closer links with Europe. During the 1980s extreme right-wing groups routinely used appeals to a patriotic nationalism to exclude minorities from the idea of a British nation, and Gilroy pointed out that the concept of national belonging used militaristic and patriotic metaphors of war and invasion to describe immigrant minorities. Particularly after riots in urban areas 'the enemy within, the unarmed invasion, alien encampments, new commonwealth occupations' were all used to describe the black and Asian presence in cities (Gilroy 1987: 45). An Immigration Act in 1988 claimed 'control of settlement' by restricting the right of men and women from New Commonwealth countries to bring marriage partners into the country, while allowing for free movement of European citizens. Meanwhile the settlement of minorities in areas where there was employment, with spatial segregation by both constraint and choice in poorer areas of cities and towns, and white flight from these areas, was ensuring that notions of assimilation on a geographical level had more or less disappeared. Schools in 'high minority' areas were de facto becoming separate schools, although at the primary level a large number of these schools were Church of England voluntary-aided schools, which at this time welcomed all faiths to fill places.

Political anxieties that the society was indeed fracturing along racial lines became acute in the early 1980s. There had been numerous suggestions in the 1970s that the lack of attention to the disadvantages faced by young black people could lead to rioting. In 1980 the CRE had drawn together studies of the disadvantages experienced by black youth in inner cities, making use again of James Baldwin's metaphor of fire in *Youth in Multiracial Society: The Fire Next Time* (CRE 1980). In April 1980 young black men were indeed involved in rioting in the St Paul's area of Bristol, with the local National Union of Teachers reporting in *After the Fire* (Avon NUT 1980) that black frustration over poor schooling and discrimination in employment were major causes of disorder. In June 1980 some 40 minority groups established a National Council of Black Organisations and caused anxiety for press and politicians with a call for black and Asian people to withdraw any cooperation with the police. In January 1981 a fire broke out in a house in New Cross, London in which 13 young black people died. After police discounted a racial motive 15,000 black people marched from New Cross to Westminster, London demanding an end to racial murders. In April 1981 police launched 'operation swamp' to check on black people in Brixton, London, after which rioting broke out, to be followed by riots in Toxteth, Liverpool, Manchester, Birmingham, Coventry, Leeds and other towns and cities. Home Secretary William Whitelaw appointed Lord Scarman to hold an inquiry into the events and possible causes. He noted that rioting in London and Liverpool was mainly by young black men versus the police, in Birmingham and Coventry white youths were involved, and the Coventry disorder was sparked by the murder of two Asian men. Just as some 14 years earlier the Kerner Report on civil disorders in cities in the USA (Kerner 1968) had reported that negative policing practices, unemployment, poor education and inadequate housing were major reasons for riots, the Scarman Report blamed poor police methods, unemployment, poor education and youth services, and discriminatory housing policies in areas where 'unemployment is high and hopes are low' (Scarman Report 1982: 15). Recommendations included more focus on the special problems and needs of ethnic minorities and included training teachers to understand minority cultures, more involvement in schools by parents, and more police liaison with schools. Fryer (1984: 399) took the view that 'the persistent bullying of black people was bound, sooner or later, to provoke rebellion'.

Urban rioting forced governments to give priority to racial disadvantage and discrimination. Cabinet minister Michael Heseltine recommended a major coordinated attempt to combat racial disadvantage in inner cities and was made Minister for Merseyside; in addition, spending on the Urban Programme increased to £338 million in 1984, the Youth Training Scheme was expanded and reforms to policing were suggested. In the 1983 Conservative election campaign, posters featured a young black man with the caption 'Labour says he's black, Tories say he's British'. Further riots took place in Handsworth, Birmingham in 1985, again blamed on poor education, unemployment and policing, and in Tottenham, London a police officer was stabbed to death in a riot following the death of a black woman during a police raid. All this meant that a focus on inner cities continued during the 1980s. In 1988 an Action For Cities programme was initiated with public and private funding, the intention being to regenerate inner-city areas and make them more attractive to business. While some businesses began to pay attention to equal opportunities in employment and training, there was not much evidence that education, training and employment for young black people improved. While the decade began with conflicts and assertion of rights by mainly black communities, the end of the decade was marked by Muslim assertiveness and new antagonisms. This was exemplified by the burning of Salman Rushdie's book, *The Satanic Verses*, in Bradford in 1988, after which the notion of 'tolerance' become a subject for debate. As Robert Winder put it, the notion of a 'benign elite graciously tolerating the outlandish habits of its inferiors' was now severely challenged (Winder 2004: 415). By the end of the decade Norman Tebbitt MP, who to some extent had taken on the mantle of Enoch Powell, suggested the now well known cricket test for new citizens; minorities were to be judged for acceptance based on whether they cheered on the English cricket team. This suggestion became interesting when Caribbean and Asian immigrants played in and even captained the English cricket team.

The newly founded Social Democratic Party (eventually to merge with the Liberal Party) had the most coherent policies on race, suggesting that the Equal Opportunities Commission and the Commission for Racial Equality merge to become one Equality and Human Rights Commission, a move which took place in 2007. In 1989 the Labour Party produced a document for debate on multicultural education, claiming that

> Britain is manifestly a multiracial society with a plurality of cultures. We believe that any education system, . . . must ensure that all children develop an understanding of and a sensitivity towards this plurality of cultures and traditions . . . secondly it must ensure that pupils of all races achieve their full potential.
>
> (Labour Party 1989: 2–3)

Certainly by the end of the decade, despite enduring hostilities, 'Anti-racist politics had made deep inroads into public life. It was no longer easy to cast aspersions on "bloody foreigners" with a clear conscience' (Winder 2004: 416).

Education policy in the 1980s

The core focus of social policy under Mrs Thatcher was an emphasis on the use of markets and free enterprise to produce the goods and services wanted by consumers. Although other countries, notably New Zealand and the USA, were experimenting with the introduction of market forces in education, a precondition for consumer choice in England was to be the partial dismantling of a democratically controlled education system via local education authorities, and its replacement by more autonomous individual schools, but with centralised funding, curricula and examinations. Education was, from 1980, intended to be a commodity, with parents supposedly free to choose the quality, location and amount, and the best quality of schooling was to be a positional good which must be competitively sought. Values of competitive individualism and separatism were extolled and knowledge itself regarded as a commodity for private consumption. But knowledge was to be regulated and controlled by central government, a national curriculum finally being introduced in 1988.

Some ten Education Acts were passed during the decade, with a 1980 Act allowing parents to 'express a preference' for their children's schooling. Mrs Thatcher's first Education Secretary, Mark Carlisle, announced that from October 1979 comprehensive education was no longer national policy and local authorities were free to retain their selective grammar and secondary modern schools or return to this pattern. Several did so and others attempted the reversal but were defeated by local objections. The move towards comprehensive education continued during the decade but this form of secondary education was on the defensive and various forms of selection and specialisation crept in. The 1980 Act provided for assisted places at private schools for academically able children from poor homes, to provide them with a supposedly better education than state schooling, or, as one headteacher put it to Edwards and his colleagues, 'pluck embers from the ashes of comprehensive schools' (Edwards *et al.* 1989: 1). In fact, the children selected came from 'educationally advantaged homes' and very few ethnic minority children were offered places. Some £70 million was spent on this scheme in the first seven years, with the Labour Party pledged to abolish it. The successes of comprehensive schools were glossed over and Mark Carlisle was sacked for suggesting that more pupils passing public exams and staying in education was evidence of this success. He was replaced by Keith Joseph, who was committed to a return to selection and differentiation between an academic and vocational curriculum. In 1984 Joseph set up a curriculum project for the 40 per cent of lower attaining pupils (LAPP), with many black children falling into this category.

A 1986 Act reduced the influence of LEAs in school governor appointments and gave governors responsibility for the conduct of the school and its curriculum. There had been particular right-wing anxieties that the curriculum in some schools was now including such areas as world studies, peace studies, health studies and sex education, and governors were now urged to take responsibility for ensuring that any 'political' education was balanced and not indoctrination. A clause in a 1988 Local Government Act (Section 28) did forbid LEAs to support any teaching in schools relating to homosexuality, a suggestion largely supported by Muslim parents. Section 28 caused much furore and was finally abolished via a 2003 Local Government Act. The 1981 Special Education Act, which changed the law on special education, was something of an anomaly, given the pressures for selection by ability. The Act followed the report of the Committee, chaired by Mary (later Lady) Warnock, set up by Mrs Thatcher in 1973 to inquire into the education of handicapped young people and reporting in 1978. This report argued that children formerly segregated by categories of handicap or disability should be regarded as having special educational needs (SEN) and be progressively integrated into mainstream schools. The issue of black children's over-representation in special schooling was ignored. As pressure on teachers to raise standards increased, the need to remove troublesome or needy children increased and led to considerable professional and political conflict over notions of integration and inclusion, particularly where disaffected black pupils and second language learners were concerned. Raising standards at all levels became a major objective and a major task for schools was to

> create the human capital which is the raw material for industry, providing a differentiated curriculum preparing pupils for management or labour but with skills, attitudes and technological competences equal to international competitors. . . . Industry and Commerce are among the school's main customers.
>
> (DES 1985b: 15, 82)

However, in 1986 Joseph introduced the GCSE examination at 16 to replace the O level and the lower level CSE (Certificate of Secondary Education). A complaint among ethnic minority pupils had been that they were often entered for this lower level exam. At this point, the national average of those pupils gaining five O level passes was 23 per cent, a figure which began to rise significantly when the GCSE was introduced (five A–C GCSE passes being equivalent to the O level benchmark). Government needed new policies to cope with youth unemployment within an economy in which unskilled labour was no longer needed, and higher levels of skills were demanded. The Department for Employment set up a National Council for Vocational Qualifications in 1986, with National Vocational Qualifications (NVQs) providing an occupational route. Responsibility for youth training schemes was devolved to Training and Enterprise Councils (TECs), employer dominated organisations set up in 1986 and abolished in 2000, when a Learning and Skills Council (LSC) took over much responsibility and funding for post-16 training. A further attempt to link education more firmly to employment, and increase private involvement in schooling, was the creation of City Technology Colleges in 1986. Only 15 were ever set up, and were mainly state-financed as employers were unwilling to provide money.

Moves to curtail the professional autonomy of teachers were made during the decade and those who argued that teachers should be reflexive practitioners were presented by the radical right as enemies of good practice. Teacher trainers were accused of Marxist bias in their courses, especially those courses 'concerned with the politics of race, sex, class and even anti-imperialist education . . . the nature of these courses appear designed to stir up disaffection, . . . preach a spurious doctrine of equality and subvert the entire curriculum' (Hillgate Group 1989: 5). Madan Sarup's book, *The Politics of Multiracial Education* (Sarup 1986), came in for particular criticism, as did a course offered at Brighton Polytechnic examining class, race and gender issues. Mrs Thatcher was moved to mention in her memoirs (Thatcher 1993), how shocked she was at the Brighton course. A Council for the Accreditation of Teacher Education (CATE) was set up in 1984, effectively removing responsibility for teacher education courses from institutions of Higher Education, and a bitter teachers' pay dispute took place in 1985–87, after which a Teachers Pay and Conditions Act led to an imposition of pay structures and conditions of work on teachers. Keith Joseph was replaced by Kenneth Baker in 1987, but by this time there was considerable dissatisfaction with the Conservative reforms, particularly the under-spending on education which had left school buildings crumbling, especially old schools in inner cities. Education expenditure as a proportion of GDP had fallen from 5.5 per cent in 1981 to 4.8 per cent in 1987. Teacher morale was low and even the Chair of the Conservative Education Association was critical of the state of the service and what he described as 'some fairly bizarre individuals' advising the Prime Minister (Ball 1990: 42). However, Baker undertook a major piece of education reform which initially created even more dissatisfaction.

The 1988 Education Reform Act made a decisive break with the welfare state principles that had underpinned the 1944 Education Act. It was concerned with individual entrepreneurism and competitiveness, rather than equity and social justice. Although 20,000 mainly negative replies had been received during a brief period of consultation, including anxieties expressed by the CRE and the Afro-Caribbean Education Resource Project (De Haviland 1988), the Act, giving the Secretary of State 451 new powers, was law by July 1988. Ignoring advice from HMI and others that a curriculum based on the subjects laid down by the 1904 Board of Education regulations might need rethinking, the Act introduced a national curriculum of three core and seven foundation traditional subjects. The collective 'act of worship' and religious education laid down by the 1944 Act were to be of a 'mainly Christian' character. There was to be testing at Key Stages 7, 11, 14 and 16 and ten levels of performance were drawn up by a Task Force on Attainment and Testing. A National Curriculum Council and a Schools Examination and Assessment Council were set up in place of the existing curriculum and assessment bodies. School admissions procedures were to provide for open enrolment and more parental 'choice', with schools receiving delegated budgets based on pupil numbers. School could also opt out of local authority control to be grant-maintained, with funding direct from central government. The Inner London Education Authority was abolished and Higher and Further Education responsibilities removed from local authority control. During the passage of the Act through Parliament race-specific concerns were raised in the House of Lords. An amendment put forward by Lord Pitt, Britain's first black peer to sit in the House of Lords, asked for the first clause of the Act, which required the National Curriculum to 'prepare pupils for the opportunities, responsibilities and experiences of adult life' should continue 'in a multicultural and multiracial society'. The amendment failed, as did a further proposal that the Act should incorporate a sentence from page 61 of *Better Schools* (DES 1985b) that all pupils be educated to acquire positive attitudes to all ethnic groups. Labour Lords, in conjunction with the legal section of the CRE, also sought to amend requirements on open enrolment and parental choice, to prevent such policies leading to racial segregation. Ministers had already admitted such a possibility existed, Lady Hooper, Minister of State for Education, concluding in an interview that 'racial segregation may be the price we pay for giving some parents more opportunity to chose' (*Times Educational Supplement* 1987). This amendment also failed. Others were more optimistic, suggesting the National Curriculum and testing would give black parents reassurance that their children were being offered equal curriculum opportunities, and that new provisions for schools governors could allow black parents more active roles in school management.

Educational needs in a multi-ethnic society

By the early 1980s, subsuming minority children under the blanket notion of disadvantage was becoming untenable. The Rampton Committee noted that 'within the DES we have been concerned to note that the needs of ethnic minority children are so often seen only as an aspect of disadvantage, or even . . . just a form of handicap' (DES 1981a: 73). A combination of riots and reports eventually persuaded government that while inner-city disadvantage was part of the problem, racial discrimination was an added disadvantage. There was also a more overt recognition that the racism and ignorance of the majority society needed combating and that education for an ethnically diverse society was now of importance. Concerns about public order and egalitarian recognition that minorities needed more equal educational and employment opportunities, were matched by more recognition of the interdependence of the world economy and trade. Joint ventures with a Commonwealth of former colonies was making it uneconomic to hold arrogant or hostile attitudes to ethnic minorities either in Britain or abroad. Despite the determined attacks of the new right on any curriculum change and the nervousness of politicians to address the issues openly, advances were made during the Conservative government tenure in the 1980s in bringing the changing realities of 'the nature of British society in a global context' (DES 1985a: 324) to the fore. Policies were shifting towards an understanding that education had a crucial role to play in determining the relations between ethnic minorities and the white majority society. The Labour Government's Green Paper in 1977 had noted that 'the curriculum should reflect a sympathetic understanding of the different cultures and races that make up our society' (DES 1977: 41) but gave no guidance on how this could happen. It was the Conservative government in the 1980s which supported policies for curriculum development, supplied education support grants and grants for in-service teacher training for a multi-ethnic society (DES 1987).

An HMI paper on the school curriculum in 1981 concluded that learning in a multicultural society should help all pupils develop respect for religious values, tolerance of other races and knowledge of the interdependence of individuals and nations (DES 1981b). This meant a focus on schools in white areas as well as multiracial inner-city areas, where efforts had so far been concentrated. The work of Gaine (1987), perceptively entitled *No Problem Here*, described the prevailing attitudes in areas with few or no ethnic minority children where many LEA officials, schools and teachers believed there was no serious racism in their region, and regarded multicultural and anti-racist initiatives as threatening or stirring up trouble. By 1984 literature began emerging relating education for a multicultural society to a majority white society that was not much interested. Gaine recorded that his white pupils 'did not listen to distinctions between Sikhs and Muslims, Gujeratis and Bengalis, West Indians and Indians, because they are not interested . . . The important thing to them is that these people are not white and the students believe they are responsible for unemployment and bad housing' (Gaine 1987: 86). However, both the Anglican and Catholic Churches endorsed a broader education for diversity and a multi-faith approach to religion (Working Party on Catholic Education 1984, Archbishop of Canterbury 1985) and the Swann Committee included in its report a description of visits to schools in white areas (DES 1985a: 224–314). In 1987 NAME held its annual conference in Sussex on the theme of anti-racist education in white areas, and practitioners, both white and ethnic minority, contributed to the debates through articles in journals, notably the journal *Multicultural Teaching*, and descriptions appeared of attempts to change practice in areas from Cumbria in the north of England to the Scilly Isles in the far south-west (Tomlinson 1990).

Lord Swann's Committee continued the work of the committee chaired by Anthony Rampton, which was set up in 1979 to report on *The Education of Children from Ethnic Minority Groups.*[3] This become, under Swann, a report on *Education For All* (DES 1985a). The 807-page report, complete with much evidence and consultation, constituted a high point in positive recommendations for offering 'all pupils a good, relevant and up to date education for life in Britain and the world as it is today' (ibid.: 315). The report was clear that meeting the needs of ethnic minority pupils and broadening the education offered to all pupils were inter-related, and it recognised that, in common with world-wide debates, there were problems inherent in promoting shared values within a nation-state, while accommodating cultural and religious diversity. Chapters covered the theory and practice of racism, minority school achievements, educational policies to date, the development of multicultural education, language and religious issues, and teacher education, and also briefly reviewed the needs of Chinese, Vietnamese, Ukrainian, Cypriot, Italian and travellers' children, and the long established black community in Liverpool. The crucial Chapter 6 covered 'Education for All' and optimistically described the role of education in laying the foundations for a 'genuinely pluralist society' in which shared values and appreciation of diversity could co-exist. In their discussion of achievement issues, however, the committee did still feel it necessary to commission a review of research on IQ testing and innate 'intelligence', as a sop to the Jensen-Eysenck assertions of a lower black IQ (DES 1985a: 126–63). They also overviewed research which compared various test and performance scores using the blanket labels of 'West Indian, Asian and Indigenous' and the recommendations on raising the achievement levels of black children were remarkably vague (ibid.: 768). The main suggestion was further research on the academic success of black pupils. The ILEA research and statistics branch had originally proposed such research after the Rampton Committee reported, but was opposed by NAME and some black groups.[4] The committee also briefly considered the call for separate schooling from some black parents and, while sympathetic, dismissed the suggestion as fragmenting the school system on racial grounds. They were more sympathetic to Muslim parental requests for single-sex schooling for girls.

Before the Swann Report was published various false assertions were made as to possible recommendations, the most extreme probably being an article in the *Daily Mail* (Kenny 1984), which claimed that every school would be obliged to offer the entire curriculum in Gujerati and Punjabi, end morning assemblies so as not to 'favour Christianity over Hinduism, Islam or presumably witchcraft', and hire minority teachers in preference to white. On publication, the Swann Report was attacked from both the right and left. Among others the Deputy Chair of the Conservative Monday Club considered that the report was 'contemptuous of the rights of the native inhabitants of the UK' (Pearce 1986), while academic Barry Troyna,[5] accused the committee of 'political chicanery' for failing to consider how racism operates through the education system and for providing comfort for those who were only committed to cultural tourism in the curriculum (Troyna 1986, 1993). Having access to the Swann Report before publication, the government had decided to respond by offering Education Support Grants initiated by a 1984 Education (Grants and Award) Act. The purpose of the grants was to target resources on educational problems that government considered were of national importance and needed national solutions, and *Educational Needs in a Multi-ethnic Society* was one such area. Between 1985 and 1989 some £3 million went to fund ESG projects – largely in areas with few or no ethnic minorities. Curriculum development, school twinning, teacher and headteacher training in race awareness and race equality, parent involvement, pre-school education, business courses for minorities and many others, were some of the projects which continued into the 1990s, the annual project reports being sent to the DES, and filed away (Tomlinson 1990). Many of these recommendations were repeated in the 2000s with schools being exhorted to bring about community cohesion. On leaving office six months after the Swann Report was published, Keith Joseph, Education Secretary of State, issued what was reported as an important statement of the objectives of government action on education for an ethnically mixed society. He noted that the report had been followed by much talk and some action, and made what was becoming a familiar disclaimer, that 'Action on this sensitive subject is difficult . . . the subject arouses deep emotions' (Joseph 1986: 200). He reiterated that objectives of policy were to prepare all children and young people for life in an ethnically mixed Britain and raise the achievements of all children, especially ethnic minorities. He also deplored the polarisation of debate into those who denied that any change was needed in education or the society, and those who argued for a complete transformation of the system.

Although Joseph had nothing to say on funding, there was considerable anxiety that Section 11 grants, totalling some £100 million by the mid-1980s, were mismanaged and not benefiting ethnic minority communities as intended. Scrutiny of the grants was undertaken in 1987 by ministers and officials from both the Home Office and the DES, and a report was published in 1988 (Home Office 1988). The recommendations were that local authorities should have primary responsibility for administering the grants and money should be targeted at meeting 'ethnic minority needs arising from racial disadvantage'. Minority communities should be more involved in grant use, as should the voluntary sector, the references to 'Commonwealth immigrants' should be abandoned, and the grants directed towards opening up mainstream services for all ethnic minorities. The report did not placate critics and arguments continued over Section 11 grants and their application. Teacher training for a multicultural society became something of a priority from the early 1980s, as there was a growing awareness that many teachers were ignorant or unsure of the issues. Training for trainers was needed, and in 1981 Maurice Craft organised a seminar at Nottingham University on this theme, and subsequently obtained funding from the DES, Shell and Boots to run courses in training-the-trainers at six institutions. By 1986 over 40 colleges were running such courses (Craft 1986). Teacher unions agreed that teachers needed information and training, with the NUT and AMMA publishing booklets on combating racism, race equality and multicultural and anti-racist education. Nursery nurse teachers of pre-school children, aware that racial attitudes were incorporated at an early age, supported the formation of a Nursery Nurse Tutors Anti-Racist Network (NNTARN), which held its first national conference in London in 1988. The Council for the Accreditation of Teacher Education, set up in 1984, was required to make sure that all students received training for a multicultural society, and in 1986 and 1987 'Teaching and the Curriculum in a Multiethnic Society' was made a national in-service training priority. The DES issued consultation papers on increasing the supply of ethnic minority teachers, and there was also a requirement from 1986 that Examining Boards for the new General Certificate of Secondary Education (GCSE) have regard for cultural and linguistic diversity. The Council for National Academic Awards (CNAA) required all the higher education institutions it validated to permeate their teacher training courses with multicultural understandings, and set up a working group in 1982 to promote good practice. The group produced a document in 1984 which had wide circulation in polytechnics and colleges and caused the University Council for the Education of Teachers (UCET) to set up its own working group. However, the CNAA document was rewritten on the advice of DES officials, deleting any reference to the term 'anti-racist'. The defensiveness many central government officials demonstrated in admitting that policies were actually designed, not just to provide more realistic information on the backgrounds, cultures and life experiences of minorities, but also to combat racism and deal with racial hostility in the majority society, was evident well into the 1990s. They were certainly influenced by a powerful lobby opposing anything under the label of multicultural or anti-racist education (Lewis 1988, Lawlor 1990).

Local authorities and schools

Although local authorities had their responsibilities reduced by a 1980 Local Government Act, by which central government decided on the level of service for each LEA, gave a block grant, capped powers to raise money through local rates, and required 'bids' for extra money, the 146 LEAs did retain considerable influence over schools, teachers and the curriculum. During the decade most authorities began to produce policies described as multicultural or anti-racist, or combining the two. By the end of the decade some two-thirds of authorities had produced some kind of policy document, either glossy booklet or mimeographed sheets, and the theme of race equality was becoming part of the vocabulary in public services generally. Whatever the label, the policies, together with LEA responsibility for in-service teacher education, did provide schools with a framework for changing and developing the curriculum, and educating teachers. They were spurred on by the requirements of the 1976 Race Relations Act, by the urban riots and the Scarman Inquiry, by a 1981 requirement to review the curriculum (DES 1981b) and by the Rampton Committee, which had suggested that the DES should invite all LEAs to define their policy and commitment to multicultural education and describe how this was put into practice in schools. A Home Office circular in 1986 also recommended that local authorities adopt guidelines on racial incidents in schools, although a CRE survey two years later reported that many ethnic minority children suffered racial harassment from nursery school to college, the perpetrators being ordinary fellow members of the learning community, not extremists (CRE 1988). By the early 1980s a survey of 70 local authorities and 255 schools found significant advances in curriculum development and English Language teaching in schools with large numbers of minority pupils, but those with few or no such pupils still claiming there was no need for change (Little and Willey 1981). Those authorities who were most responsive appointed multicultural advisors, set up teacher in-service courses, encouraged school initiatives, and engaged with parents and community groups. Pioneers in the field were the ILEA, the Greater London Boroughs of Haringey and Brent, and Bradford, Berkshire and Manchester LEAs. Pioneers in all or mainly white areas included Cumbria, Wiltshire and Lincolnshire. As the decade progressed it became clear that the production of these policies by local education authorities and schools was proving contentious in the extreme, whichever political party was in control in the authority. In the meantime, black parents continued to develop what was a recognisable black supplementary school movement, particularly in the West Midlands and London, with Chevannes (1979) having documented one of the first supplementary schools in Wolverhampton, and Clark (1982) describing a Saturday school in Peckham.

The Inner London Education Authority was the first to produce written guidelines on education in a multi-ethnic society in 1977, setting up a special inspectorate and writing an aide-memoire in 1981 (ILEA 1981). Francis Morrell, Leader of the ILEA from 1981 to 1987 commissioned a series of reports and research to improve the quality of education in London schools and colleges, including the report of a committee chaired by David Hargreaves, which documented school practices that could disadvantage minorities, and she encouraged written policies for equality on race, sex and class (Morrell 1989). She took the view that 'Equal opportunity, once intended to provide equality irrespective of social class, had become associated with the elimination of discrimination against the black and ethnic minority communities and against the female majority' (ibid.: 39). The internationally known ILEA Research and Statistics Branch, under the direction of Peter Mortimore, produced research and evaluation of the examination results of all groups in the authority, noting the complexity of this as the decade progressed. Throughout the decade the examination results of pupils of Afro-Caribbean, Bangladeshi, Turkish and ESWI (English, Scottish, Welsh and Irish) were lower than those of East African Asian, Indian and Pakistani, although all groups improved over time. The lower white scores were largely explained by social class factors, many of the middle class having fled parts of inner London by this time. Of all groups black students were most likely to go on to study in Further Education Colleges. As with other research during the 1980s, there was a focus on 'school effectiveness', which was demonstrating that some schools proved more successful than others in encouraging student success whatever their social class, ethnicity or gender (Smith and Tomlinson 1989, Drew and Gray 1990). It remained the case, however, that schools which incorporated a mix of middle- and working-class children had more educational success, and minority children were more likely to be attending predominantly working-class schools where it was more difficult to obtain the qualifications black and Asian parents expected.

The attempts by the ILEA, the largest education authority in the country with the largest and most diverse school population, to ensure a more equal education for all led to criticism from central government, and from teachers and parents – both black and white. Criticism of both curriculum innovations and the inequalities in examination preparation, entry and success, continued to assume that a focus on the former somehow created less focus on the latter. Schools that local inspectors and HMI considered were under-performing generally were often singled out by the media for their anti-racist activities. One such school, Highbury Quadrant, with 70 per cent ethnic minority pupils, was widely reported for its poor quality of teaching and a reported public row between teachers over an assembly to honour Nelson Mandela (gaoled leader of the African National Congress), after which some teachers were redeployed (Wilby 1988). A black parents association in South London published its first special issue in 1985, attacking the Hargreaves Report on secondary education (Hargreaves 1984), the Swann Report, and the black and Asian members of the Swann Committee, including Bhikhu (later Lord) Parekh, and Professor G.K. Verma, long-established academic researcher, as not focusing sufficiently on black achievement (Black Parents Fight Back 1985). Outer London Boroughs, even those that had been at the forefront of educational change and employed ethnic minority staff in senior positions, were also targets for criticism. In Haringey, a black pressure group on education sent letters to headteachers and officials blaming them for poor examination results, but opposing the keeping of records of exam scores and school suspensions by ethnicity (Venning 1983). In Newham a 1986 inquiry reported that black parents felt that white teachers had hijacked anti-racist policies for their own career benefit. In Ealing a report drew attention to the small numbers of ethnic minority teachers and their lack of promotion, with Chair of the Education Committee Hilary Benn (later an MP and Minister for International Development) promising action. Brent Borough set up a Brent Development Programme on Racial Equality, which was criticised in the *Daily Mail* as introducing 'race spies in the classroom', and the Home Office was instructed to set up an inquiry into the programme. Central government, especially Mrs Thatcher and her close circle, were not enamoured of the attention local authorities and some schools were paying to race equality, and subsequent political decisions influencing the 1988 Education Act expressed this distaste. The decision to abolish the ILEA and split it into

13 separate boroughs, each with control of education, was taken on political grounds. Mrs Thatcher recorded in her memoirs that despite increases in public spending on education, standards had not improved – 'a classic case being the left-wing dominated ILEA' (Thatcher 1993: 590). However, three of the first Chief Education Officers appointed to the new boroughs were black, notably Gus John, education officer and co-author of the MacDonald Report on Burnage School, and Beb Burchill, who announced that her appointment must not be seen as a personal triumph but a 'breakthrough to combat racism at the very top' (Hughill 1989).

Bradford LEA in Yorkshire, with a large Asian population, was one of the first outside London to produce a memorandum in 1982 suggesting that schools seek ways of preparing all young people for life in a multicultural society and countering racist attitudes, inequalities and discrimination. The memorandum covered information for parents on religious assemblies and education, special provision for Muslims, uniform, meals, recording of names, dealing with racist behaviour, graffiti, bullying, and curriculum development. Ray Honeyford, a local headteacher of a middle school with a large number of Asian pupils did not share the council's aspirations for curriculum reform and ethos in a multicultural or anti-racist direction, writing in an article in the *TES* in 1982 that 'the responsibility for the adaptations and adjustments involved in settling in a new country lies entirely with those who have come to settle and raise families' and suggesting that West Indian pupils' lower achievements were due to family problems rather than school (Honeyford 1982). After the publication of a further article in the right-wing *Salisbury Review* in which he complained about 'multi-racial bigots augmented by a growing bureaucracy of race in local authorities', the poetry of Linton Kwesi Johnson, the 'hysterical political temperament' of the Indian subcontinent, and dispossessed indigenous parents (Honeyford 1984), a campaign was launched against him, and two years later he accepted an early retirement settlement. Bradford and the 'Honeyford Affair' were much publicised, with protest and writings from left and right, from supporters and opponents of multicultural and anti-racist policies and from white and Asian parents. Dozens of articles on Honeyford and Bradford were written over the next six years, Honeyford himself publishing his views (Honeyford 1988) and a succinct and balanced account of the political, legal and social implications being provided by Halstead (1988). Halstead pointed out that some of the issues highlighted by the affair concerned the long-running debate between the need for social cohesion and the rights of minority groups, and debate over the aims of education from liberal and religious perspectives, issues which surfaced sharply in the 2000s. Berkshire LEA, the second to produce a policy in the early 1980s (a policy that concentrated more on racial equality than curriculum change and advocated race-awareness courses for teachers and administrators) also ran into trouble. In 1988 the council, alarmed by accusations of left-wing influences, suggested that the policy be abrogated and new guidelines for schools substituted. The proposed new guidelines worried that 'we are in danger of losing our British heritage and national pride', and declared that race-awareness training was socially divisive. Opposition to scrapping the original policy united a range of groups including Berkshire heads and teachers, teacher unions, the CRE, 30 other LEAs and the Education Board of the Church of England, and eventually the council decided to retain the original (Tomlinson 1988).

A year-long battle between white parents and another Yorkshire LEA began in August 1987. Twenty-two parents in Dewsbury, Kirklees, objected to their children being allocated to a school where 85 per cent of the children were of Asian origin and requested they go to a predominantly white school, both schools being Church of England primary schools. The parents educated their children privately in a room above a local pub and challenged the council in a High Court action. Supported by a newly formed Parental Alliance for Choice in Education, which asserted that the parents 'have a natural desire that their children be educated in a traditional English and Christian environment' (Naylor 1988), the parents won their action on the technicality that the council had not provided sufficient guidance on catchment areas. A report on the affair, advised by a solicitor and Hermann Ousley, then Chief Executive of ILEA, suggested that councillors were determined to defend multicultural developments against parents they perceived as racist. The defeat of the council was regarded as a vindication of 'those white and Muslim parents who make legitimate demands for separate schools and distinctive education'. The Dewsbury case gave wide publicity to white parental claims that school standards were lowered by a focus on Asian pupils, although no evidence was ever produced to support this claim. However, in 1988 in Cleveland LEA in the north-east of England, a parent requested that her daughter be transferred to a predominantly white school on the grounds that she was 'learning Pakistani'. Cleveland had produced a policy statement on multicultural education and race equality in 1985. After taking legal advice Cleveland Council decided that it had a statutory duty under the 1980 and 1988 Education Acts to comply with the parental request and a subsequent investigation by the Commission for Racial Equality highlighted the contradictions between the 1976 Race Relations Act and the Education Acts.

In Manchester a working group of staff at Birley High School produced one of the first school policies, endorsed by the Chief Education Officer, on changing attitudes and practice (Birley High School 1980). The school was filmed for BBC television by John Twitchen, who produced a series of films during the 1980s on the role of the media in reducing racism (Twitchen 1988), and was also chosen for a research study which became the focus of a controversy over the extent of teacher racism (Foster 1990).[6] In 1986 a disturbed 13-year-old white boy stabbed fellow pupil Ahmed Ullah in the playground of all-boys Burnage High School. This school had an anti-racist policy, and sensationalist media coverage following the murder gave the impression that the policy was to blame. A committee chaired by Ian MacDonald QC presented a report on the murder in 1988, which concluded that there had not been sufficient consultation by senior management with all staff, parents and pupils on the policy, and criticised the macho culture of an all-male school and the wider manifestations of racism in society. Manchester LEA declined to publish the whole report on the grounds of possible libel, and the committee eventually published it themselves (MacDonald *et al.* 1989). The report noted that following the murder the national media had mounted a sustained attack on anti-racist policies, 'looney-left' councils with such policies and anti-racist approaches in education generally. As a result 'Burnage was suddenly writ large as a question mark against anti-racist education' and Education Officers in other LEAs who had resisted any notions of multiculturalism or anti-racist education were able to claim vindication for the view that it was all a dangerous activity (MacDonald: xix).

Exclusion and achievement

The media was less interested in the information that during the 1980s a disproportionate number of black pupils were being suspended from schools, particularly in Birmingham and inner London, and that this was of great concern to black parents. It appeared that the ESN issue had been overtaken, after the 1981 Special Education Act had abolished the category, by the speedier removal of children from mainstream schools by suspension and exclusion, although black children were still over-represented in special schools for the emotionally and behaviourally disturbed (EBD). Despite a focus on policies that were described as anti-racist or encouraging race equality, there was little evidence of an examination of school structures and organisation which reconstructed inequalities by social class and race. The data on school leaving qualifications obtained for the Swann Report (DES 1985a: 110–18) was much quoted as demonstrating the lower school leaving qualifications obtained by West Indian pupils, although the previous year the third PSI study (Brown 1984) had shown that African-Caribbean students persisted in study at Further Education Colleges and eventually obtained similar O level qualifications to whites. In a study of pupils passing through their five years of secondary schooling in multiracial urban schools, Smith and Tomlinson (1989) found that while the national average for those passing in the last year of the O level examination was 22 per cent (the O level exam having originally been designed for the 20 per cent most academically able), in the 20 schools studied only 10 per cent of pupils overall achieved the required five subjects. There was clear evidence of what has been noted above, that these urban schools were never designed, resourced or staffed to levels that could offer all pupils higher academic achievements, a message that eluded policy makers, who preferred to focus on pupil and family deficiencies. The differences between minorities were not large, and the West

Indian pupils gained the highest number of passes in English, although this was not highlighted in subsequent comment. Media and political interest in the publication of this study was considerable, almost every national and many regional newspapers devoting an editorial and other comment to it, mainly commenting on the finding that some schools were more effective than others in helping children through examinations, and 'what school a child goes to makes far more difference than which ethnic group he or she belongs to' (Smith and Tomlinson 1989: 281). Other messages, that schools were more likely to teach and enter pupils from higher social classes for higher level exams, and that school processes such as choosing subjects to study after 14, even though operated by liberal and well-intentioned teachers, could have the effect of disadvantaging black pupils, were not so readily absorbed. While during the 1980s attention was paid to curriculum, organisation and expectations that produced gender inequalities, after which girls' school achievements began to rise, there was less attention paid to raising the achievements of ethnic minorities overall. The disadvantages associated with placement in a lower status curriculum, leading to lower level credentials, which was where a majority of black pupils were placed, was becoming increasingly obvious as employment possibilities dwindled and higher level credentials were required for higher levels of education and training. By the end of the 1980s debate about the educational performance of ethnic minority groups and the way they were treated by schools was firmly on the agenda, although still with the familiar central government nervousness over what were regarded as controversial race and education issues. The Smith and Tomlinson DES-sponsored research, ready for publication at the end of 1987, was held up for publication for almost two years by officials, with questions eventually being asked in Parliament about its non-publication.

Multi and anti brigades

An outpouring of literature and comment expressed in writings from just about every academic, practical and political viewpoint on the subject of multicultural and anti-racist education during the 1980s far surpassed any actual action in schools, LEAs or the DES. However, it was a teacher-led movement that, from the 1970s, recognised that a curriculum which took no account of the presence of minorities led to the perpetuation of stereotypes and misinformation and fed popular racism. In the 1980s more practitioners began to write about their changing practice and define what a curriculum based on non-racist and multicultural approaches would look like. The notion of curriculum permeation became popular. Teachers, textbook writers and publishers gave serious thought to the incorporation of multicultural and global approaches to subjects. Visitors to schools, as one teacher working on an Education Support Grant project pointed out, would not find a 'subject' of multiculturalism on the timetable, but would find teachers in schools in multiracial and white areas working 'to help pupils acquire the intellectual skills and emotional maturity in areas such as the humanities, science and languages, to recognise that there are many interpretations of the world and all children need to open-mindedly examine them' (Brown 1988: 41). Much of the literature up to the mid-1980s was summarised in Craft and Klein (1986). Hemming, for example, pointed out that the universality of mathematics made it an obvious contributor to a multicultural curriculum (Hemming 1984), while black teachers documented the contributions black scientists had made, contradicting the common view that science was a white European monopoly and demonstrating, again, the nonsense of psuedo-scientific claims of a biological base for racial differences in intelligence. English teachers documented and evaluated successful innovations in literature, language and media studies and made links with dance and drama, and were also involved in heated debates over the removal of racially derogatory literature from libraries and classrooms (Klein 1985). The Bullock Report in 1975 had encouraged a broad approach to language, and support for bilingual and ESL learners encouraged more study of the nature of language. The teaching of history, always a contentious area, took on new antagonisms during the 1980s. A large literature discussing the political and nationalistic bias in history teaching now included an examination of an Anglo-centric focus, considered to be limiting in the modern world. HMI supported the teaching of history in a global context and by 1987 a World Studies project (Hicks 1987) had developed materials used in over half of LEAs. The notion that there was an unproblematic British past and heritage to be taught came under question and, in turn, provided a focus for those defending a traditional view of history. Professor (later Lord) Skidelsky was a prominent critic of the GCSE history syllabus, refuting the suggestion that historical themes should relate to the development of a multicultural society.

The Swann Committee took the view that the aims of a multicultural anti-racist curriculum were synonymous with a good education designed to produce decent, tolerant and knowledgeable citizens. More understanding of the origins and values underpinning the curriculum was required rather than arguing about the content of subjects. The report stressed that 'we are not primarily concerned with changing the content of the curriculum but rather with bringing about a fundamental reorientation of the attitudes which condition the selection of curriculum materials and subject matter and which underlie the actual teaching and learning process' (DES 1985a: 324). But well before the Swann recommendations an antagonistic debate had developed between academics and practitioners over the ways in which attitudes could be reoriented. This took the form of presenting multicultural and anti-racist curriculum aims as alternatives, rather than mutually supportive. Radical supporters of the anti-racist stance argued that, as the fundamental response of the education system towards ethnic minorities was marked by racism and a denial of resources, power and equal opportunities, any change labelled multicultural could only be tokenism. Work from the Marxist oriented Institute of Race Relations, from Mullard (1984),[7] Brandt (1986) and Troyna (1987) claimed that what they termed 'multicultural education' was assimilationist and unsupportive of racial justice. There were few return claims from those practitioners who, with minimal help or training, were attempting to offer a curriculum that would reflect their multiracial classrooms or inform their all-white classes, while still offering equal opportunities for learning to all pupils. Troyna's dismissal of 'saris, samosas and steel bands' as tokenism, actually first quoted by Canadian Kogila Moodley (1983), was widely repeated. It is noteworthy that by the 2000s sari-making and selling was a multi-million pound business in the UK, samosas were in every supermarket, and steel bands continued to entertain in schools, community and city centres. However, it soon became clear that this debate set up a false dichotomy and diverted attention from right-wing political critiques. There was little evidence produced by committed anti-racists to support their contention that teachers were putting into practice multicultural aims which did not also challenge the racist beliefs of their pupils. For example, the observations by Brandt (1986) of what he described as anti-racist teaching and curriculum, were similar to those described by teachers in Craft and Bardell (1984) as curriculum in a multicultural society. By 1987 the central debate was actually between those who supported any kind of multicultural anti-racist curriculum innovation and policies at central and local level, against powerful opponents who opposed any changes and were successfully marginalising and vilifying any change.

Opposition to any multiculturalist anti-racist curriculum development from the political and education right was relatively muted until the 1980s. Once it became apparent that innovation in all schools was advocated, opposition became more vocal. Change advocated by Marxist-oriented academics or Labour-controlled local authorities could be dismissed as looney left subversion, but a Department of Education Report from a committee chaired by a Liberal Lord was more threatening. Politicians, academics and educationalists who could be described as educational nationalists[8] either formed new pressure groups or redirected the efforts of groups such as the Hillgate Group and the Salisbury Group to argue against tampering with a 'traditional' school curriculum. They were able to influence legislation and the new National Curriculum, and received much sympathetic media coverage. Opposition came to focus on the charge that multicultural anti-racist education was associated with left-of-centre egalitarianism, political subversion and posed a threat to traditional British values and culture. At the 1987 Conservative Party conference the Prime Minister, introducing the forthcoming 1988 Education Reform Act, specifically noted that

> In the inner cities, where youngsters must have a decent education if they are to have a better future, that opportunity is all too often snatched away from them by hard-left education authorities and extremist teachers. Children who need to be able to count and multiply are learning anti-racist mathematics, whatever that may be.
>
> (Thatcher, reported in Hughill 1987)

Baroness Cox, later Deputy Speaker of the House of Lords, criticised the contents of an ILEA teaching pack on Auschwitz and the Holocaust as 'crude indoctrination', denying children information about other genocides. Holocaust studies were eventually introduced into the National Curriculum. World Studies, Peace Studies and maths were also singled out as indoctrination with the political purpose of fostering disaffection, social tension and inter-group conflict (Cox 1986). Any possible multicultural incursions into mathematics seemed to excite much political opposition, even teaching Chinese and Arabic number systems. Mrs Thatcher appointed Professor Sig Prais, a supporter of the Dewsbury parents noted above, as a member of the Mathematics Working Group which produced proposals for the National Curriculum in 1988. Unsurprisingly this group vetoed any inclusion of multicultural mathematics. History teaching became a major focus for those opposing a changed curriculum, with any alternative views of Britain's relationship to Empire colonies or the Third World being condemned. Hastie, a former head of an ILEA studies centre, had written in 1981 criticising the activities of the ILEA inspectorate and the 'Multicultural Education (ME) Brigade'. In 1986 he again published a critique of the 'race industry's presentation of slavery and colonialism' as stirring up 'needless resentments in the minds of black readers' (Hastie 1986). It was not until 2007 that discussion of slavery became a mainstream topic, with the Mayor of London issuing a public apology for British slavery.

The Education Reform Act became law in July 1988 and in August Kenneth Baker offered the post of Chair of a National Curriculum Council to Duncan Graham, together, as Graham noted, with a malt whisky (Graham 1993). He appointed working groups to develop subject content and attainment targets in ten subjects, with cross-curricular themes intended to take care of race, gender and other inequalities. The Council and its working groups consulted hundreds of educational and business organisations and were required by Baker to 'take account of ethnic and cultural diversity and the importance of the curriculum in promoting equal opportunity regardless of ethnic origin or gender' (Tomlinson 1993). Graham responded by setting up a working group (the author being a member) to suggest ways of incorporating this aim into all subjects. The group reported in 1990, although its proposals were ignored. There was considerable political interference with the work of the curriculum subject groups from right-wing organisations and politicians. Mrs Thatcher took particular exception to the history curriculum, which she felt did not contain enough traditional British history, and considered the history group proposal 'comprehensively flawed' (Thatcher 1993: 596). As the National Curriculum developed during the 1990s (it having been acknowledged that its introduction was too hasty), the Cambridge Professor of Education recorded that 'The 1988 Act . . . should have looked forward with confidence and determination to a better multicultural, multilingual and multi-faith Britain entering a new relationship with itself and with the rest of the world. But it did not' (Hargreaves 1993).

Religion and Muslim assertion

The Education Reform Act contained more sections on religious education than any previous Act, these sections being heavily influenced by Baroness Cox (referred to above) and the Bishop of London. The daily act of worship in schools was to be 'wholly or mainly of a broadly Christian character' and new religious syllabuses were to be in the main Christian faiths. Local Standing Advisory Committees on Religious Education (SACRE) were to make local decisions on treatment of other faiths. Parents were given a right to withdraw their children from religious education or assemblies and could request alternative religious education. In Manchester two white mothers promptly requested the High Court that their children be taught only Christianity, and the Muslim Education Trust prepared a leaflet on 'What can Muslim parents do to protect their children from the effect of compulsory Christian worship'. The 1980s was certainly a decade when the assertion of a Muslim identity ensured that religion was incorporated into race and multicultural debates. While attention had previously focused on race as exemplified by the black community, the relations between Muslims, estimated in 1981 as some 650,000, and British society now assumed greater importance.

Although religious issues generally had not yet assumed the importance of later decades, Muslims were challenging the secular basis of British society, and asserting a particular religious, as distinct from a black or non-white, identity. Studying Muslims in Bradford in the 1980s, Philip Lewis (1994) noted that the communities in Britain, whether in the large cities or smaller northern towns, were large enough and geographically separate enough to sustain social and economic infrastructures and perpetuate religious and cultural values. He noted the proliferation of and investment in mosques as an indication of a determination to pass on these values to their children. But he also referred to research by a Muslim educationalist into what was to become an issue in the 2000s – the importation of non-English speaking Imams, a fact that was already worrying some Muslim parents. They were concerned that some Imams were inculcating children with 'a germ of anti-western education' (Din in Lewis 1994: 142). Din also recorded that the supplementary schooling in mosques was a focus for criticism by Muslim parents and educationalists over the authoritarian styles and content of teaching. By 1991 there were nine elected Muslim Councillors and the Authority had become largely sympathetic to Muslim concerns over education, but Bradford continued to be a centre of attention over Muslim disputes during the 1980s. In 1983 a Bradford Muslim Parents Association requested that five Bradford schools be classified as voluntary-aided Islamic schools on the same basis as the Christian and Jewish faiths. The same requests were made in other authorities, notably in Kirklees, and an Islamic Schools Trust sought publicity for such schools (Hewitt 1988). Their case was supported by right-wing groups who were enthusiastic about the separation of Muslim and white Christian children, but refused by the Secretary of State for Education.

Bradford remained in the news during the mid-1980s over the Honeyford affair (as documented above) and in 1988–89 many Muslims in the city and elsewhere complained that Salman Rushdie's novel, *The Satanic Verses* (1988), was offensive. The book was publicly burned in January 1989 with the approval of the Bradford Council of Mosques, and the Iranian Ayatollah Khomeini issued a *fatwa* (death sentence) on Rushdie, who was forced to hide and seek police protection. What Modood later described as 'public rage against Muslims' (Modood 2005) was intense, although other interfaith organisations attempted to moderate hostility. Karen Armstrong, in her book *Muhammad* (1991), also pointed out that at a meeting of the 45 Member States of the Islamic Congress shortly after the fatwah, 44 condemned the Ayatollah's ruling.

Summary

This chapter has demonstrated that the 1980s were a high point of awareness that the education system needed radical change in order to accommodate what was manifestly a racially and culturally diverse society; although this assertion was still denied by prominent politicians claiming to represent a majority of the white British. Intense conflict surrounded the acceptance of former colonial immigrants and their children, now recognised in law as black and Asian citizens or potential citizens. The assertion of black youth willing to enter into open conflict with the wider society to complain about inequalities and discrimination, was matched by Muslim assertion of a religious identity. While all this worried mainstream politicians and the white majority, it drew an intense reaction from influential right-wing groups, who, formerly campaigning against immigration, now turned their attention to a denial of inclusion of non-whites and 'alien cultures' into their version of the British heritage. Education became a central focus of concern, and attention turned from subsuming minorities under the label of disadvantage, to considering the educational needs of a multi-ethnic society. While some in central government and local authorities and some practitioners were making serious, if often misguided, attempts to create the optimistic Swann hope of a 'genuinely plural society' while attending to racial inequalities and discrimination, attacks and criticism of policies and practice came from all sides. The antagonisms voiced by committed anti-racists against supposed multiculturalists were unhelpful in the extreme. It slowly became clearer that while liberal and left-wing educationalists were engaged in arguments about multicultural education and the extent of racism and racial inequality, the white majority and the media were not particularly interested. There was more attention paid to those who supported the notion of an unproblematic white British national identity. In particular, there was antagonism to any suggestions that majority cultural values expressed in the school curriculum needed scrutiny, or that education should play a part in diminishing racism in the society. It was not surprising that into the 1990s government became less willing to examine education in a multicultural society more closely or develop more initiatives to promote race equality.

Notes

1. Political concentration during the early 1980s was on the black Afro-Caribbean community but a 'divide and rule' strategy was evident as cultural links with India were stressed, and the political label of black was not endorsed by South Asians generally. By the later 1980s Muslim religious assertion was worrying politicians. However, by 1990 Modood *et al.* were of the view that the society had 'not collapsed into a plurality of cultural separatisms, but ethnic identity has become of considerable significance' (Modood *et al.* 1997: 7).
2. The Campaign for Real Education was set up in 1987 by a Yorkshire businessman Nick Seaton, the first secretary being Yasmin Ahmed. It was not an accident that the initials CRE could be confused with those of the Commission for Racial Equality. The aim was to ensure higher standards via a traditional curriculum in schools in which 'sociology, peace studies, world studies and political education have no place' (Campaign for Real Education 1989). The group published a series of papers, and was particularly critical of any multicultural or anti-racist approaches. The organisation was dedicated to the teaching of British culture and the Christian religion and supported the right of minority groups to pursue their own cultures 'separately'. They had some Muslim support for this.
3. Anthony Rampton was a mail-order company businessman, a member of Lambeth CRC, a Trustee of the Runnymede Trust and a founder of the charitable Hildern Trust. With no particular education knowledge he was a curious choice for Chair of an inquiry into the education of West Indian children, and resigned in 1981. However, his obituary in 1993 noted that he 'received no official recognition for his work but earned the gratitude of millions of ordinary black and white men and women' as the Rampton report was the first to refer openly to racism being a cause of West Indian children's school performance. Lord Michael Swann, appointed to Chair the committee on Rampton's resignation, was a distinguished academic and public servant, being Vice-Chancellor of Edinburgh University and a Chairman of the BBC. He incurred the displeasure of Margaret Thatcher when

he widened the scope of the inquiry to examine what a good 'Education for All' in a multi-ethnic society should look like. He died in September 1990.

4. The ILEA Research and Statistics Branch, under Peter Mortimore and later Desmond Nuttall, was responsible for reviews and evaluations of minority achievement in London during most of the 1980s. The proposed research on successful black pupils was opposed by ALTARF, NAME and Haringey Black Pressure Group on Education, the objection being that it would concentrate too much on families rather than schools. It was not until the 2000s that research on this topic began to appear.
5. Barry Troyna remained an indefatigable supporter of anti-racist education and regarded what he described as token multiculturalism with suspicion. He was internationally recognised for his work on social justice and equality, and after his untimely death in February 1996 colleagues produced a book of essays in his honour (Sikes and Rizvi 1997).
6. Foster's study of 'Milltown High' (in reality Birley School) found little evidence of negative teacher attitudes or low expectations of the Afro-Caribbean students due largely to positive school policies and experienced teachers. (The author examined his PhD.) Other studies asserted that teachers' ethnocentric perceptions could lead to actions that were racist in their consequences (Wright 1986, Gillborn 1990). Debate on the extent of teacher racism continued although Peter Foster died in 1998.
7. Chris Mullard, as a lecturer at the Institute of Education, London University, was an influential critic of multicultural education and described himself as 'the father of anti-racism'. He was appointed Professor of Ethnic Studies at the University of Amsterdam, Holland in 1984, and in 1991 began a legal action against the university when his department was closed. He eventually took a retirement package and became an educational consultant, and the organiser of the Notting Hill annual carnival.
8. In Tomlinson (1990) I suggested that 'Educational Nationalism' could describe the ideological and policy reaction of those groups committed to a defence of mono-cultural British values, and who blamed ethnic minorities themselves for their failure to obtain educational qualifications. Pilkington (2003) later suggested this was overstating the case as, during the 1990s, there was evidence of successful multicultural and race equality initiatives.

four

The absent presence (1990–1997)

> Unspoken anxieties about ethnic differences underlie several bits of educational policy, all of which are beginning to show a pattern. There seems to be a definite though unformulated intent to starve multicultural education of resources and let it wither on the vine.
>
> (*Times Educational Supplement*, Editorial, 23 June 1990)

> Historians may probably decide that not much of lasting significance happened in Britain during John Major's seven years.
>
> (Hastings 2007)

After a rumbustious decade for race relations in the 1980s, the early 1990s appeared to go quiet as John Major, lampooned as a 'grey man' of politics, took over as Prime Minister from 1990 to 1997. In reality, several things happened which were crucial to the future of race relations in Britain, and it was also a period of consolidation of right-wing successes in preventing issues of race, culture, religion, spatial segregation, discrimination and inequalities from being more openly discussed. During the period issues and tensions concerning immigration surfaced again, this time not overtly concerned with New Commonwealth immigration, but with the arrival of economic migrants from former communist East European countries and refugees and asylum seekers from civil wars world wide, notably from the old Yugoslavia after 1992. Despite the creation of a single European market and a European Union in 1992, the British public seemed as equally unenthusiastic about closer links with Europe as they were about accepting that their empire had disappeared. Globalisation was becoming a buzzword among politicians, and the realities of global markets, instant communications and transactions, more migrations, and cultural convergences were becoming more obvious. There was now more public understanding, as Stuart Hall pointed out, that the tea and sugar for the traditional British cup of tea actually came from India and the Caribbean (Hall 1991). The 1991 Census was the first census in Britain to include an ethnic question, asking for a subjective identification by either country of origin, colour or cultural affiliation,[1] after which the geographical spread and extent of ethnic segregation became clearer. The fourth PSI survey, questioning a representative sample of over 8,000 people in 1994, demonstrated that the political notion of a 'black–white' divide, which had provided a focus for minority solidarity during the 1970s and 1980s, was now more complex. By the 1990s 'the differences between minorities have become as important and significant to life chances as the similarities' (Modood *et al.* 1997: 8). This survey and other research in the early 1990s particularly illustrated the problems young Asians experienced in alternating between Western liberal individualism and ethnic assertion. The more open identification with a Muslim identity, particularly after the first Gulf War in 1990, created the conditions whereby popular racism began to be directed towards the demonisation of Islam as a world religion.

In education, USA scholar Michael Apple rightly noted (1999) that 'race became an absent presence' as the government ignored rising racial tensions and problems in schools, the actual lack of school places for Bangladeshi children in parts of London, and, notably, the murder of a black A level student, Stephen Lawrence, by young white racists in 1993. The working out of the 1988 Education Reform Act created more disadvantages for minorities, helping to increase social and ethnic segregation and, after reneging on promises made by Education Secretary Kenneth Baker, there was open hostility by ministers to making changes in the National Curriculum to reflect a multi-ethnic society. Section 11 money was scaled down and new criteria required that it was mainly used for English language teaching. During the period 1988–1997 the Conservative government legislated on almost every area of education from early years to higher education, with one or more Education Acts appearing each year. The Secretary of State for Education was handed over 1,000 new powers, and local authority autonomy was progressively reduced. However, entry and success in public examinations, and numbers entering higher education, continued to rise among all groups, and a more promising picture of school achievements among minorities began to emerge, although with a growing gap between African-Caribbean, Pakistani and Bangladeshi pupils, and those of white, Indian and Chinese origin, and with distinct variation by social class and gender. This chapter documents the working out of the 1988 Education Act and other Conservative Acts, and the effect on minorities, noting that blame for low attainment now included the deficits not only of individuals and families but also 'failing' schools. It also documents the continued negative treatment of black pupils in schools particularly via increased suspension and exclusion, ethnic minority achievements and the effects on employment, and school attempts to incorporate increasing numbers of refugee children arriving during the early 1990s. The terminology of this period reflected a growing preference for a language of ethnic minority, although the terms black and Asian, and delineating groups by country of origin and religion continued. Afro-Caribbean and then African-Caribbean became more common. 'Immigrant' now largely referred to European migrant workers, refugees and asylum seekers, the term illegal immigrant entering popular and media discourse.

Chronology of Acts and issues

1990 (November) John Major takes over as Prime Minister from Margaret Thatcher. Schengen Agreement signed between nine European countries to create common rules for asylum seekers.

1990 Section 11 rules revised. Education Secretary turns down a request for a private Muslim school in Brent to become voluntary aided. Report of the NCC Working Group on a multi-ethnic curriculum ignored.

1990 Over 500 Bangladeshi pupils in Tower Hamlets, London known to be without school places. Court removes blame from the local authority.

1991 General National Vocational Qualifications (GNVQs) introduced. (January) First Gulf War in Kuwait/Iraq.

1991 Culloden Primary School, Tower Hamlets, with large numbers of Bangladeshi children, attacked in the tabloid press as giving too much attention to second language speakers and the disabled. Feud between (Asian) governors and white headteacher at Stratford School, Newham.

1991 (September) Rioting by white youths in Newcastle and South Shields. Economic deprivation and heavy policing blamed.

1992 Maastricht Treaty establishes a European Union (EU), allowing more movement of citizens between countries. Conflicts in Europe and elsewhere brings in asylum seekers.

1992 White Paper on *Choice and Diversity* (DfE). Education (Schools) Act creates an Office for Standards in Education (Ofsted). Inspectors not required to have training for understanding a multi-ethnic society. DES becomes DfE. Higher Education Act allows polytechnics to become universities. Further Education Colleges to be independent of local government.

1992 National Union of Teachers produces anti-racist curriculum guidelines. 'The NUT has long accepted that it is the responsibility of the education service to prepare pupils for life in a multicultural society' (NUT 1992: 2).

1992 (October) Prime Minister Major tells the Conservative Party conference that 'teachers should learn to teach children how to read, not waste their time on the politics of gender, race and class'. DfE report indicates that black pupils are four times more likely to be excluded from schools than white pupils. CRE inquiry finds ethnic minority pupils assignment to low ability sets and bands was unlawful discrimination (CRE 1992).

1993 Stephen Lawrence, a black A level student, stabbed to death in Lewisham by white youths. No police conviction. Government refuses an inquiry. First Chair of NCC confirms that ministers made clear to him that multicultural anti-racist education was a 'no-go' area in the National Curriculum (Graham 1993). Mrs Thatcher's memoirs make clear her distaste for multicultural education and non-traditional history (Thatcher 1993).

1993 Education Act introduces the notion of 'schools requiring special measures' (failing schools). A majority of these schools turn out to be predominantly those serving poor, high minority areas, with large numbers of second language speakers and children with special educational needs.

1994 Teacher Training Agency set up. No special brief for training teachers for a multi-ethnic society. A new model syllabus for religious education in schools approved by faith leaders. Leader of Opposition Tony Blair sends his son to a Catholic grant-maintained school. Herrnstein and Murray publish *The Bell Curve*, claiming that members of a black underclass have lower IQs.

1995 House of Commons Education Committee Report, *Performance in City Schools*, notes the negative effects of schools choice, and teacher anxiety that Section 11 grants were to be cut. Hackney Downs School (80 per cent ethnic minority) becomes the only 'failing school' to be closed down by a Conservative appointed Education Association after a judicial review. Transfer of Section 11 funding from Home Office to Department of the Environment and a Single

Regeneration Budget. (June) Riots in Bradford between young Asians and whites.

1996 Ofsted report on the achievement of ethnic minorities (Gillborn and Gipps 1996) noted African-Caribbean, Pakistani and Bangladeshi pupils were still less likely to achieve well, but minorities were more likely to stay in education than white pupils. Government proposes ten measures to deal with minority educational performance. Dearing Review of Qualifications 16–19 contains only three paragraphs on ethnic issues (Dearing 1996). Benn and Chitty publish *Thirty Years On*, showing that black and Asian pupils were mainly attending schools with high working-class intakes.

1996 (November) Two Education Acts consolidated much of the previous extensive legislation, one clause reiterating that religious education should reflect mainly Christian traditions while taking account of other religions, with a collective act of worship wholly or mainly Christian (however, parents could still opt to take their children out).

1997 Fourth PSI report *Ethnic Minorities in Britain* published, noting the differences in educational and vocational qualifications between ethnic groups and their different life chances.

1997 (May) New Labour elected.

Politics and ideology

Despite Hastings' view that not much of significance happened under John Major's premiership, events occurred that proved crucial to British race relations over the next decades. In 1990 Saddam Hussein invaded Kuwait, and in January 1991 military from 30 countries, led by the USA and assembling in Saudi Arabia, attacked Iraqi troops and forced a withdrawal. A subsequent United Nations resolution required Iraq to rid itself of weapons of mass destruction. The first Gulf War led directly to the second in 2003, which had severe consequences for all Muslims and indeed all citizens in Britain (Ramesh 2003). During this first Gulf War the Bradford Council of Mosques sent a letter to the Queen and Prime Minister criticising the deployment of British troops in Iraq and there was evidence that some secondary school Muslim pupils were pro-Iraq (Lewis 1994). Young Muslims felt their communities under attack once again, after the Honeyford and Salman Rushdie affairs, a situation not helped by the decision to ban two Muslim girls from wearing headscarves in a school in Altrincham, Cheshire in January 1990 (Spencer 1990). In East London boroughs, and centred round the East London Mosque,[2] young Muslims were joining radical Islamic groups, particularly via a Young Muslim Organisation (YMO). Mutual fears surrounding the presence of Muslims in European countries had led, as Rex pointed out, to 'Islam' being a 'focus for racist hostility at least as important as colour' (Rex 1996: 8), and the term 'Islamophobia' to describe this phenomenon became popular in Europe (Karakasoglu and Luchtenberg 2006).

It was also of importance that in the early 1990s political attention switched back to immigration, this time to the economic migration of Eastern Europeans from former communist countries, and refugees and asylum seekers from conflicts and civil wars around the world.[3] The 1992 Maastricht Treaty created the European Union – containing, at that time, 15 Member States – with rights of movement for employment between States. Political asylum seekers from civil wars included Kurds of Turkish origin and groups from Iraq, Somalia, Somaliland, Southern Sudan, Sierra Leone and Zimbabwe, as well as East European Roma and, during the Balkan wars, refugees from Bosnia, Kosova and Albania. While treaties were passed enabling Europeans to move more freely, the Member States became increasingly anxious to reduce the entry of non-Europeans, and in 1990 the Schengen Agreement provided for increased border policing, and a database on criminals, asylum seekers and visitors. One consequence of the European-wide efforts to control immigration and asylum seeking, was a resurgence of fascist neo-Nazi parties, especially in France, Germany and Austria. The British National Front Party, turning itself into the British National Party (BMP), continued its recruitment of young white racists. During the early 1990s housing and welfare benefits were gradually restricted for asylum seekers and by 1997 a Treaty of Amsterdam allowed the UK to determine its own asylum policy. Numbers of refugee children have always been difficult to establish, but estimates were of around 40,000 by 1997, mainly living and attending schools in the London area – the schools receiving no extra assistance.

Despite the small number of asylum seekers allowed entry (fewer than 20,000 in the year Major became Prime Minister), the tabloid press in Britain kept up a steady stream of denigration of asylum seekers as welfare 'bogus scroungers', as stealing British jobs and 'swamping' Britain all over again. The British National Party also exploited fears of both legal and illegal immigration. When the British overseas territory of Montserrat in the Caribbean, with the same status as the Falklands Islands, suffered a volcanic eruption in 1995 and its citizens were forced to leave, with over half coming to Britain, they were treated as 'homeless citizens' and offered little help; and when the British overseas territory of Hong Kong was returned to China in 1997, the government ensured only a small number of Chinese citizens had entry to Britain. In the event, many went to Vancouver, Canada and helped create a booming economy there. The media denigration and political panics over immigration in the 1990s and beyond had the serious consequence of confusing the presence of settled British citizens – children and grandchildren of those long settled from the Asian sub-continent, the Caribbean, and East and West African countries – with refugees, asylum seekers and anyone who did not appear to be 'white British'. It certainly helped set the scene for what developed by the mid-2000s into a 'siege mentality of wartime' (Winder 2004: 436) against anyone assumed to be 'immigrant', which made subsequent political pleas for national and community cohesion difficult and contradictory.

Class politics and ideologies also surfaced in the early 1990s as an 'underclass' made its presence felt. But this time it was the white socially deprived who came to public and political attention. In 1991 there was rioting on white housing estates in Newcastle-on-Tyne and South Shields in the north of England, in Cardiff, Wales and on the Blackbird Leys estate in Oxford, where thousands of workers had been laid off from the local car factory. Explanations for the riots resurrected 19th-century theories of a 'dangerous new class of alienated poor' (Murray 1994),[4] with Charles Murray, a US academic who was influential in the formulation of American social policy, blaming lone parenting, family collapse and community disintegration, and the former Education Secretary Kenneth Baker, now Home Secretary, blaming the Society of Motor Manufacturers for enabling easy car thefts and calling for extra police in deprived areas (MacIntyre 1991). George Carey, Archbishop of Canterbury, was one of the few who suggested that poverty, unemployment and segregation on housing estates or in inner cities might create the conditions for social unrest. There was little mention of the market conditions local authorities now functioned under, by which urban aid was denied to some deprived areas through a competitive process of 'bidding' for money, and the developing education market whereby 'choice' policies were further segregating minorities in inner-city schools. In the media discussion following white rioting there was no suggestion that however morally feckless the white underclass might be, their innate intellectual capacities were deficient, they were merely undeveloped by poor education! In contrast, the 1994 publication of Herrnstein and Murray's book, *The Bell Curve*, resurrected pseudo-scientific racial theories of intelligence, claiming that on IQ tests, African-Americans scored 15 points less than whites, and in particular black women of 'low cognitive ability' became chronic welfare payment recipients and produced babies with low IQs (Herrnstein and Murray 1994: 201). In the UK overt racial discourse suggesting black students had lower innate capacities was by now absent, but a 'new IQism' (Mirza 1998, Gillborn and Youdell 2000, 2001) covertly connected lower 'ability' with lower intelligence and affected teacher perceptions of black children's potential. Rioting between young Asian and white men did occur in Bradford in June 1995, and Asian community leaders pointed to underlying problems of unemployment, bad housing and low expectations among teachers as alienating a younger generation, who were no longer prepared to tolerate the racism and abuse their parents had suffered (Donegan 1995).

However, one effect of rioting by both black and white young people was more recognition that education and employment chances really did need improving, and a political focus on the low levels of education and skills in the British workforce generally. A developing ideology centred around the notion that the preparation of a skilled, flexible, competitive workforce, through improved education and training, would transform Britain's position in a competitive global market economy. All young people were urged by what was now called the Department for Education and Employment to 'learn to compete' and make themselves employable by acquiring skills and knowledge, being adaptable and managing their own careers throughout their lives (DfEE 1996). Although the idea of individual effort and entrepreneurship was attractive to many young people, the problem for minorities was that there was no level playing field. All young people were affected by economic restructuring, particularly the loss of low-skilled manufacturing jobs, but ethnic minorities were likely to pay an 'ethnic penalty' (Heath and McMahon 1997) as research continued to document racial discrimination in employment, even for those young people with higher level qualifications. The fourth PSI survey (Modood *et al.* 1997) noted that while some Asian groups were better educated and skilled and able to be socially and economically mobile, they still suffered discrimination. East African Asians, who had arrived in Britain with higher levels of education and business skills, and the relatively small number of Chinese were more successful, but still discriminated against at higher levels in employment; other Indian and Caribbean groups found discrimination in both obtaining jobs and gaining promotion, while Pakistani and Bangladeshi groups were the most severely disadvantaged. This was despite improved qualifications, as research continued to demonstrate that that all groups of ethnic minority students tended to stay in education beyond 16 more than white students. A study following young people from 34 schools in six LEAs into their post-school careers found that despite gaining qualifications, half of the black students and a third of Asian students noted their unfair treatment in training and employment, and all those who gained apprenticeships were white (Shaw 1994).

Political interest in racial harassment and violence was minimal during the early 1990s, although evidence mounted as to its extent and nature. In discussing the 'education for white supremacy' which many children still seemed to absorb, Tomlinson (1990: 44–70) noted the 97 derogatory names that white children in Manchester schools directed against their racial and religious school peers. The Runnymede Trust, the 1990 Trust and the London Research Centre[5] were among organisations publishing information on racial violence and harassment. In June 1992 the House of Commons held its first debate on racial equality for six years, introduced by Roy Hattersley, then shadow spokesman for Home Affairs. The Home Secretary replied that the government 'has forceful policies to tackle racial discrimination and racial disadvantage' and 'we have done a great deal of work in combating racially targeted crime' (Hansard 1992). Two months later a black Chelsea football player was attacked with an iron bar by a white youth and the Chair of the CRE requested new legislation against racial violence, a request refused by the Home Office. In April 1993, a black 18-year-old A level college student, Stephen Lawrence, was attacked and killed by five white racist youths at a bus stop in Lewisham, south London. Although the murder of Stephen Lawrence and the results of the eventual inquiry into his murder became a defining moment in the history of race and racism in Britain, leading to an amended Race Relations Act, the Conservative government initially refused an inquiry. It was left to his parents, Doreen and Neville Lawrence, to pursue a private prosecution, and the New Labour government finally to allow an inquiry in 1997 (Macpherson 1999, Lawrence 2006). In 1994 pupils at a school in east London were moved to other schools as racial harassment increased after the election of a BNP councillor in the area, police reporting a 33 per cent rise in racial violence (Martinson 1994). Antagonisms between all groups continued in the east London area – a black Christian youth was killed by a young Muslim at Newham FE College in 1995. The extent of racial hostility and harassment in white areas of the country was documented in a CRE study in rural Norfolk, where all the small numbers of minorities interviewed, including black, Asian, Japanese, Cypriot, Irish, travellers, Jewish and mixed race groups, had experienced some form of racism and harassment (Derbyshire 1994).

Education policies 1990–1997

During the period 1988–1996 the Conservative government legislated on almost every aspect of education, and those working in education were overwhelmed by the reforming zeal as everything from early years to higher education, through school structures, curriculum, assessment, inspection, parental influence, ancillary services and teacher training were all subject to scrutiny, criticism and legislation. The aims were: to consolidate a market ideology in schooling by parental 'choice' of school; establish central government control over the curriculum and assessment; erode the powers of local authorities, teachers and their trainers; require accountability from individuals and institutions, including universities; and increase selection under a rhetoric of school diversity.[6] The influence of right-wing individuals and organisations on politicians and civil servants in breaking up a national state education system moving slowly towards more egalitarian structures and outcomes, and replacing it with a competitive, divisive and fragmented system has been well documented (Ball 1990, Lawton 1994, 2005, Tomlinson 2005), but left-wing and liberal politicians and commentators were also castigating the low levels of education performance of the mass of young people, and blaming schools. There was certainly a case to be made for the view that carefully planned change, in consultation with all partners in the education process, including minority parents, could have built a 'magnificent modern system' (Lawton 1994). Instead 'The legislation has been a mix of attempts to enforce ideological prejudices and out-of-date traditions, with more legislation to patch up overhasty drafting, the result is a system that demoralised teachers who had to cope with too many changes in too short a time' (ibid.: 102).

The 1988 Act gave parents the right to 'express a preference' for a school of their choice for their child with no guarantee of a place. Local authorities could no longer fix admission limits, and schools were to be delegated their budgets – money following pupil numbers – with governors given powers to manage the budget and hire staff. Schools were to publish their examination results, and by 1992 newspapers were eagerly publishing the results of GCSE examinations by school in football style 'league tables', to be followed by league tables of test results for children aged 11 and 14. The intention was that parents would chose schools with good examination results and underperforming unpopular schools would close, a competitive market supposedly ensuring that consumers of education gained power over producers. In the event, oversubscribed schools rapidly began 'choosing' their pupils, via both overt and covert strategies, and schools that did not achieve good results were 'blamed, named and shamed' but were not able to close. Choice was to be enhanced by the reintroduction of schools directly funded from central government, renamed as grant maintained (GM) schools. Mrs Thatcher appeared on television to say she hoped all schools would opt out of LEA control, an ambition reiterated by John Major in 1994, the year that future Prime Minister Blair sent his eldest son to a grant-maintained Catholic school. Although opting out was slow to take off, by 1997 over 1,000 out of 3,500 secondary schools in England were grant maintained, with control of their own admissions. The label of grant maintained disappeared under New Labour in 1997 but the policy was continued with the introduction of foundation school status. Voluntary-aided faith schools continued to be allowed to control their admission of pupils.

After a White Paper extolling the virtues of choice and diversity (DfE 1992a), a 1993 Education Act attempted to increase these for parents by encouraging more opted-out schools and it also introduced the notion of failing schools, defined as inadequate schools identified by inspectors and placed in 'special measures', the intention being to remove them from the local authority control. In the event, the only school that had a 'hit squad' sent in to close it – a school taking 80 per cent black and other minority pupils – had its actions questioned by a judicial review in the High Court (O'Connor *et al.* 1999). The failing schools subsequently identified were predominantly in inner-city areas, taking large numbers of poor, minority, second language speakers, and those with special educational needs, which did not inhibit the media from mounting negative and derisory attacks on them, or the government attempting any positive suggestions as to how to improve all schools other than by the market mechanism. The accolade of the 'worst school in Britain' was handed out to different schools every few months and politicians competed to demonstrate their zero tolerance of failing schools (Tomlinson 1997, 2005). In contrast to policies removing powers from LEAs, they were given more responsibility for children with disabilities and special educational needs. The inclusion of the children in mainstream schools, which was cheaper than keeping open special schools, was advocated, and a 1995 Disability and Discrimination Act and Code of Practice placed more requirements for inclusion on LEAs and schools, while other legislation made it easier for schools to exclude pupils on behavioural grounds. Schools were to be held more accountable by a new system of inspection, with a partly privatised inspectorate set up under the control of an Office for Standards in Education (Ofsted). The inspectors were not required to have any training in understanding education in a multi-ethnic society. Ofsted reports on schools, initially taking little account of the social and economic circumstances in which schools functioned, quickly became another tool by which parents were encouraged to 'chose' schools. From 1993, following the creation of the handful of City Technology Colleges sponsored by business, schools were encouraged to specialise in a subject area, despite the introduction of a national curriculum intended to give all children a broad and balanced education up to 16. Although slow to take off, the specialist schools policy eventually resulted in almost all secondary schools boasting a curriculum specialism.

The government had by now taken unprecedented control of the school curriculum, with high levels of prescription for subject content and testing of all children at 7, 11, 14, and via GCSE at 16. Teachers struggled to implement an overloaded curriculum, and attempted to put in place market-oriented strategies which were largely at odds with their own professional beliefs. A multicultural working group, set up to ensure that multicultural and global perspectives were spread across subjects, (the author being a member) received short shrift, the Head of the NCC eventually recording that 'it was made starkly clear to NCC that whatever influence it might have would be rapidly dissipated by entering what was widely seen as a no-go area' (Graham 1993: 132). Honeyford, the Bradford headteacher referred to above, wrote in *The Salisbury Review*, that continued reference by the NCC to cultural diversity, equality for women and the handicapped and to personal and social education, was evidence that the curriculum was dominated by left-wing extremists and progressive zealots (Honeyford 1990). Prime Minister Major made his contribution at the Conservative Party conference in October 1992, asserting that 'teachers should teacher children how to read, and not waste their time on the politics of race, class and gender', and

Mrs Thatcher's efforts to influence history in a more nationalistic direction became public (Thatcher 1993: 596). Eventually even one of the 'Black Paper' writers, in charge of developing the English curriculum, complained of extreme right-wing influence on curriculum development (Cox 1995).

The overloaded curriculum became unworkable after three years and Ron (later Lord) Dearing was appointed to slim it down with shorter courses and lower level 'tiers' of entry to GCSE being introduced, an issue later for black pupils when it transpired that many were entered for lower levels without parental knowledge. Dearing recommended a three-track system of an academic route leading to A levels, a vocational route leading to the General National Vocational Qualification (GNVQ) introduced in 1991, and National Vocational Qualifications (NVQs) leading to craft or occupational levels (Dearing 1993). Many of the latter courses were to run in Further Education colleges, which after a 1992 Further and Higher Education Act became independent of local authorities and were encouraged to obtain more private funding. The colleges were also by now taking in disaffected and problem pupils 'disapplied' from the National Curriculum from 14 for part of their education. This Act also allowed polytechnics, the higher education institutions many minority students were enrolled in, to take the title of university and be funded by a Higher Education Funding Council, part of the funds to be determined by performance in a Research Assessment Exercise. Students were to take out loans for their keep from 1990, but their tuition was still free at this time. Teachers and their training were further controlled via Acts in 1991 and 1994, which centralised pay and conditions and handed teacher training over to a Teacher Training Agency, with a chief executive and members appointed by the Secretary of State for Education. During the early 1990s the shadow Labour government was preoccupied with repudiating 'Old Labour' commitment to free comprehensive education from nursery to higher education, embracing instead the competitive and divisive school structures and funding of the Conservative governments, and the centralist control. Although Labour produced a host of policy documents during the early 1990s, the last paper supporting comprehensive education (Taylor 1994) was ignored, as was any commitment to removing an academic–vocational divide in the 14–19 curriculum. Individuals were to be responsible for their own learning and the 'young unemployed have a responsibility to seek work, accept reasonable opportunities and upgrade their own skills' (Labour Party 1996). The major political parties went into the 1997 General Election with very similar education manifestos.

New disadvantages

Although the Major government attempted a return to subsuming minorities under the general rubric of disadvantage, it was clear that they suffered disadvantages over and above class disadvantage. Major claimed, in a foreword to a White Paper on *Choice and Diversity* (DfE 1992a), that he 'was not prepared to see children in some parts of the country having to settle for a second class education', but the creation of an educational market, driven by the self-interest of primarily white, knowledgeable parents and schools seeking desirable customers, was leading to a first and second class division. While numbers of individuals below the official poverty line in Britain had risen from four million in 1979 to over ten million in 1993, the 1991 Census and other data demonstrated overcrowded housing, especially among Pakistani and Bangladeshi groups, high levels of unemployment for these groups and among black Africans, a prison population with four times the number of young blacks than their numbers in the general population warranted and high rates of long-term illness, including mental illness and poor health among minorities in general. Minorities were located primarily in urban areas and an HMI study on *Access and Achievement in Urban Areas* (Ofsted 1993) concluded that 'schools in disadvantaged areas do not have the capacity for sustainable renewal. Beyond the school gates are underlying social issues such as poverty, unemployment, poor housing, and inadequate health care' (Ofsted 1993: 45). The House of Commons Education Committee, examining performance in city schools in 1994–1995 pointed out that choice policies, especially when influenced by league tables of exam results, could lead to 'a flight of more mobile, better-off parents, which creates empty places to be filled by pupils excluded from other schools' (House of Commons 1995: 1 vii). While white flight from high minority areas was nothing new, the education market encouraged it, creating the conditions of school segregation later deplored by politicians. Although initially it appeared that there was an absence of reference to racial minority issues in the choice legislation, Michael Apple rightly pointed out that 'While race talk may be overtly absent in the discourse of markets, it remains an absent presence that I believe is fully implicated in the goals and concerns surrounding support for the marketization of education' (Apple 1999: 12).

It was apparent by the early 1990s that a major result of choice policies globally had been to increase social class segregation in schools, an OECD study suggesting that privileged groups and those in prosperous areas were more active and able to chose schools (OECD 1994) and choice in the UK was encouraging middle-class parents to seek entry to the remaining 164 grammar schools in England, and to buy housing in areas near comprehensive schools high up in league tables. Ethnic minorities continued, on the whole, to be part of lower socio-economic groups, and their class position continued to disadvantage them, as did their predominantly urban location. It has been documented above that the urban schools most minority children moved into from the 1960s to the 1990s were, although nominally comprehensive, intended for a working class who were not taught higher level academic work. In a study of 1,560 comprehensive schools carried out in

1994, Benn and Chitty found distinct class differences between schools with and without minority students. Thus 81 per cent of schools with West Indian groups had predominantly working-class intakes, as did 71 per cent of schools with Indian, Pakistani and Bangladeshi groups (Benn and Chitty 1996: 175). While the resistance many white parents exhibited to sending their children to schools with minorities had been well documented from the 1960s, choice policies gave white parents a legitimate means of avoiding high minority schools. In the research Ball, Gerwirtz and their colleagues carried out between 1993 and 1995, they concluded that racially informed choosing took place, and while white privileged choosers were skilled at disguising their concerns, white working-class parents were often less reticent. One parent (echoing the racist comments made to the 1973 Select Committee on Race Relations and Immigration, see Chapter 2) asserted that his son was not going to one school because 'It's all nig-nogs, isn't it? It's all Asians and it's a known fact they hold ours back . . . the kiddies while at home speak Punjabi or whatever it is and when they come to school they can't understand a bloody word . . . there's no way he (son) is going there' (Gerwirtz *et al.* 1995: 490). However, while almost all minority parents held values about the worth of education that were distinctly middle class, the choices of an emergent black and Asian middle class mirrored white middle-class choice, some parents preferring to send their children to private schools if possible, selective schools or predominantly white schools.[7] But research suggested that despite expressed preferences and high aspirations, minority parents during the 1990s were less likely to get their children into schools with higher examination performance (Noden *et al.* 1998). Permitted selection of 10 per cent of pupils by 'aptitude' for the specialist schools encouraged by the Conservatives, and later by New Labour, further affected minority choice of schools, although it was noteworthy that schools opting to specialise in technology attracted high numbers of Asian applicants, while those opting for sport were mainly inner-city schools with higher numbers of black children.

An education market also worked to encourage schools to get rid of pupils who disrupted the smooth running of the school or interfered with the teaching of other pupils. Thus, while black pupils had previously been removed from mainstream schools by special educational procedures, and were over-represented from the 1980s in Pupil Referral Units (special units nominally attached to mainstream schools), the early 1990s saw the use of straight exclusion from school as a way of rapidly removing the troublesome, with black pupils disproportionally represented. In 1992 black students constituted 2 per cent of the school population but 10 per cent of those excluded from school were black (DfE 1992b). Gillborn, after researching the issue that exclusion operated in a racialised fashion, concluded that a disproportionate number of black pupils of both sexes aged 5–16 were excluded and denied access to basic education (Gillborn 1995). In 1995–

1996 school exclusions were at a peak of 12,467, with variations around the country in terms of race. Black pupils in Trafford and Surrey schools were 15 times more likely to be excluded than whites, and in Bolton and Bury Pakistani boys were also more likely to be excluded than whites (Thornton 1998). The Institute of Race Relations commented that a government which had declared its indifference to the potential effects of open enrolment on racial segregation was not likely to consider the impact of its policies on schools and the subsequent rejection of children through exclusion (Bourne *et al.* 1994). The media was more interested in linkages made between exclusion and truancy from school and youth crime than in the rights of all young people to an education. In 1991 a black mother used race relations legislation to challenge the right of a school to suspend then exclude her four-year-old son from a reception class, two weeks after he started school. Her seven-year-old son had previously been excluded from the same school (Hughill 1991). The nonsense of excluding children who had barely begun their school careers mirrored the situation in the 1960s when black children were removed to ESN schools before they had even settled into mainstream school. But by the mid-1990s social class, race and ethnicity, special needs and behaviour problems were becoming filters through which the desirability of admitting pupils to schools was understood, and on most counts minority students, especially black African-Caribbean, were less likely to be regarded as desirable. The market, as Apple had predicted, was certainly racialised.

LEAs and schools

A major reason for the disappearance of multicultural anti-racist education (now described in some publications as MC/ARE) during the early 1990s, was, as the *Times Educational Supplement* editorial quoted above indicated, a removal of funding. The Education Support Grant funding and money for in-service training courses came to an end, and after yet another Home Office review of Section 11 grants funding was only to be given to LEAs who could demonstrate that the money was to be used 'to compensate for linguistic and cultural deficiencies of minority ethnic communities', which would in turn promote more equal opportunity (Bagley 1992: 9). English language support was to be a priority and there was to be no funding for the kind of multicultural anti-racist initiatives, policies or processes set in train during the 1980s. The reform of Section 11 continued into the 1990s, and by 1994 over half the money was handed over to a Single Regeneration Budget, a programme requiring bids for locally created regeneration efforts in urban areas. Regeneration funds were not specifically directed towards schools or ethnic minorities, although initiatives were required to enhance the employment prospects, education and skills of local people, and promote equality of opportunity. Those Section 11 teachers employed with the remaining money often felt they had low credibility with other staff, and were not encouraged to assist in curriculum developments for black and other minority young people.

Information on what was happening in LEAs as the constraints and requirements of the Education Reform Act put an end to multicultural anti-racist developments was provided by a study carried out at the National Foundation for Educational Research. Some 119 LEAs replied to a questionnaire and 'A general perception that the national educational and political climate was ideologically unpropitious for MC/ARE', as the NFER delicately put it, was revealed (Taylor 1992: 5). While over two-thirds of local authorities had claimed to have a MC/ARE policy in 1989, by 1991 less than half claimed a policy was in use, and a fifth had the policy under review or were revamping it. There was more consultation with school governors who had been given more responsibility for school affairs under the 1988 Act but whose levels of awareness and sometimes negative attitudes to diversity and equality issues caused concern. Although there was considerable variation between LEAs, 'many recently developed policies are proclaimed as equal opportunities policies' (ibid.: 14) and were usually linked to gender and disability and a few included racial harassment. Casualties of funding cuts included local authority multicultural advisors and inspectors who lost their jobs, while those remaining worried about a marginalisation of racism and explicit curriculum strategies to deal with cultural diversity. As Taylor pointed out, the development of policies had always been highly political, varied between authorities, had seldom included minority ethnic organisations, parents or pupils in their development, or set out strategies for curriculum development or school organisation. It is worth noting again, in the light of subsequent attacks on multiculturalism in the 2000s, that no strategies or policies developed by local authorities or schools included support for separatism by race, religion or cultural group. Local authorities felt that a policy lead was necessary and deplored the failure of central government to produce any national policy or guidance. The DES did require LEAs from September 1990 to collect information from schools on the ethnic origin of pupils, and it was hoped that this would allow for a monitoring of pupil achievements, language, religious or other needs. However, as with the collection of statistics on immigrant pupils from 1966 to 1972, the information was never put to any central use and the requirement was scaled down in 1995. The education officer at the Association of Metropolitan Authorities commented that 'this is a deeply disappointing climb down from a policy which we have always supported but which has never been enthusiastically embraced by the Department for Education' (Pyke 1995). There was no requirement for local authorities to collect information on the numbers of refugee children arriving in their areas. Some decided their needs were the same as other minority children, and as Rutter (2006: 71) noted 'There were no explicit directives on refugee education by central government between 1954 and 2001'. Most refugee children were excluded from Section 11 money and a split between refugee education and the education of ethnic minority children developed.

More accurate information would have been of use in a situation that developed during the 1980s and early 1990s in Tower Hamlets, London, when hundreds of Bangladeshi children were denied a place at *any* school in the borough, then under control of the ILEA. The borough included some 44 per cent of families of Bangladeshi origin, and despite building three new primary schools during the 1980s, admitted to a school place shortage which had become critical. A 1989 ILEA paper referred to 500 mostly Bangladeshi children known to have no school place, although this was an underestimate, and forecast that by 1992 there would be a shortfall of 2,228 secondary places. Despite a number of campaigns from Bangladeshi and Race Equality organisations, and the Tower Hamlets Law Centre submitting a complaint to the Secretary of State for Education, children continued to be out of school, with ILEA blaming the size of Asian families, their reluctance to travel out of the area for fear of racial attack, continued migration and frequent changes of housing. In 1990 the Tower Hamlets Law Centre applied for a Judicial Review of the situation, and Lord Justice Woolf gave the extraordinary judgment that the duty of a local education authority to provide school places, under the relevant Acts was 'not absolute', absolved ILEA and the Secretary of State from blame and noted that as ILEA was about to be abolished, no further action could be taken. It appeared to be the case that 'if the authority with such a large number of children out of school had been in Solihull or Surrey, and the children predominantly white, the judgment would have been very different' (Tomlinson 1992: 445). The authority had certainly created a situation of unequal opportunities, which negated its own policies on equal opportunities. There was no national media coverage of this issue, in contrast to attention the right-wing media gave around the same time to Culloden Primary School, a Tower Hamlets school which took large numbers of second language speakers from Bangladesh, Somalia and Vietnam, and had an excellent centre for the hearing-impaired. The headteacher allowed the school to be filmed for the BBC, demonstrating how the school coped with racism, bullying, and the integration of children with special needs and while the series was much praised, the right-wing press began a campaign of vilification of the school. The *Mail on Sunday* attacked the school for its supposedly 'trendy' teaching methods which lowered standards, and claimed support from a some parents. The Education Secretary, Kenneth Clarke, then sent in inspectors whose report was leaked to the press before presentation to the school governors. While there was no evidence of lowered standards, attacks on the school continued from the right-wing media and self-styled parental groups. The Advisory Centre for Education, a long-established and respected body advising parents, commented that 'operating under a number of different "parent" groups, the same hard-core of activists can be found behind every flare-up from Dewsbury onwards. Loudly supported by swathes of the Thatcherite press, these educational luddites have lambasted modern educational methods and made dirty words of terms like multiculturalism and equal opportunities' (ACE 1991: 1). Another school attacked and vilified in the press was Hackney Downs Boys School in what was widely acknowledged to be the educationally troubled borough of Hackney. After closure proposals, a fierce community campaign to keep the 80 per cent black school open was successful, with the Education Secretary Gillian Shepherd announcing on 4 July 1995 that closure proposals had been terminated. A week later on 14 July she announced that an 'Education Association' would take over the school, one of the five Association members being Michael Barber, later an influential figure in Labour education policy. It is still unknown who influenced the Education Secretary in that crucial week but the Association recommended closure of the school and after a hasty Judicial Review the school was closed in December. The boys were transferred to a nearby school where exam results were no better than at Hackney Downs, their education was disrupted, and Gus John, the black Chief Executive of Education in Hackney took early retirement (O'Connor *et al.* 1999). It was ironic that Hackney Downs School was later demolished and one of Labour Prime Minister Tony Blair's semi-privatised Academy schools built on the site at a cost of some £25 million to the taxpayer.

The opting-out and choice policies were beginning to affect schools in highly political ways, combined with the demographic need for fewer school places. In the Borough of Newham, London, where reorganisation required the closure of some schools, governors at Stratford Secondary School, attended by pupils of mainly Asian origin, decided, after a small majority in a parental ballot, to opt-out of local authority control to become grant maintained, a decision supported by the Education Secretary. The local Labour MP later asserted that 'the school was allowed to opt out because of Tory party dogma, not on its own merits' (Rafferty 1992), and there was trouble at the school when the Asian chair of governors called for the dismissal of the white female headteacher. Subsequent court actions involved the DES, the Education Secretary, MPs, the National Association of Headteachers, the London Collective of Black Governors, the Grant Maintained Schools Trust, the former head of HMI and others. One Asian governor was reported as saying that 'Our dream of setting up a multicultural multi-racial school has been shattered by the controversy . . . we never wanted a Muslim school, we wanted one that would reflect the community' (ibid. 1992). The right-wing Parental Alliance for Choice in Education supported the governors and was all in favour of separate Muslim schools, as 'more attuned to the philosophical requirements of parents' (Naylor 1992). Meanwhile the Education Secretary had approved GM status for a school in the borough of Brent, while refusing a request (led by Yusuf Islam, formerly the pop star Cat

Stevens) from the private Islamia school, which had been campaigning for ten years to become a state-aided Muslim school. The DES/DfE had always adopted the view that while other religious schools were not divisive, Muslim schools would be regarded as separate on racial as well as religious grounds. However, without formal faith separation or opt out from local authorities, school admission by location and parental choice was increasing segregation in some areas, with consequences not envisaged by politicians, civil servants or educationalists. By the 1990s Stepney Green Boys School in Tower Hamlets, attended almost entirely by Muslim boys, was becoming a place for the recruitment of radicalised young Muslims. Remarking on his time at the school in the early 1990s, Husain noted that

> In the multicultural Britain of the 1980s and 1990s we were free to practise our religion and develop our culture as we wanted . . . but British values of democracy, tolerance, respect, compromise and pluralism had no meaning for us. We attended a British Academy but there was nothing particularly British about it, it might as well have been in Cairo or Karachi. Cut off from Britain, isolated from the eastern culture of our parents, Islamism provided us with a purpose.
>
> (Husain 2007: 73)[8]

Educational achievements

With more attention paid to the need to acquire educational credentials, minority parents were becoming acutely aware that their children needed good GCSEs and A levels to progress into higher education or professional training, or take up good vocational courses that would reduce the chances of them remaining in unskilled employment or becoming unemployed. Black parental anxiety about the education of their children continued into the 1990s, with much disillusionment that despite the hopes generated after the Swann Report and the development of equal opportunity policies, there had been little change. Parents at the mainly black Seventh Day Adventist John Loughborough School in north London encapsulated the view that written policies asserting equal opportunities were worthless unless good teachers and resources were offered. One parent noted that 'State schools think that if Afro-Caribbean youngsters attend a school standards will drop . . . the two things that will promote equality for us, speaking for black people, is high quality education and economic independence. The best equal opportunity anyone could give us is to educate us properly' (Steiner 1991). The view that schools continued to regard black Caribbean children in potentially negative ways was supported by Shotte, a teacher from Montserrat, who followed the fortunes of pupils relocated and moved into inner-city London from 1995 after the volcanic eruption. She recorded that the pupils, doing well in Montserrat, lost motivation and achieved badly, to much parental dismay. She also recorded that some of the London teachers did not initially know where the island was, but on hearing that it was a Caribbean island, made negative assumptions about the children. Those who were relocated to the USA, by contrast, continued to do well in school (Shotte 2002). Earlier in the 1990s Sewell, a black academic studying one inner-city school, tried again to explain why black boys were excluded from school or did not achieve well. He observed that teachers apparently feared the physical size and attitudes of black youths, and some blamed Afro-Caribbean subcultures, others acknowledging that it was their school which could not provide a high standard of education. His conclusions, however, were that while teachers stereotyped the boys, this was not one-sided, 'The boys in many cases saw themselves in stereotyped constructs . . . the school was not a world of evil racist teachers and innocent Afro-Caribbean boys' (Sewell 1997: 66). In contrast, Mirza (1992) found that second generation African-Caribbean girls had high expectations of their schooling and future employment. This despite the constraints of negative teacher expectations and a racially and gender determined labour market. Black parents and community groups continued to develop self-help strategies. In Lewisham, London, where in 1991 50 per cent of boys excluded from primary school were black, a 'Positive Image project' run under a youth programme, worked with black boys and men to improve educational and employment prospects, and the supplementary school movement continued to develop nationwide. Although some schools, teaching mainly on Saturdays, had been entering pupils for O level/GCSE examinations via Further Education Colleges from the 1970s, an Afro-Caribbean Supplementary Education Service in London arranged for GCSE examining in maths and English to be available to all its pupils. Support for separate schooling for black pupils came from visiting black Harvard educationalist Majors, whose 1992 book detailing possible solutions to the education of young black males in the USA had included the suggestion of separate education as a way of raising self-esteem and achievement. He reasserted the view that Eurocentric education undermined black pupils and there should be more focus on black pupils' experiences, history, culture and identity (Majors 1992, 2001), a view the supplementary schools had been promoting from the 1970s.

The main evidence for the relative achievements of minorities over ten years to 1995 came from a review of research commissioned by Ofsted, after requiring competitive bids from academics. Gillborn and Gipps reviewed past research and also carried out their own survey of LEAs and were able to point to significant differences between achievements of different ethnic groups in different local authorities (Gillborn and Gipps 1996). The review noted that while overall levels of achievement, as measured by GCSE examination results, had risen over a decade, all ethnic minority groups had not shared equally in this. African-Caribbean, Bangladeshi and Pakistani pupils continued to achieve below other groups, while pupils of Indian origin performed best in some, but not all, local areas. Overall white pupils had the highest educational attainments at 16. The review pointed out yet again that social class was strongly associated with higher achievements, and that there were significant gender differences in achievement between all groups. The report noted, as the fourth PSI survey (Modood *et al.* 1997) and Shaw's work at the Policy Studies Institute (Shaw 1994) had shown, that most ethnic minority students showed greater persistence and motivation to stay in education beyond 16, usually in FE colleges. Young Asians tended to study academic courses and consequently had the highest qualifications of any group by 18. Young black men were more likely to follow vocational courses and by 24 had more vocational qualifications than other groups. Entry to FE colleges, as MacCrae *et al.* (1997) demonstrated, was however, also structured by class and race, with some colleges 'niche marketing' themselves to appeal to minority students, while others targeted the white middle class.

Gillborn (1998) documented that, like the Smith and Tomlinson research, Ofsted and the DfEE held up publication of the Gillborn and Gipps review for over a year, although on the day of publication the DfEE announced a ten-point plan for raising the standards of ethnic minority pupils, the Junior Education Minister who announced the plan claiming that the lower achievements of some minority groups was a real cause for government concern (DfEE 1996). On publication the media highlighted again the 'underachievement' of black pupils, presenting an alarmist view of black children as failures and part of an 'alienated underclass'. The regional newspaper the *Yorkshire Post* (1996) used the research to attack the 'misguided liberalism of the race equality industry' and portrayed black children as an underclass. It was ironic that, at the time, young Muslims who would later become suicide bombers were currently in Yorkshire schools. It also did not seem of interest to politicians or the media, that it is not possible to pass examinations if pupils are not prepared and entered for them. In the foreword to a study of the allocation of white and Asian pupils to different sets (ability groups) in one comprehensive school, carried out by the Commission for Racial Equality, the then Chair, Sir Michael Day, commented that 'teachers decided that many pupils for whom English was not the first language were unable to learn successfully in the higher ability groups and placed them in non-examination sets' (CRE 1992: foreword). This study quoted Tomlinson (1987) who had noted from the study of 20 multiracial schools the effects of class, race and gender on allocation to examination groups, 'pupils of Pakistani, Bangladeshi and Afro-Caribbean origin were less likely to say they were directly entered for O levels than UK, East African Asian or Indian origin' (CRE 1992: 12). Despite the large numbers of students studying in FE colleges, the Dearing Review of Qualifications (1996) which recommended a three-track route for over 14 year olds – the academic route being A level, with, GNVQ and NVQ as vocational and work-related routes – only made a brief reference to minorities.

Overall though, the persistence and motivation of ethnic minority students in education was beginning to pay off, particularly in terms of entry to higher education. During the 1980s FE colleges had begun to develop access courses by which students termed 'non-traditional' could be prepared for higher education in addition to the A level route. Polytechnics and some universities, notably the newer campus universities, began to accept access students and this became another way in which minority students could enter higher education. From 1990 the University and Polytechnic Admissions Councils requested applicants to state their ethnic origin and from 1992 were able to record differences in the representation of minority groups in higher education and between institutions. Data showed considerable differences between ethnic groups, although all minorities were more likely to be studying in polytechnics than in universities. East African Asian, Indian and Chinese students were represented in both types of institution, with Caribbean, Bangladeshi and Pakistani students under-represented in HE generally and more likely to be in the city polytechnics. From 1992 polytechnics and some colleges could take the title of university and award their own degrees, the CNAA being abolished. Minorities were now over-represented in what came to be called the 'new universities'! However, applications from minorities confounded social class expectations, as more from manual working-class homes entered higher education than whites, Modood (1993) arguing that the drive for social and economic mobility led them to use higher education for higher status and professional jobs. Black women, always realistic about the need for educational qualifications, were particularly keen to acquire higher qualifications, the 1993 Labour Force Survey showing that 61 per cent of all black women aged 16–60 had higher or other qualifications (Mirza 1997a). However, the well documented 'ethnic penalty' that minorities suffered in employment also applied to those with higher qualifications; for example, the legal profession and high-status city firms recruiting predominantly white graduates from old universities (Shiner 1997).

Teachers and the curriculum

Further control of teachers and their training continued to be a feature of policy and legislation during the 1990s, a period when teacher morale and recruitment to the profession were at a low ebb. Newly qualified teachers were to be subject to competence-based assessment and new schemes for training teachers developed, including school-based initial training. The government was keen to minimise the influence of teacher trainers in universities and colleges, influenced by right-wing views that these institutions were hotbeds of left-wing theory, and progressive methods, producing incompetent teachers who did not know their subjects (Lawlor 1990, Thatcher 1993). An HMI report in 1991 criticised courses at Manchester

University and South Bank Polytechnic, specially designed to encourage ethnic minorities into teaching, as being of 'poor quality' and they were later closed down (DES 1991). In 1993 proposals for the reform of teacher training were published and in 1994 a Teacher Training Agency was created, with the head and members appointed by the Education Secretary, effectively detaching teacher training from higher education. This agency, later to become the Teacher Training and Development Agency, also eventually took control of all professional development (formerly in-service) courses, all of which were to be inspected by Ofsted. One result of these reforms, plus the concentration on 'delivering' the Nation Curriculum, was that courses specifically designed to prepare all teachers for teaching in a multi-ethnic society virtually disappeared. The eventual Ofsted inspection framework for schools (Ofsted 1995) did require inspectors to check for equal opportunities, attainment of minorities, curriculum innovations, second language learning, and parental and community contacts but inspectors had little or no training in the issues as they affected either schools or teacher training institutions. The recruitment of more minority teachers had been a declared government aim since the Swann Report in 1985 had noted the under-representation of ethnic minorities in the teaching force – by the later 1980s only some 2 per cent of teachers were from minority groups – but recruitment continued to be problematic. Assumptions were made that minority teachers would provide role models, be able to communicate better with pupils and parents, or, if Asian, be bilingual. But as Osler remarked, 'the evidence suggests that black and ethnic minority teachers are seen as a cheap commodity by their employers, more likely to be employed at lower pay levels and on temporary contracts' (Osler 1997: 49). The NUT was also worried about the problems faced by black teachers and support workers, including conflicts with white teachers and difficulties with both black and white pupils. However, in 1992 the Higher Education Funding Council set up a group to widen access and participation in higher education and money was given to 17 one-year projects designed to encourage ethnic minorities into teaching, with evidence showing that these projects did increase minority participation (HEFC 1995).

Meanwhile an overloaded and controversial National Curriculum continued to be criticised from all sides and 'slimmed down' in 1993. The Education Secretary had originally decided that history would come to an end in 1970, and leading black educationalists expressed disquiet that history in the National Curriculum was still Eurocentric, with few references to migration and population changes in the 20th century, particularly the cultural diversity developing from the 1950s. Brian Cox, Chair of the National Curriculum English working group, wrote that the battle for the English curriculum 1991–1995 resulted in an uninspiring, slimmed down curriculum reduced to basics and clichés, on which millions of pounds had been wasted (Cox 1995). There were endless arguments over what constituted standard English, and what should be included in a 'canon' of literature – the result being that much world literature was excluded. There was certainly no response to 30 years of black disquiet that the curriculum excluded their history and voice. The religious education curriculum continued to be influenced by local Standing Advisory Committees on Religious Education (SACRE), with the Muslim Education Trust complaining that some headteachers were dissuading parents from withdrawing their children from Christian or multicultural assemblies and not providing for Muslim worship. Islam appeared to be taking advantage of modern technology, the National Muslim Education newsletter reporting in 1991 that the Islamic computing centre had databases for the Qur'an and the Hadith (Islamia 1991). Any radical developments in schools and universities attended by Muslim students in the 1990s remained undocumented until the 2000s.

Summary

This chapter has briefly documented both general and educational policies and practices that affected ethnic minorities in Britain in the early 1990s, noting continuities and changes which, in contrast to the view that not a lot of significance happened under John Major, were crucial for the incorporation of ethnic minorities into the British nation-state. A new factor in the 1990s was the arrival of refugees and asylum seekers fleeing war and political conflicts and, with the creation of a European Union, the entry of economic migrants from Europe seeking work. One result of this was that the acceptance of long-settled minorities and their children into what was unquestionably if controversially a multicultural society, was set back as they were lumped together with other groups as 'immigrants' again. Class politics reared its head in England with riots by the white working class, and the government attempted once again to subsume ethnic minorities under the label of disadvantage. While many black and some Asian parents had good reason to complain about the quality of education offered to their children, and the negative views held by some schools and teachers, minority school achievements overall had begun rise, and their mode of incorporation into the labour market was an improvement on the past decades. The use of exclusion mechanisms by schools to rid themselves of black and other pupils regarded as undesirable continued, and there was a continued media focus on so-called failing schools, which were predominantly attended by minorities, special needs children, second language speakers and refugees. It was during the 1990s that, following Modood *et al.*'s (1997) empirical work, the different trajectories of the variety of groups labelled Asian, Muslim, black, refugee and others became more obvious, with different claims to a cultural or religious identity. There was also a rise in support for fascist groups and anti-Muslim sentiment throughout Europe. Muslim educators and community leaders kept up pressure for recognition of religious and cultural requirements, although a particular brand of anti-Western radical Islam was beginning to influence some young Muslims. With education being turned into a market by the 'choice' and opting-out policies of the 1988 Education Act, more licence had been given for racial segregation in schooling, and the social class and location of minorities meant that more schools became 'high minority'. Funding cuts and a political climate hostile to any organisational or curriculum change to improve education for all in a multicultural society meant that local authorities' policies and practices did not develop further, and training for teachers for a multi-ethnic society in universities, colleges and through in-service courses began to disappear. There was sufficient dissatisfaction with Conservative policies, encapsulated in John Major's outgoing assertion as he left office in 1997 that 'policies must be colour-blind, they must just tackle disadvantage', to enable the incoming New Labour government to create a new ideological and policy climate.

Notes

1. The 1991 Census recorded some 5.5 per cent of the population as ethnic minority. Actual numbers were: White 51,874,000, Black Caribbean 500,000, Black African 212,000, Black other 178,000, Indian 840,000, Pakistani 477,000, Bangladeshi 163,000, Chinese 157,000, Other Asian 198,000, Other groups 290,000.
2. The East London Mosque was eventually recognised as a centre for radicalising young Muslim men, especially influenced by the cleric Omar Bakri, later deported from Britain.
3. The term refugee became a legal construct in 1951 after a UN Convention. A 1967 Protocol defines a refugee as one who has fled a country of origin owing to fear of persecution. Most refugees apply for political asylum. The Convention and Protocol were accepted into British law in 1993, which should now prevent refugees and asylum seekers being returned to persecution. The 1989 UN Convention on the Rights of the Child requires that refugee and asylum-seeking children receive protection and assistance. Once the Home Office has granted Refugee Status to asylum seekers they had, until the 2000s, rights to work, benefits, housing and five years' right of residence. A temporary protection was 'exceptional leave to remain' in the country.
4. For a discussion of theories of the underclass see Pilkington (2003: 52–5).
5. The Runnymede Trust was set up in 1968 to study issues concerning racial justice and equality. It publishes a monthly bulletin and sponsors and carries out research. The 1990 Trust was established as the first National Black Trust to promote good race relations from a black perspective. Its first bulletin, *Black to Black* (July 1993), included an article 'Racist Attacks and Harassment: the epidemic of the 1990s'. The London Research Centre, an offshoot of the Office for National Statistics, publishes census analyses and other information on London's population.
6. In an interview with the then Education Secretary, Kenneth Baker, ten years after

the 1988 Education Act, he claimed that the aims were to 'punish the teacher unions, kill off the local education authorities and wipe out comprehensive schools by stealth' (Davies 1999: 1).

7. The option of private schooling is available for minority parents who can afford this kind of privileged schooling. Black MPs Diane Abbott and the late Bernie Grant (both London Members of Parliament) and Trevor Phillips, Chair of the Equalities and Human Rights Commission, were high-profile figures who sent their children to private schools.
8. A testimony from a former student at Stepford Green Boys School and then Newham FE College described his Islamic radicalisation via the Young Muslim Organisation, then the more militant Jamat-e-Islami and finally Hizb al-Tahrir, one of the groups calling for an Islamic state and eventually banned in other European countries but not the UK (Husain 2007). Other young Muslims disputed his account.

Race, education and New Labour (1997–2003)

> Education, education, education, will be the top three priorities of a New Labour Government.
>
> (Tony Blair, Campaign speeches, April 1997)

> Nations that succeed will be tolerant, respectful of diversity, multiracial, multicultural societies.
>
> (Tony Blair 1999b)

A giddy rush of public enthusiasm greeted the election of a New Labour government in May 1997, centring around the charismatic person of Prime Minister Tony Blair. More women (119) and eight minority MPs were elected and the government initially embraced an ideology of a Third Way, a marrying of neoliberal market competition with social democracy and a reformed welfare state (Blair 1998, Giddens 1998, Tomlinson 2005b). A Third Way was also intended to incorporate commitment to values of equal worth and opportunity for all. The new government, as the Prime Minister asserted, was committed to social justice and to education as a means to help create a socially just society. In particular, social justice would embrace all backgrounds, creeds and races and 'the attack on racial discrimination now commands general support, as does the value of a multicultural society' (Blair 1998: 3). New Labour inherited an increasingly unequal society from the Conservatives, with the highest proportion of children living in poverty than any in Western Europe, especially minority children, but domestic policies appeared set to tackle inequalities. In the first two years these included more regeneration programmes: a Neighbourhood Renewal Unit under the Deputy Prime Minister; a New Deal for Communities; a Social Exclusion unit within the Cabinet office, with a first brief that included an inquiry into black pupil school exclusions; a National Skills agenda; a National Childcare Strategy; and a Human Rights Act incorporating the European

Convention on Human Rights into UK law. Grappling with some long-standing grievances, the Home Secretary Jack Straw set up an inquiry into the 1993 murder of Stephen Lawrence, gave Muslim and other faiths the right to state-funded schools, and replaced the Section 11 grant with an Ethnic Minorities Achievement Grant (EMAG). Education was promised as a passion and priority of the new government, and there was no shortage of education legislation and initiatives, including the setting up of a Schools Standards Task Force. In fact, much education policy was based on a continuation of Conservative beliefs in choice and competition in schooling, with education developing as a market commodity driven by consumer demands. There was a continued focus on 'raised standards' as measured by tests and examinations, particularly the achievement of five A–C passes at GCSE, further central control of the curriculum and its assessment, and teacher training. There was a further diminution of local authority powers and more private incursion into public education.

In national policy race again became a presence rather than an absent presence, as New Labour was demonstrably eager to affirm the view of a modern national identity that valued cultural diversity and recognised the citizenship rights of settled minorities. However, by the second New Labour term of office from 2001 it was clear that the government had not grasped the scale of the problems inherent in creating some kind of what was now termed a diverse society that was conflict free and actually based on equal treatment.[1] Rioting in northern towns in April 2001 forced a reappraisal of conditions and policies which had worked against what was now referred to as 'community cohesion', and ushered in another round of examination of notions of what constituted a British identity and conditions for equal citizenship. There were many assertions that 'multiculturalism' had failed to create a cohesive society and education was deemed to be both a cause of separation of ethnic groups and a possible solution. Despite this there were further moves to encourage separate faith schools.

Domestic race policies were influenced by foreign policy, as Blair took the country to war five times in six years up to 2003 (Ramesh 2003), and the events of 11 September 2001 in New York[2] led to a declaration by US President Bush of a 'war on terror', which at times seemed to demonise all Muslims. Although military intervention in Kosovo in 1999 was to protect Muslims from non-Muslim Serbs, the invasion of Muslim Afghanistan in 2001 and Iraq in April 2003, plus alignment with increasingly unpopular US foreign policy, led to much disquiet among many citizens in Britain, and further helped to radicalise some young Muslims. This chapter discusses in more detail the policies and ideologies that affected race relations generally in the period 1997–2003, covers general education policies, and goes on to examine the various programmes intended to incorporate minorities into general educational improvements, but with contradictory policies having the effect of increasing racial and religious segregation. The chapter covers the continued exclusion of black children, negative policies towards refugee children, the achievements of different minority groups and the disquiet of black parents, the curriculum changes, especially citizenship education which was intended to teach rights and responsibilities in a multicultural society, and the continued lack of adequate teacher education to achieve declared aims. The language used in this period referred more to diversity, race equality, ethnic minority and Black and Minority Ethnic groups (BME). The Office for National Statistics used minority ethnic groups to record that in the 2001 Census, 4.5 million people (8 per cent of the population) had defined themselves minority ethnic, including a category of 'mixed' (Social Trends 2003: 30–2).[3]

Chronology of Acts and issues

1997 (May) New Labour wins General Election. John Major leaves office asserting that: 'Policy must be colour blind. It must just tackle disadvantage.' European Year Against Racism.

1997 Social Exclusion Unit set up in Cabinet Office. First brief is to inquire into school exclusions and truancy, with special reference to black pupils. Qualifications and Curriculum Authority (QCA) set up out of merged School Curriculum and Assessment Authority and the National Council for Vocational Qualifications.

1997 Sir William Macpherson asked by Home Secretary Jack Straw to chair an inquiry into the killing of Stephen Lawrence (Macpherson 1999). Muslim schools to be offered state funding on a par with other faiths.

1998 Crick Report on *Education for Citizenship and the Teaching of Democracy in Schools* recommends mandatory citizenship education. It contains just two paragraphs on multicultural issues.

1998 Human Rights Act incorporates the European Convention on Human Rights into UK law (implemented October 2000). Government sets up a task force to deal with the implementation of the Act. Crime and Disorder Act incorporates more penalties for crime motivated by racial antagonism.

1998 Education Action Zones (EAZs) set up to improve education in mainly inner-city areas (eventually subsumed into the Excellence in Cities programme).

1998 (July) School Standards and Framework Act. Ends grant maintained schools but schools are allowed to opt to be foundation, voluntary-aided or community schools (the first two controlling their own admissions). Herman Ousley, Chair of the CRE, criticises the government over the effects of education policy on minorities. Government sets up an inquiry on ethnic minority achievement.

1998 Enoch Powell dies. Many tributes to his patriotism.

1999 Devolution of powers from Westminster to a Scottish Parliament and a Welsh Assembly. Hopes for an end to the religious conflicts in Northern Ireland and the return of powers to a government there.

1999 Excellence in Cities programme includes identifying the gifted and talented in cities, and offering learning support units and mentoring programmes. Emerging black and Asian middle classes adopt similar strategies to whites in choosing schools, white parents continue to move children away from high minority schools. Sure Start programme set up, which focuses on disadvantaged children aged 0–3.

1999 Macpherson Report into the murder of Stephen Lawrence suggests there is institutional racism in the police force and makes four recommendations on education. The QCA responds that reforms from 2000 will ensure that 'pupils become healthy, lively, inquiring individuals capable of rational thought and positive participation in our ethnically diverse society'. NUT passes a resolution against racism at its annual conference.

1999 Ofsted reports that the educational performance of African-Caribbean, Pakistani and Bangladeshi pupils still gives cause for concern.

1999 (April) Ethnic Minority Achievement Grant (EMAG) replaces Section 11 of the Local Government Act 1966. *1990 Trust and Race on the Agenda* (ROTA) outlines its concerns about this grant. Revised National Curriculum document put out for consultation (QCA/DfEE 1999), with citizenship education to be a statutory requirement in the National Curriculum from 2002.

1999 Immigration and Asylum Act introduces vouchers instead of cash benefits for asylum seekers, enforced dispersal and detention on arrival.

2000 Race Relations (Amendment) Act. Requires all local authorities to prepare race equality schemes and all schools to have race equality policies. Ofsted introduces new inspection regime for monitoring race legislation. TTA produces guidelines for teachers in place of face-to-face courses on teaching in a multi-ethnic society, which no longer exist in most teacher training courses.

2000 Torture and death of eight-year-old West African child Victoria Climbié leads to a public inquiry, a 2003 Green Paper *Every Child Matters* (HM Treasury), and a 2004 Children Act.

2000 Gillborn and Mirza report a rise in achievement in all groups in school public examinations, but black, Pakistani and Bangladeshi groups improving at a lower rate.

2000 A Report by a Commission on the Future of Multi-ethnic Britain (Parekh 2000) is derided in the press and received with hostility. One suggestion in the report is that the separate commissions on race, gender and disability be merged.

2001 Allied forces invade Afghanistan to remove the Taliban regime.

2001 Census shows that 4.5 million people, 8 per cent of UK population, identify as minority ethnic, with a younger age structure for those of Pakistani and Bangladeshi origin. Leicester, a city rejuvenated by the settlement of minorities, forecast to be majority of minorities by 2010.

2001 (June) New Labour re-elected for the second time, with nine black and Asian MPs. DfEE becomes DfES. Riots in northern English towns, Oldham, Bradford and Burnley. Home Office report (Cantle 2001) complains of loss of community cohesion, school segregation and communities living 'parallel lives'.

2001 (September) Attacks on the World Trade Center and the Pentagon in the USA increases hostility to Muslims. The perpetrators had been educated in Western universities.

2002 White Paper (Home Office 2002) outlines new policies on citizenship and nationality, suggesting that future British citizens should pass an English Language test and a citizenship test. Also proposes accommodation centres for asylum seekers with separate schooling for their children. A Nationality and Immigration Asylum Act 2002 implements some of this paper and further border controls are set up to prevent the arrival of asylum seekers, with an increase in detention facilities and deportation orders. DfES sets up a Vulnerable Children Fund. Citizenship courses mandatory in schools from September.

2002 Education Act continues to reform the legal framework of schools and encourages further diversity. Academies, a hybrid between state and private schools, to be sponsored by business or faith groups.

2002 Data available from first Pupil Level Annual School Census (PLASC) on achievement of individual pupils, also their gender, ethnicity and free school meals (FSM) take up.

2002 (September) 14-year-old pupil Shabina Begum informs Denbigh High school of her wish to wear the jilbad. School refuses, court cases continue until 2007.

2003 DfES paper on *Transforming London's Secondary Schools* (DfES 2003a) promises to reduce achievement gaps by class, gender and ethnicity. DfES White Paper *Aiming High* (DfES 2003b) notes the differential education performance of different ethnic groups.

2003 (April) Invasion and war in Iraq leads to national division of opinion and hostility to the government, especially from Muslims. Cardiff School of Journalism finds media coverage of refugees and asylum seekers to be characterised by stereotyping, exaggeration and inaccurate language.

2003 (October) Secretary for Trade and Industry announces government decision to set up a Single Equality Body which would also promote human rights.

Politics and ideologies

New Labour initially faced the dilemmas of creating some kind of unity within a diverse society in a more informed and realistic manner than previous governments. There was some recognition that past assumptions of white supremacy and hostility to immigration were not appropriate in a globalised world where movement of capital and labour were permanent fixtures, and that neo-Conservative beliefs still assuming the subordination of racial groups were outdated. There was also an acceptance that people living in regions that had considered themselves to be internally colonised by the English should be given a measure of independence, hence in 1999 powers and responsibilities were devolved to a Scottish Parliament and a Welsh Assembly, and there was much negotiation towards resolution of the religious conflict between Catholics and Protestants in Northern Ireland. There was more open recognition that what was still the United Kingdom was now composed of large numbers of ethnic minority groups with different migration histories, economic positions, religious and other group affiliations whose claims to be part of the society could not be ignored. There was also recognition of supra-national influences on the way European nation-states treated their citizens, and the European Convention on Human Rights was incorporated into UK law in 1998. The ideology of the Third Way, as noted above, was intended to signal that social institutions could be reformed to pursue both profit and racial justice. Early signs were positive. Shadow Home Secretary Jack Straw met Doreen Lawrence, mother of the murdered black student Stephen Lawrence in April 1997, at a meeting organised by black MP Diane Abbott, and as Home Secretary in June 1997 Straw ordered a public inquiry into the murder chaired by former High Court judge William Macpherson. The publication of the Macpherson Report (1999) was a defining moment in British race relations, as criticism of the metropolitan police over their handling of the murder brought the notion of institutionalised racism to public attention. This was defined as collective failures in public institutions to provide equal, fair and just services to all groups.[4] The report made 70 recommendations, four specifically concerning education, the Home Secretary produced an action plan for implementation, and the Race Relations (Amendment) Act in 2000 put the onus on all public institutions, notably the police service and education, to work towards and monitor race equality treatment and outcomes. At the same time, Osler and Morrison were reporting their research on Ofsted, which showed that Ofsted inspectors failed to report on race equality as the 1995 inspection framework required, and inspectors were untrained and unprepared to meet race equality requirements (Osler and Morrison 2000).

However, the government had moved beyond simplistic attempts to subsume minorities under disadvantage, had some awareness of the politics of ethnicity, and was attempting to discover ways of creating unity within the society. There was a flirtation with ideologies of communitarianism (Etzioni 1988), and the government also seized on social capital theories, which attempted to articulate why social networks and social ties could bind individuals into a stronger civil society. Helena Kennedy's 1997 report on further education noted that law, contract and economics provided a basis for social values but should be leavened with reciprocity, moral obligation, duty towards community and trust, and building social ties that took precedence over individual, familial or class interests. Kennedy considered that education had a powerful role in creating social capital as 'education strengthens the ties that bind people, takes the fear out of difference and encourages tolerance' (Kennedy 1997: 6). The pragmatic reality was that communitarian philosophies of the common good were utopian in a society structurally divided along class, race and ethnic lines, and that in a competition for scarce resources, groups divide along ethnocentric, religious and class lines. Despite a raised awareness of race issues, the government continued to take account of a right-wing media which was assumed to represent a white majority. Home Secretary Jack Straw initially supported the committee set up by the Runnymede Trust in 1998 to inquire into the future of a multi-ethnic Britain, but after negative press attacks on the day it was published, misrepresenting its final report as attacking 'Britishness', he repudiated the findings (Parekh 2000). Even *The Times* newspaper, criticising the findings of the commission (the author was a member), asked 'Who do these worthy idiots think they are?' (Kaletsky 2000). The report actually suggested that the government find better ways of nurturing diversity while fostering a common sense of belonging and a shared identity among its members,[5] a theme that was repeated in most of the subsequent academic and official literature. Proof that shared identity was lacking was provided two weeks after the publication of the Parekh Report when a young Asian prisoner was killed by his white cell mate who admitted that he was racist and resented being in prison with people 'whose race and origin he despised' (Kelso 2000). The BNP continued to gain influence in some high minority areas, using more subtle tactics to influence white voters, and gaining three council seats in Burnley in the 2002 local elections, and by 2003 gaining some 18 council seats in England overall. The Commission for Racial Equality expressed concern that the BNP was successfully exploiting hysteria over asylum seekers.

New Labour went into the June 2001 General Election with a manifesto committed to Britain as a multicultural, multiracial, inclusive society in tune with (unspecified) British values. It promised a reduction in barriers to opportunity for black and Asian people in public services and other institutions, and connections with interfaith communities. However, more sophisticated policies and ideologies defining a multicultural society reverted back to simplistic assumptions asserting the failure of minorities to 'integrate' after riots in the northern towns of Bradford, Bolton, Oldham, Burnley and others in July 2001. The destruction of the World Trade Center towers and part of the Pentagon in the USA on 11 September signalled more general hostility to Muslims, and unpopular wars and foreign policy began to intrude on domestic policies concerning race and ethnicity. In July 2001 an inter-departmental Ministerial Group on Public Order and Community Cohesion was set up and a review team chaired by Ted Cantle visited northern towns and also Southall in London, as well as Leicester, Birmingham and Sheffield. The Cantle team, while acknowledging existing segregation in housing and in inner cities, expressed surprise at the depths of polarisation of communities where people lived 'parallel lives' (Cantle 2001). The team recommended the promotion of community cohesion based on a greater sense of citizenship but with value placed on cultural difference. For education the report placed much faith in joint ventures and twinning between schools with 'different cultures', more parental involvement and interfaith networks, virtually repeating recommendations made by the ESG projects in the later 1980s, with the added claim that citizenship education would improve the situation. There were also reports from the Lords Clarke, Ritchie and Ousley, the latter a former Chair of the CRE, on the riots in Oldham, Burnley and Bradford, and the final report of the Ministerial Working Group drew the findings together in December 2001 (Ministerial Working Group 2001). This report again stressed that citizenship education would improve understanding, and suggested that all schools, including faith schools should take 25 per cent of children from other 'cultures or ethnicities' – a suggestion considered and blocked from incorporation into legislation in 2006 by Catholic bishops. The report implicitly laid the blame for disturbances on the failure of minorities to integrate and put responsibility for action onto local authorities, a tactic to be repeated in other reports. Issues largely out of the hands of local authorities – notably lack of employment opportunities, lack of money for sufficient social housing, education policies which encouraged segregation, and lack of political leadership in demonstrating that minorities were not taking unfair shares of resources – were notably underplayed. By the 2000s textile mills in the northern towns, which had originally brought in minorities and in which they worked with white employees, had closed down, and a major avenue of community mixing disappeared. Policy reversals were also evident in legislation on law and order. A 1998 Crime and Disorder Act had brought in more penalties for racially motivated crime, but legislation after 2001 made it more likely that young people of Asian origin would be regarded with suspicion by the police, in a manner reminiscent of the 'sus' laws against black youth in the 1970s. In 2002 there was a 40 per cent increase in Asian people stopped by the police, and a 30 per cent increase for black people, compared to an 8 per cent increase for whites.

Notions of community cohesion, and citizenship education supposedly aimed at preparing all pupils for an ethnically diverse society, were at odds with more punitive immigration and asylum legislation. A White Paper (Home Office 2002) outlined new policies for citizenship and nationality, and a Nationality, Immigration and Asylum Act required future British citizens to pass an English Language and a citizenship test. This Act also proposed to build 'accommodation centres' for asylum seekers, which would provide separate schooling for their children, a move which led to campaigns and arguments that such separation could breach children's human rights (Rutter 2003). One argument presented in support of this was that some schools were overwhelmed by the presence of refugee pupils, although evidence indicated that schools taking the children worked hard to incorporate them despite lack of funding. Conservative policies restricting the welfare entitlements of asylum seekers were extended by New Labour, and policies of dispersal of those awaiting decisions on asylum applications meant that families were often housed in areas hostile to their presence. Refugee agencies reported an increase in racist abuse and attacks and 'the majority of perpetrators of racist harassment are young' (Rutter 2003: 141). Despite the 2001 Census demonstrating that there were some 4.5 million settled British citizens who identified themselves as ethnic minority, David Blunkett, Home Secretary after his four years as Education Minister, had, after the 2001 riots in northern towns, managed to conflate the presence of long-standing minority citizens with newer migrants and refugees, asserting that there were norms of acceptability and 'those that come into our home . . . should accept these norms'. Familiar patterns of playing to public fears of immigration continued, with even the Director of the London School of Economics, famed for its overseas student intake, urging the Labour government to be 'tough on immigration' although also tough on the causes of hostility to immigrants (Giddens 2002). The Shadow Home Secretary Oliver Letwin told the Conservative Party conference in 2003 that asylum seekers would be deported to a 'far, offshore processing island', although the island was never specified. Ministers were, however, quick to embrace the 'Britishness' of 17-year-old Amir Khan, a college student from Bolton, who won a silver medal for boxing at the 2004 Olympics.

Education policy to 2003

New Labour settled into office in May 1997 and continued the avalanche of policy initiatives, legislation and guidance that had characterised 18 years of Conservative rule. One or more Education Acts were passed each year, apart from 2003, a year free from legislation but not of inquiries, White and Green Papers, Codes of Practice and Regulations. Education continued to develop as a market commodity notionally driven by consumer demands, with market competition between schools, fuelled by the publication of league tables, school choice, specialist schools and failing schools. There was a continued assertion that raising standards was crucial, as the global economy now required improved skills and qualifications of all young people. There was a continued commitment to academic selection with policies searching out the supposed gifted and talented, and a continuing academic and vocational divide, and there was a continued emphasis on state regulation and control of the curriculum and its assessment, teachers and their training and local authority activity. The services of Chief Inspector, Chris Woodhead, were retained until 2000, and government advisor Michael Barber made Head of a Standards and Effectiveness unit in the DfEE, which became the DfES in 2001.[6] There was an adherence to the belief that all educational institutions should be managed along the lines of private business, with enhanced business funding and influence, and the traditional Labour belief in free higher education ended with a Teaching and

Higher Education Act in 1998 which, while supporting wider participation, introduced tuition fees for all students. The contradictions of pursuing competitive market policies in education while affirming commitment to social justice quickly became obvious. While New Labour preached inclusiveness and developed strategies to deal with disadvantaged children and young people, market and selective forces were demonstrably excluding large sections of the working and non-working class, many ethnic minority children, and those with learning difficulties, from the more desirable schools and universities. On the wider welfare front, a range of policies to reduce poverty among those on low wages, and 'lift children out of poverty' was accompanied by increasing disparities in wealth and income. Continued criticism of the education service left unremarked the situation that, by the 1990s, British society was actually benefiting from the relative success of education policies from the 1960s and 1970s, when for the first time a generation of people under 35 had experienced five years of secondary schooling, comprehensive schools had actually taught and entered more young people for public examinations, including girls and minority students, and prepared more for higher education. There was instead denigration of comprehensive schooling, with the Prime Minister's communications director in 2001 famously labelling some schools 'bog-standard', and the Shadow Home Secretary claiming that he would rather go out and beg than send his children to the local comprehensive. This was in spite of the OECD Programme for International Student Assessment (PISA) demonstrating in 2002 that countries with comprehensive school systems produced the best examination results.

The first major Education Act in 1998, which although presented as raising standards, was concerned primarily with school structures. Grant maintained schools, notionally abolished, were reincarnated as foundation schools, which together with voluntary-aided religious schools, could control their own admissions and funding arrangements, local authorities being left to maintain community schools, prepare education development plans, and establish school organisation committees which would include Catholic and Anglican nominees. The declared aim was to create a diversity of schools and to modernise comprehensive schools. The diversity at secondary level soon included private schools still educating elites, the remaining 164 selective grammar schools over which fierce battles were fought, the 15 city technology colleges, all secondary schools now foundation, voluntary-aided, or community, plus special schools for those with disabilities and learning difficulties, and an increasing number of Pupil Referral Units for those with what was now referred to as 'challenging behaviour'. Modernisation largely meant adhering to the specialist school programme initiated by the Conservatives, which was expanded with announcements that eventually every school was expected to have one or more specialisms, with the school raising £50,000 from business or the local community and the government paying in the same amount. Despite a National Curriculum still promising all pupils a broad and balanced education, most secondary schools did eventually adopt a specialism in a subject – technology, sport, arts and languages, being the most popular, with some headteachers noting that the attraction was the extra money rather than any educational aims. Specialist schools could select 10 per cent of pupils by aptitude for the declared specialism, although the House of Commons Select Committee on Education asserted that they could see no clear distinction between ability and aptitude. Disaffected pupils could be disapplied from part of the National Curriculum and from the age of 14 to take up a work-related curriculum at FE colleges.

Although initially ending the Conservative policy of assisted places at private schools, these schools taking some 7 per cent of children but providing 26 per cent of those taking A levels, New Labour abandoned any serious plans to bring private schools closer to the state sector and indeed produced policies to privatise state schools. Religious or faith schools, already educating nearly a quarter of all children at both primary and secondary level, were further encouraged by a 2001 White Paper which announced that 'the government wished to welcome faith schools, with their distinctive ethos and character, into the maintained sector' (DfES 2001: 5, 30) and the 2002 Education Act gave schools and LEAs the right to 'innovate' and gain 'earned autonomy'. Following a review commissioned by the Archbishop of Canterbury's Council in 2001, and carried out by the ubiquitous Lord Dearing, the Church of England announced that it planned for over 100 more church secondary schools, taking pupils from predominantly Christian backgrounds. The notion of extended schools, opening from 8am to 6pm, a legacy from attempts in the 1960s to develop genuine community schools, was introduced in the White Paper and Act, this time more concerned with assisting with childcare for the increasing numbers of working mothers. Academies, making a first appearance in a 2000 Learning and Skills Act as City Academies, were to be a new type of school independent from the local authority, and sponsored by business, faiths or voluntary bodies. Set up as limited companies with charitable status they were, in effect, private schools publicly funded. Sponsors were to contribute up to £2 million, with central government paying what turned out to be between £20 and £30 million per Academy for the 46 opened by 2006, and sponsorship money, never reliable, scaled down despite the sponsors having control of the school, its staffing, curriculum and admissions (Beckett 2007).

Unsurprisingly this diversity produced an even more rigorous hierarchy of schools, with a pecking order of those regarded as desirable or undesirable, and schooling continued to mirror the social class structure. The housing market was increasingly affected by parents buying near 'good' schools, and despite codes of admission to which schools until 2007 were only to 'have regard for', the admissions procedures became a source of anxiety and anger for many parents, as 'choice' rapidly became 'selection' by schools. Middle-class parents, eschewing any meritocratic notions, soon developed a range of strategies to privilege their children in the search for a good school. Schools placed in special measures after inspections continued to be demonised as failing schools, and a naming and shaming of these schools continued. One headteacher of a predominantly black school in a poor area noted bitterly that 'we have had a Herculean task to improve in a climate of hostility' (Gardiner 1997: 7). A policy of closing schools and reopening them as 'Fresh Starts' was soon abandoned, although the Academies programme was originally presented as a repackaging of failing schools in inner cities. Beacon schools, eventually becoming at secondary level part of a Leading Edge Partnership scheme, were intended to share good practice, but a competitive market acted as a constraint on collaboration. On instruction from the Secretary of State, the curriculum was once again subject to scrutiny by the Qualifications and Curriculum Authority, a body created in 1997 from the former School Assessment Authority and the National Council for Vocational Qualifications. Changes were to ensure further concentration on the teaching of literacy, numeracy and key skills, including Information and Communications Technology for all pupils, and education was to ensure that

> all pupils respond as individuals, parents, workers and citizens to the rapid expansion of communication technologies, changing roles of employment and new work and leisure patterns resulting from economic migration and the continued globalisation of the economy and society.
>
> (QCA/DfEE 1999)

However, apart from a stress on citizenship education, the content of much of the curriculum, particularly that leading up to the GCSE examination at 16, remained unchanged, and the testing of children at ages 7, 11 and 14 remained in place with results published in league table format and schools using all possible strategies to show up well in the tables. The GCSE examination was now 'tiered' for entry, research eventually demonstrating that black students were more likely to be entered for lower 'tiers' (Gillborn and Youdell 2000). Despite consultation papers and much advice on the reform of 14–19 education from both the DfES and the Learning and Skills Council (LSC) an academic–vocational divide remained in place. Skills for employment were to be strengthened and a National Skills Strategy developed, with the Education Secretary claiming that learning and skills were crucial both for social justice and economic success. A General Teaching Council was created in 1997 to register all teachers and produce professional codes of conduct, a private firm was hired by the DfEE to assess teachers for performance pay, teacher training became even more controlled and a National College for School Leadership was set up. Education was to further emulate business and management, although in 1999 the DfES funded a Centre for Research into the Wider Benefits of Learning at the London University Institute for Education, as there was some concern that education could not be concerned solely with employability and economic purpose.

Policy effects

New forms of inequality emerged with the creation of education markets and a diversity of schools, not least because markets create winners and losers, and competition from minorities can be regarded as illegitimate competition by the majority. If some minorities are successful in the competition xenophobia then racism can increase, especially if the familiar but untrue perceptions that minorities take more than a fair share of resources and teacher time are not countered. Equally, if some minorities continue to achieve less well they can be further stigmatised and blamed as groups or individuals. The urban location and social class of most ethnic minorities dramatically affected their 'choice' of schooling, previous chapters having demonstrated that they were most likely to attend schools that had previously been under-resourced and not set up to enter pupils for examinations. Both ethnic and social segregation was exacerbated by choice, as it became more apparent that this offered white parents even more legitimate ways of avoiding schools with high minority intakes. Faith schools, especially those Anglican and Catholic schools which, during the 1980s and 1990s, had taken pupils from a range of faiths became more selective by Christian faith, as the middle classes rediscovered their Christian religious roots. Choice policies generally were allowing schools, either centrally or locally funded, to become more selective and choose their pupils in a variety of overt or covert ways (West and Hinds 2003). In the school market place those regarded as valuable commodities who would enhance league tables were desirable customers. Pupils valued above others were likely to have higher measured ability levels, be motivated and have supportive parents, and thus fitted the pattern of selection by social class. While qualitative research studies had indicated from the early 1990s that choice and a diversity of schools increased social segregation, quantitative studies also showed the extent of sorting and choice by social class and ethnicity in England (Burgess and Wilson 2003, Taylor *et al.* 2005), although with different patterns in different local areas.

The socio-economic position of some minorities, particularly Caribbean, African, Pakistani, Bangladeshi, Somalis and newer migrant groups, made it more likely they would be excluded from desirable schools. But evidence also showed that an emerging black and predominantly Indian middle class, together with determined aspirational working-class minority parents, were adopting similar strategies to white parents, with expressed preferences for selective or private schooling, seeking out the 'best' schools, often defined as those with small numbers of minority pupils, and paying for private tutoring. Abbas' study in Birmingham in the later 1990s found that Indians from higher socio-economic positions were able to take more advantage of selective education, whereas the Pakistani and Bangladeshi parents had little choice apart from their local schools where educational resources were limited (Abbas 2004: 137). Given high minority parental aspirations it was not surprising that many supported selective schooling, and politicians representing high minority constituencies were reluctant to support ending selection if the area had grammar schools. In Birmingham by 2004 the remaining grammar schools overall took in 68 per cent white children, 14.4 per cent Indian, 6.9 per cent Pakistani, 3.2 per cent African-Caribbean and 1 per cent Bangladeshi, although the grammar school located in Handsworth, a high minority ward, took in 35 per cent Indian pupils. There was evidence that some schools were favouring highly-motivated Asian girls as easier to teach and achieve well in examinations. But minority parents of whatever social class, as noted in previous chapters, have always aspired for their children to do well in education, and by the 2000s some black parents were so discouraged by the system that they were sending their children back to the Caribbean for secondary schooling (Goring 2004). Black parents were also initially supportive of the Academies programme, but it rapidly became clear that these schools too, would be over-subscribed and thus selective of pupils, rather than helping all black pupils. Mindful that London included the largest proportion of ethnic minority pupils in the country, and that parents were dissatisfied with the education offered to their children, the DfES produced a strategy for a 'London Challenge', appointing a Commissioner for London Schools, and setting targets for raised achievement by social class, gender and ethnicity (DfES 2003a). However, the 'challenge' included further school diversity, with more Academies and specialist schools, and competitions for new schools to be open to churches, parents and voluntary groups. Rather than supporting notions of school diversity, campaigns continued for a good local school in every area.

The New Labour government set in train a number of initiatives designed to combat disadvantages suffered by low socio-economic groups, but included minorities in more careful ways, recognising long-standing grievances of minority parents about the poor quality of their children's schools, their achievements and other issues. Much of the policy was to be delivered by way of announcing targets to be attained by LEAs, schools and teachers. A Social Exclusion Unit was set up in the Cabinet Office in 1997, launched by the Prime Minister as helping 'our national purpose to tackle social division and inequality'. The Unit was to concentrate initially on schools exclusion and truancy, 17 per cent of those excluded from school in 1996 being of ethnic minority origin. One of the two black members of the Unit, Assistant Chief Probation Officer Reardon, asserted that there would be a specific focus on minority concerns. A second programme that was intended to benefit all those living in disadvantaged areas was that of Education Action Zones, set up with much publicity in 1998 and with 73 zones in operation before their amalgamation into an Excellence in Cities programme in 2004. Education Action Zones were intended to bring schools, community and business influence and funding together in local areas to improve schooling and achievement. The results of this intended cooperation were variable and inspectors did not find significant raised achievements in the schools involved. The Excellence in Cities programme, set up in 1999, was more clearly intended to reassure minority parents who could not take flight from inner-city areas that attention would be focused on attainment and behaviour. There were to be programmes for the 'gifted and talented' and eventually all schools were required to identify a percentage of children under this label, in addition there were to be more learning support units for the disaffected and slow learners, and learning mentors for pupils. This last was taken up with enthusiasm among city and business employees who enjoyed time off work to mentor selected pupils, but mentoring programmes for black pupils were regarded as helpful for individual pupils. An academy for the gifted and talented was set up at Warwick University, with payment required for summer schools, and although the Director of the Academy claimed that it served social justice, the majority of those identified as gifted were from white middle-class homes (Tomlinson 2008).

Childcare strategies

The New Labour government was particularly concerned to focus on child-care for the increasing number of mothers going out of the home to work, and this included minority mothers. In 2003, 84 per cent of black Caribbean women were in work, and 80 per cent of 'Asian', mainly Indian women, with lower employment rates for Pakistani and Bangladeshi women (Social Trends 2003). In 1998 a National Childcare Strategy was launched with an ambitious goal of creating five million childcare places, 20,000 after-school childcare projects and 60,000 new care jobs. While more public, private and voluntary sector pre-school places became available, the House of Commons Public Accounts committee reported in 2004 that parents in high minority areas were less likely to find or afford places. Childcare policies were treated with more urgency after the torture and death of an eight-year-old child of West African origin, Victoria Climbié, which led to a public inquiry, chaired by Lord Laming, into the failure of children's services to help her. In 2003 a Green Paper *Every Child Matters* appeared (HM Treasury 2003), followed by the appointment of a Minister to lead a Children's Directorate in the DfES and a Children Act in 2004 which required education, health and social services to work more closely together. The Education Secretary announced that schools were to act as community hubs offering 'educare', early years provision and health services. A Children's Commissioner,

Directors of Children's Services combining education and social services, and lead members of local councils were all to be appointed. Children's Centres were to open for all children offering full day-care, 3,500 being envisaged by 2010, and extended school days were to be adopted by schools. A Sure Start project was set up in 1999, the architect of this being Treasury civil servant Norman Glass. This programme was to bring together midwives, health workers, play workers and others in a £425 million project for 0–3 year olds and by 2004 there were 524 Sure Start local programmes in operation. Despite Norman Glass eventually worrying that a project designed to benefit children was in danger of becoming child-minding while poor mothers worked at low-paid jobs, government enthusiasm continued for links between the various projects for early years and childcare provision. Some Sure Start centres became part of children's centres, some were separate centres, and some located on school sites. The intention was to serve the most disadvantaged wards in the country, which by definition included those with large ethnic minority populations, but it was not until 2006 that research was commissioned to inquire whether the programmes were actually benefiting black and minority ethnic (BME) populations and contributing to social cohesion in local areas. The research concluded that while the project was, on the whole, successful in its aims, both the local Sure Start programmes and a national evaluation of Sure Start had 'failed to address the question of ethnicity with sufficient rigour or sensitivity' (Craig 2007: 9). In one area white parents had told Bangladeshi parents that they could not use the Sure Start facilities.

Achievement, EMAG and exclusion

The long saga of the lower educational attainments[7] of some minority groups continued into the later 1990s and the 2000s, particularly regarding black Caribbean, African, Pakistani, Bangladeshi, traveller and refugee pupils. The differential attainment of groups was now becoming clearer, but with different patterns emerging in different local authorities, and affected by social class and gender in different ways. The Open University was commissioned in 1997 to research the teaching and learning strategies in those multi-ethnic schools regarded as successful. Eleven primary and 18 secondary schools were studied and the researchers produced a list of factors that apparently made these schools more successful, which included high expectations, strong leadership, language support, curriculum changes, and staff who listened and responded to parents and students (Blair and Bourne 1998). In 1997 the DfEE asked Ofsted to inspect school initiatives in raising attainments, and inspectors duly looked at 48 schools in 25 LEAs with 12 selected for special case study, and with information on racial tension and harassment in schools being included in the report. This study noted the 'long standing reluctance of schools and LEAs to monitor pupil performance by ethnic group' (Ofsted 1999: 54). The inspectors' conclusions were that while the attainments of all groups were improving, Pakistani, Bangladeshi and travellers' children were less likely to attain well and black students made a good start in primary school with a decline in performance at secondary level. Partly as a response to this, the government finally made the decision to abandon Section 11 funding which, with central government paying for 75 per cent of approved schemes for what was now mainly for teaching English language, had remained the only extra funding for minority education. It was replaced in 1999 with an Ethnic Minority Achievement Grant (EMAG), briefly EMTAG for a year when travellers' children were added, and an Ethnic Minority Achievement Unit was set up in the DfEE. Announcing the grant, ministers asserted that they wanted a 'step change' in raising the attainments of ethnic minority pupils but the onus was again on local authorities to bring this about, with less funding and teachers still largely untrained in educating minority pupils. The 1990 Trust and numbers of other black and ethnic minority organisations and academics expressed concerns over EMAG (Race on the Agenda and 1990 Trust 1999). In particular, mainstream staff were expected to take up the work of teachers formerly paid under Section 11 grants, without support or training. Tickley *et al.* (2005), commissioned to examine whether EMAG had been successful in helping to raise minority achievements, concluded that although the government had recognised the complex issues surrounding minority attainment, the grant had failed to deliver as far as black students were concerned and there had been little consultation with black parents and community organisations.

Gillborn and Mirza (2000), again commissioned by Ofsted, were able to draw on 118 LEA submissions for EMAG and on information from the government-sponsored Youth Cohort study, which tracks a national sample of young people through into their post-school careers (DfES 2005). While the ethnic classifications used by LEAs often differed, the information gathered showed again that overall standards, as demonstrated by pupils achieving five A–Cs at GCSE level, had improved for all groups; white and Indian pupils had largely enjoyed a year-on-year improvement, with African-Caribbean, Pakistani and Bangladeshi pupils less likely to improve yearly. Attainments of minority pupils varied between LEAs, in one urban authority African-Caribbean pupils entered their schooling with the highest measured attainments but emerged with the lowest numbers of GCSEs. The data also demonstrated gender inequalities in attainments, with white, Indian and Chinese girls attaining more than other groups, but overall ethnic inequalities persisted even when controlling for social class and gender. The study pointed out that ethnic inequalities in attainments were not new but nor were they static, black pupils in all social classes had not shared in rising levels of GCSE attainments.

By 2002 the introduction of ethnicity codes based on the 2001 Census into the Pupil Level Annual School Census (PLASC) made it possible for central and local authorities to know more precisely how all pupils in local areas were attaining year on year. However, rather than clarifying achievements, the amount of statistical information available by social class (using the unreliable measure of free school meals as a proxy for class) and by gender and by ethnicity, led to much argument over the inter-relationships between these, and to what Archer and Francis termed 'complacent commentary' by the DfES. Any improved achievements or otherwise by minorities were assumed to be located in their own work ethic (Archer and Francis 2007). An Ofsted report on six schools which had raised black achievement did however, stress the need for dialogue between schools, parents and communities (Ofsted 2002). The DfES and Parliamentary Select Committees[8] focused particularly on 'achievement gaps' between white and minority groups, a term much used in the USA and which eventually recorded over 11 million citations on the Google search engine. Gillborn demonstrated that following a six-year trend, closing the gap between white and black students could take up to 83 years!

Gaps in achievement by social class exacerbated longer standing debate on the lower school performance of white boys from lower socio-economic groups, with much media presentation giving the impression that 'white students may be the new race victims' (Gillborn 2008). Political debate on race inequalities in achievement quickly turned to zero-sum assumptions that any concentration on race inequalities meant less focus on working-class white boys, and the 1990s' media anxieties of an alienated black underclass now changed to worry about poor white boys 'left behind' by the education system.[9] More information also focused attention on what had for some time been referred to in the USA as 'model minorities'. The higher achievements and progress of Indian and Chinese minorities were used as a stick to beat black and Muslim students with, even the Chair of the CRE asserting that since these groups also suffered from racism, other groups could not blame racism for their lower performance. The government followed this line of argument in their consultation document, *Aiming High* (DfES 2003b), on raising the achievements of pupils of Caribbean and Pakistani backgrounds, mixed race, traveller/gypsy and other 'vulnerable' groups. These groups were again noted as more likely to be recorded as lower achievers and as having special educational needs. The document claimed that African-Asian and Chinese communities had developed after the Pakistani communities but had better exam results, implicitly blaming the other communities for their children's educational performance. In fact, the higher social class position, education and entrepreneurial skills many East African Asians (a group which included Hindu and Muslim), Indians from the subcontinent and Chinese enjoyed had much to do with their children's achievements. The relatively small number of Chinese pupils, for example, were more likely to be in private schools or higher achieving white schools. Black pupils from West Africa achieved better than black Caribbean pupils, but mainly arrived from Nigeria and Ghana, countries with well developed school systems. Both *Aiming High* and subsequent guidance documents focused particularly on the education of African-Caribbean pupils as a tool of behavioural control, in order to prevent their involvement with the youth and criminal justice system. Meanwhile, black parents and communities continued their 50-year-long efforts to improve the education offered to their children. It was becoming very obvious that the presentation of some groups as model minorities included such stereotypes as Asian parents in particular encouraged their children more than black or other minorities. In fact, the long history of supplementary schooling, parental and community action and protest demonstrated that black parents were as interested in their children's education as any group and were increasingly frustrated by the system. Lorna Cork (2005), for a Cambridge doctorate, studied five organisations committed to supporting black parents, and demonstrated the wider issues of institutional racism, cultural stereotyping and the impact of race and class on home–school relations. She also showed the ways the school exclusion of black boys extended to the marginalisation of their parents. Black churches and other groups were also prominent in support for parents and a 'National Black Boys Can' Association, founded in 1999 by a group of black professionals and church leaders, aimed to provide black boys with more equal educational opportunities, life skills and confidence to succeed.

However, a determined right-wing had not given up on efforts to persuade the world that black people had lower average IQs than whites. The magazine *Right Now*, with several English lords and professors as patrons, recorded an interview with 77-year-old Arthur Jensen in 1999, in which he again asserted that black people had an IQ on average 15 points lower than whites, and that some 'high level' politicians in both the USA and Britain agreed with him that compensatory education programmes did not work (Turner 1999). While such views were not mainstream among most politicians in Britain, there was a linkage in most policies directed at black youth between low educational attainment, exclusion from school and potential criminality. Black boys were still the group most likely to be demonised as potential problems for school and society, – at least until Muslim youth vied for the demon label after 2005. Black boys continued to be four times over-represented in exclusions from school, although with variations between schools and LEAs. Following the first report from the Social Exclusion Unit in 1998, the government had set targets for reducing exclusions and introduced Behaviour Support and Improvement plans. Initially numbers of exclusions dropped but began to rise again after 2001. Maud Blair (2001), placing the issue in a broad social and historical perspective, showed that black pupils were criticised and excluded from school more than white children who committed similar and often minor 'offences', and Osler and

Vincent (2003) explored the exclusion from education of girls in all social and ethnic groups. The young people and parents Blair spoke to were angered by the negative racial stereotypes they felt schools and teachers attached to them, and Goring (2004) documented the very real fear even middle-class black parents felt that their children might be excluded from school and denied mainstream education.

Curriculum and teaching

Despite the plethora of initiatives, intervention and prescription concerning the school curriculum, teaching methods and teacher training, the New Labour government never indicated serious interest in the development of a curriculum that would combat cultural ignorance, ethnocentric attitudes and racism. Teachers became more of a managed profession, with 'workforce remodelling' providing more teacher numbers, teaching assistants and prescribed networking, especially via school leadership courses. They were also agents of a prescribed curriculum designed to raise standards as measured by test scores and school leaving results. While the government was unafraid to take control of curriculum delivery and assessment, it was reluctant to encourage curriculum change to prepare all young people for life in a multi-ethnic society. The work of several decades of schools, teachers, local authorities, academics, parents and communities in this direction was largely disregarded, and teachers in training were unlikely to be offered anything but a few sessions on the education of minorities. The rhetoric was that the Macpherson Report on the murder of Stephen Lawrence had galvanised policy makers and practitioners into action but the reality was different. The Teacher Training Agency produced guidelines in 2000 asserting that every trainee teacher needed to understand how to prepare all pupils to play a part in a culturally diverse society (TTA 2000). The guidance mainly took the form of indicating the tick boxes by which trainee teachers were required to demonstrate that they could deal with an inclusive education system, were aware of race legislation requirements, and were familiar with some academic writing and activist addresses. The Race Relations (Amendment) Act 2000 made it mandatory to produce and monitor policy promoting race equality in all educational institutions but CRE research two years later indicated that only 20 per cent of schools out of 1,105 responded as to what sort of policy they had and of these only a third had set aims and targets. There was, for example, some confusion when in 2002 Shabina Begum, a pupil at a school in Luton, Bedfordshire, wished to wear a jilbad (long robe) to her school, which already had a uniform policy to accommodate Muslim girls, and eventually the case was taken to the High Court and European Court of Human Rights. Despite the Parekh Report (2000) recommending that race equality and diversity be properly covered in initial teacher training and mandatory for management training for headteachers, there was little evidence that the notion of training to assist teachers and help them prepare all pupils to live in their multi-ethnic society was a dominant requirement. The Teacher Training and Development Agency from 2003 prepared a website (www.multiverse.ac.uk) as a resource for teachers and trainees, covering some academic and research information on race, class, religion, bilingualism and refugees and travellers, and materials were produced by long-standing groups and activists, but their use was optional. The Anti-Racist Teacher Education Network produced a framework for teacher education, and Richardson and Wood (1999) were commissioned by the Race on the Agenda Trust to produce a manual for teachers as to how to incorporate race and identity issues into all curriculum subjects – a task the censored 1990 National Curriculum Working Group had been set (see Chapter 4). The journal *Race Equality Teaching* (replacing *Multicultural Teaching*) continued to assist practitioners in making race equality and race issues visible in the curriculum. A community learning charity, *ContinYou*, produced information and assistance in creating 'culturally competent schools', particularly stressing the importance of Black History month, an annual initiative originally developed in the USA and popular from the 1990s with teachers and local authorities in the UK.

The government placed much faith in the development of citizenship education – a requirement for all schools from 2002 – to produce individuals capable of 'positive participation in our ethnically diverse society' (QCA/DfEE 1999), David Blunkett having appointed his old university tutor Bernard Crick to chair an advisory group on the teaching of citizenship and democracy in the National Curriculum. The subsequent report (Crick 1998) produced a framework for formal programmes of study, and the QCA followed this up with detailed guidance documents. Osler and Starkey (2005) pointed out that the Crick Report made no mention of racism, either institutional or personal, and focused on cultural differences between groups rather than issues of power or educational outcomes, and also implied that minorities see their countries of migration as their 'homeland' before Britain. Osler and Starkey, major researchers in citizenship education, suggested that education for a cosmopolitan citizenship should require all young people to regard themselves as citizens with rights and responsibilities locally, nationally and globally (Osler and Starkey 2005: 93), arguably a situation that would preclude any young person from considering action detrimental to fellow citizens anywhere! The 2002 Nationality and Immigration Act required new citizens to take a citizenship oath and be tested on life in Britain and the English language, and Home Secretary Blunkett urged all Asian families to speak English in the home. The promotion of teaching English to new citizens was somewhat ironic given the history of teaching English since the 1960s, and the general reduction of funding for this purpose. By 2000 there was already a shortage of qualified ESOL teachers, and migrants other than refugees needed to live in the UK for three years before qualifying for free classes. Blunkett specifically referred to Muslim women's need to learn English, again ironic in that ESOL funding cuts made this aim even more difficult. There was little evidence that the school curriculum or citizenship and language policies would be able to combat the racism and ignorance still illustrated by the popular press and still endemic in some institutions.

Summary

This chapter has illustrated changes in ideology and policy direction as a New Labour government came to power affirming a commitment to social and racial justice. There was an affirmation that a modern nation valued cultural diversity, and recognised the citizenship rights of settled minorities and the inequalities they faced. Race became a 'present presence' again and attempts were made to tackle some long-standing minority grievances. Some minority groups and individuals were by now demonstrably successful in educational, employment and entrepreneurial terms, particularly those with Indian, East African Asian, some West African and Chinese backgrounds. However, the race riots in northern towns in 2001 and more hostility to the Muslim population after 11 September, led to much concern over community cohesion, as minority and white groups were claimed as living segregated 'parallel lives', which in a curious twist of reasoning was blamed on 'multiculturalism'. In fact, as previous chapters have illustrated, community segregation had its roots from the 1960s in housing policies, white flight, community choices and constraints, and a reduction of mixing in employment as factories closed. Community segregation was further exacerbated by education policies encouraging choice and diversity in schooling, and the creation of a hierarchy of more or less desirable schools, including faith schools. Childcare and education policies designed to alleviate disadvantage included minorities in more subtle ways but there was little evaluation of how these policies were affecting minorities. Although the educational achievements of all young people continued to rise, the long-standing issue of the attainments of black and Muslim pupils continued to be documented by research and deplored by politicians, who, however, found it more comfortable to sidetrack the issues by reference to poor white boys, model minorities and other vulnerable minorities. Settled minorities and their concerns were conflated with problems associated with the arrival of more European economic migrants, refugees and asylum seekers. The contradictions between the teaching of citizenship as a preparation for living in a cohesive multicultural society with anti-immigrant rhetoric and more immigration control became more evident. The declared goal of preparing all pupils for an ethnically diverse society was not matched by attention to curriculum change or teacher preparation, and the support for radical religions and far right fascist parties indicated that the education system had not yet managed to teach rights and responsibilities to all citizens in a multicultural society. It was noteworthy that the publication in 2007 of the diaries of Prime Minister Blair's confidant and communications director, Alastair Campbell, documenting the period 1997–2003 (Campbell 2007), made very little reference to education, race or culture, with discussion of Cherie Blair's hairstyles seemingly being documented more often than these issues.[10] The diaries did, however, include many references to war and terror, which dominated the political background to issues of ethnicity, community cohesion and education over the next four years.

Notes

1. From the later 1990s and beyond most official documents referred to 'diversity' as shorthand for the incorporation of those who were perceived as racial, ethnic, religious, migrant or refugee groups, although the language of racial equality and race relations continued to be used in legislation. In education the term was confused with claims that New Labour wanted a 'diversity' of schools. Race equality activists and others, working on the assumption that whites were also an ethnic group, began to refer to black and minority ethnic (BME) populations.
2. Governments whose civilian population were threatened by terrorists gave the name 'Al Quaeda' (literally 'the base') to what were a variety of religious, ethnic and nationalistic groups using terror to gain political, territorial or religious advantages. Osama Bin Ladin, a Saudi Arabian fundamental wahhabist, was credited as the main leader of 'Al Quaeda'. In Afghanistan the opposition was to the Taliban (literally 'the student').
3. The 2001 classification of ethnic groups consisted of two levels. Level one being the broad categories of white, mixed, Asian or Asian British, Black or Black British, Chinese or other ethnic group, and level two breaking this down into 17 detailed categories (Social Trends 2003: 259).
4. The use of the term institutionalised racism, first used in the 1970s, and the recommendations of the Macpherson Report created much hostility from sections of the media. Sir William Macpherson eventually complained about personal attacks via hate-mail 'fuelled by articles published in such papers as the Daily Telegraph and the Daily Mail' (Verkaik 2001). However, by 2004, the failure of a further police investigation to bring the Lawrence killers to justice led the *Daily Mail* to name them in an editorial (*Daily Mail* 6 April 2004).
5. The Parekh Report (2000) identified a range of current theoretical and ideological positions relating to cultural diversity in Britain, noting that current political values still embody a liberal model where the state is assumed to be culturally neutral. A pluralist model assumes that the state will assume an active role in both the public and private sphere in promoting equality and cultural diversity and challenging institutional racism.
6. Chris Woodhead became well known for his assertions that there were 15,000 incompetent teachers and 3,000 poor headteachers, and for rewriting research and inspection reports (Tomlinson 2005, Beckett 2007). Michael Barber was a driving force behind many of the reforms to 'raise standards', which included sup-

porting the quick closure of Hackney Downs School (referred to in Chapter 5), which negatively affected the education of a number of black students. His own account of his influence on the education policies of New Labour are documented in Barber (2007).

7. The notion of 'underachievement' as a description of the lower educational attainments of minority pupils came in for academic and activist criticism from the 1980s, although it continued to be used in official literature. 'Inequality of attainment' between groups was the preferred academic description by the 1990s.
8. The author's evidence to the House of Commons Education and Skills Committee examining pupil achievement 2002–2003 pointed out again that many teachers still regard children with a Caribbean background as potential low achievers (House of Commons Education and Skills Committee 2003).
9. Gillborn and Tomlinson, meeting the then Education Minister Charles Clarke in 1999, had been presented with the white under-achievement and the model minorities arguments, when arguing the case for attention to be paid to black achievement. Gillborn (2008) has documented the way official statistics and some academics are keen to stress the importance of socio-economic factors in attainment and poor white boys problems, at the expense of race equality discussions. He also discusses in detail the notion of model minorities in the UK.
10. Campbell does, however, devote a whole page in his diaries to explaining why he used the phrase 'bog-standard comprehensives', writing that he was a supporter of comprehensive schools and that the then Education Secretary David Blunkett was 'pissed off' that he had described schools in this way (Campbell 2007: 501).

chapter six

Community cohesion, war and education (2003–2007)

> The polarising effects of terrorism and war accelerated the regression to atavistic notions of Britishness and race. As Blair leaves office he has the curious distinction of having realigned the level of public racial discourse with his own – by lowering it.
>
> (Younge 2007)

This chapter takes the narrative up to mid-2007, when Prime Minister Blair gave way to Gordon Brown. The legacy of a disastrous war in Iraq overshadowed earlier more positive race policies, as did continued scapegoating of groups including Muslims, asylum seekers, gypsies, East Europeans, black gangs and others, in which, regrettably, some politicians joined. Black journalist Gary Younge took the view that New Labour initially had the potential to create a more confident, inclusive Britain, but progressive initiatives were overshadowed by a reversal to crude anti-immigrant rhetoric, even against the EU expansion it had backed. There was now, however, more political and educational awareness that all young people in Britain would live their lives within a globalised economy, with rapid global communications and migration movements. They would also, for the foreseeable future, live with a 'war' against radical pseudo-religious movements using methods of terror against civilian populations. By the early 21st century globalisation was more clearly affecting the education and economic placement of majorities and minorities worldwide, and policy makers around the world had assigned education and skill acquisition a major role in improving the competitiveness of national economies in the global market.[1] As previous chapters have demonstrated, migrants to the UK were ahead in the globalisation game in that major reasons for their movement were to improve their own economic chances and enable their children to acquire educational qualifications and employment. Education was regarded as a key institution for incorporation into the society, and educational success was of highest importance to minority parents. However, for many parents, expectations of what the system could offer were followed by disappointment and disillusion. Limited liberal good intentions and positive policies for minorities were at odds with conservative beliefs in education as a preparation for a class-based and racialised social order and with neoliberal competitive market policies. Despite some successes, the education system into the 21st century had not been able to overcome racial exclusions and inequities. There was also continuing political and public ambivalence as to whether those perceived as 'non-white' or culturally different, or both, could ever be full British citizens. Debates about the notion of Britishness, national identity, multiculturalism and shared values had rumbled on for some years, but debates took on more urgency and more polarisation after attacks in the USA and rioting in 2001 in English towns, and after 2003 when war in Iraq increased (but did not create) the possibility of internationally sponsored terrorism by radical Islamic groups.[2] Existing hostility to the Muslim population of the UK intensified.

Education policy makers remained reluctant to make links between ongoing and new social and racial antagonisms and the contradictions created by education policies. Market competition and a 'diversity' of schools had exacerbated existing social and racial segregation. The encouragement of separation into faith schools did not appear likely to diminish segregation. Despite the decades of research and protest, the qualification levels and thus employment opportunities for many young black and Asian (especially Muslim) young people remained low, not a good situation for either the economy or social cohesion. The failure to think seriously about a curriculum for a globalised future – which would entail an understanding of the past – or to begin to agree on common values, left many schools and teachers either ignoring tensions or unable to cope with conflicts, although schools with multi-ethnic intakes were largely at the forefront in developing 'inclusive schools'. The continued devaluation and lack of proper funding for vocational training and skills, which left gaps in the labour force filled by economic migrants from an expanding European Union, led to hostility directed against the migrants. There was a continued political stress on immigration control, feeding public hostility to both long-settled migrant citizens, economic migrants and refugees and asylum seekers, and reports and recommendations on integration and community cohesion did not appear to address the issues with confidence. This chapter briefly details general education policy over the period before discussing race policies and ideologies on multiculturalism, segregation and community cohesion; the contradictions between attempts at more cohesion and policies continuing to separate children, including by religious faith; the continued issue of minority achievements; and the attempts to use citizenship education to create a national civic community linked to race equality and as preparation for a globalised world. The language used over the period continued to be diversity, race equality, multiculturalism, black and minority ethnic, with immigrant largely referring to European and other economic migrants, refugees and asylum seekers.

Chronology of Acts and issues

2004 (January) Higher Education Act allows higher tuition fees and sets up an Office for Fair Access (OFFA).

2004 (February) Editor of *Prospect* magazine 'challenges liberals to rethink their attitudes to diversity' (Goodhart 2004). (May) Chair of CRE Trevor Phillips suggests that multicultural policies have been divisive and there should be a concentration on integration.

2004 Report by the London Development Agency again documents the lower school achievements of black boys and confirms that a majority of schools identified as failing since 1993 have been high minority schools situated in deprived areas.

2004 DfES Five-Year Strategy for Children and Learners includes plans for Children's Centres, extended schooling offering 'educare' and more Sure Start centres. The Teacher Training Agency sets up a website on equality issues (www.multiverse.com) as a resource for teachers.

2004 (August) Politicians, media and public welcome home Bolton-born 17-year-old Amir Khan, winner of boxing silver medal at the Athens Olympics.

2004 (December) Ruth Kelly, a member of the Catholic organisation Opus Dei, made Education Secretary, lasting six months in post. Charles Clarke becomes Home Secretary.

2005 Leader of Opposition Michael Howard announces he intends to make asylum and immigration an election issue. Conservative calls for quotas for asylum seekers and a withdrawal from the 1951 UN Convention on the status of refugees. Government replies with a further Immigration, Asylum and Nationality Bill.

2005 (March) Court of Appeal equivocal in whether Shabina Begum's right to wear a jilbad at school had violated her human rights.

2005 (April) Education Act. TTA becomes TTDA. Competition to set up new schools can include applications from religious or parent groups.

2005 (May) Trevor Phillips, Head of CRE (and designate Head of the new Equalities and Human Rights Commission), suggests that 'we are becoming more socially polarised by race and faith'. In September he claims the UK is 'sleepwalking into segregation'. Home Secretary announces an Advisory Committee on Integration and Cohesion for British Muslims.

2005 (June) New Labour elected for a third term. Nine black and Asian MPs. The Conservatives, under Michael Howard, run a losing campaign vilifying immigrants and asylum seekers. Fourth Education Secretary in four years appointed (Alan Johnson), with Ruth Kelly made a Minister for Communities.

2005 'Desi' (countryman, Diaspora) appears in Oxford English Dictionary as a broad term to include all 'Asians'. Asian women workers strike at Gate-Gourmet, a Heathrow food supplier firm. *Social Trends* (2005) shows the British population to be 91.9 per cent white, 8.1 per cent ethnic minority, of which there are 4.1 per cent Asian British, 2 per cent Black British, 1.2 per cent mixed, 0.4 per cent Chinese, 0.4 per cent other ethnic groups. There were some 5,700 applications for asylum in 2005, and over 3,000 people removed from the country as failed asylum seekers.

2005 (7 July) Four young Muslim suicide bombers, educated in English primary and secondary schools, blow up three London underground trains and a bus, leaving 56 dead. On 21 July four more young Muslims, all initially refugees and educated in English schools, attempt a further bombing.

2005 (August) 18-year-old black student Anthony Walker axed to death in Liverpool while with white girlfriend. Police say immediately it was a racial crime.

2005 (September) DfES claims that 'Minority ethnic pupils make further progress at GCSE' (in the five A–C league black Caribbean pupils are up to 36 per cent, black African up to 43 per cent, white up to 52 per cent overall).

2005 (October) Riots in Lozells, Birmingham between black and Asian groups. Also riots in the Parisian minority-populated, outer suburbs in France. Lee Jasper (advisor to London Mayor) comments that France should adopt English multicultural policies.

2005 (November) *Tell It Like It Is: How Schools Fail Black Children* (ed. Richardson) reprints Bernard Coard's 1971 book and adds other contributions detailing the failure of the education system to educate black and Muslim children successfully. A total of 120 black supplementary schools known to be operating.

2005 (November) Education White Paper proposes reforms creating further opportunities for selection, competition and privatisation in schooling.

2006 (February) Education and Inspections Bill published, controversy over selection, admissions and faith schools clauses. An Equality Act, establishing a single commission for all strands of equality, becomes law.

2006 (March) House of Lords finds for the school in its appeal against the decision to give Shabina Begum the right to wear a jilbad.

2006 (May) In local elections BNP put up 357 candidates. Eleven are elected in Dagenham and Barking, London. Leeds University lecturer Frank Ellis suspended for claiming that whites are more intelligent than black people and describing himself as 'an unrepentant Powellite'.

2006 (August) Prime Minister Blair tells Cabinet that terrorism and immigration are the two major public concerns. The *Sun* tabloid newspaper (23 August 2006) publishes its topless Page 3 girl, Keeley from Kent, complete with speech bubble saying that 'she is very worried about immigration'.

2006 (September) Government sets up a Commission on Integration and Cohesion (CIC) Chaired by Darra Singh becomes Chief Executive of Ealing Council. (October) Trevor Philips suggests again that 'we are socially polarised by race and faith' and predicts further conflicts. Home Office study finds that a third of white pupils at mainly white schools believe one race is superior to others.

2006 (October) Jack Straw MP, former Home Secretary and former Foreign Secretary, publishes an article criticising the wearing of the niquab by Muslim women. Aishah Azmi, teaching assistant in Dewsbury, Yorkshire, is suspended for refusing to remove her niquab while in the classroom. DfES draws up proposals for universities to report on (Muslim) student 'extremism'.

2006 Education and Inspections Bill debated before and after the parliamentary recess. In October an amendment proposes that 25 per cent of places in faith schools should be given to those of other or no faiths. After lobbying by the Catholic church, there is an announcement by the Education Secretary that this will not be in the Act which becomes law in November. Nuffield Report on *The Education of 14–19 year olds* reports again that the lowest achievers in any qualification at 16 are young men of Pakistani and Bangladeshi origin.

2006 (November) MPs demand an inquiry into the Iraq war, rejected by Foreign Secretary Margaret Beckett. Ministry of Defence announces the war has so far cost £4 billion.

2006 (November) Three Pakistani-Scots men jailed for life for killing a white boy. Higher profile for antagonisms between white and minority 'gangs', and between minority groups. One third of all young black men reported as being on the national police DNA database.

2007 (January) Public drawn into a racism row over the TV programme Big Brother, when contestant Jade Goody insulted Indian-born actress Shilpa Shetty. Over 40,000 complaints were made to Channel 4 and viewers voted to evict Goody from the Big Brother house.

2007 (January) Ajegbo Report on 'Diversity in schools' highlights problems of poverty and white pupil disadvantage in creating 'community cohesion'.

2007 (March) Celebrations for the bicentenary of the abolition of the slave trade. Mayor Ken Livingstone apologises for London's role in the enslavement of millions of Africans and the legacy of racism. No events organised to celebrate the 50th year of the European Union, initially the EEC, despite the Union now embracing 400 million people in 25 countries and forming a quarter of the world economy. More internal and external border controls to prevent illegal migration between and into union countries including electronic surveillance systems.

2007 (April) Rowntree study demonstrates ethnic inequality, with two-thirds of Pakistani and Bangladeshi children raised in poverty. Jack

Straw writes an article for the *Chatham House* journal telling Muslims to subscribe to values of freedom, fairness and tolerance.

2007 (April) Baljeet Gale becomes the first minority woman (Kenyan Asian) to become President of the National Union of Teachers.

2007 (May) In local and Scottish/Welsh elections Bashir Ahmed become the first Scottish-Asian member of Scottish parliament. Political representation includes some 200 Muslim local councillors, four Muslim MPs in Westminster, five Muslim members of the House of Lords and one Muslim MEP. Fifty-six BNP local councillors are elected around the country. Margaret Hodge, Industry Minister, suggests that local white families should be rehoused ahead of new migrants.

2007 (June) Siddiqui Report on Islamic Studies in British Higher Education. Report of the Commission on Integration and Community Cohesion, *Our Shared Future*. Institute for Community Cohesion set up at Coventry University. Ofsted report on religious education in schools questions whether current RE teaching helps community cohesion. The award of a knighthood to Salman Rushdie renews the controversy over his book *The Satanic Verses*. Right-wing group Civitas suggests that the school curriculum has been hijacked into promoting 'fashionable causes', such as the environment, gender awareness and anti-racism.

2007 (June) Prime Minister Blair resigns. Gordon Brown takes over. DfES abolished and two new Ministries set up: a Department for Children, Schools and Families (Secretary of State, Ed Balls) and a Department for Innovation, Universities and Skills (Secretary of State, John Denham). Proposals put forward for raising the age of leaving education or training to 18.

2007 (July) Attempted bombings in London and at Glasgow airport. The alleged perpetrators highly educated (medical and technical) young Muslim men originally entering Britain as refugees. (August) A statue of Nelson Mandela placed in Parliament Square next to the statue of Winston Churchill.

Education policy 2003–2007

Tony Blair's government, with its education policies still largely dictated by a small group of advisors, continued its evangelical emphasis on education as a major means of improving the nation's economic competitiveness, with pupils, schools and universities subject to more accountability through testing, inspections and funding regimes, and continued support for a diversity of schools. From 2003 there were signs that many Labour politicians were concerned by the introduction of controversial measures with little consultation. Acrimonious debate concerning university funding took up much parliamentary time, with the government narrowly missing defeat in a vote in January 2004 to charge higher tuition fees to students. However, the 2004 Act did require an Office of Fair Access to encourage wider participation in higher education, and ensure bursaries for poor students. Despite the constant and often contradictory policies and initiatives, public education continued its long, slow, post-war improvement in terms of numbers of young people entering for and passing tests and public examinations, with government taking credit for improvements and continuing to blame schools, teachers and parents where improvements did not occur, especially in those urban schools attended by minority pupils. There was, however, increased public unease that policies of school diversity, competitive marketisation and privatisation of schools and services were helping to increase rather than diminish inequalities in education and society. The progressive abandonment of government involvement in social welfare and the increased role of the private sector appeared to be an electorally attractive way of enhancing choice and reducing public spending, but was creating huge anxieties for middle-class and aspirant groups, especially minorities. Competition for 'good' schools intensified, as did the increased selection of young people by overt and covert means for different and unequally resourced schools. The Academies programme continued apace, although evidence was accumulating that these expensive 'independent' schools, still funded by taxpayers, were actually increasing social segregation. The first three Academies opened in 2002, and by September 2006 46 were open, with plans for 200 in total. The United Learning Trust, an Anglican educational charity chaired by the Archbishop of Canterbury, quickly became a major sponsor of Academies, with 20 open or planned. Interestingly, a major donor to this Trust was multimillionaire Muslim Mahmoud Khayani, who also donated money to the Labour Party. An Oasis Christian Trust, founded by a Baptist minister, planned five Academies, to be rooted in 'core Christian values' which included a refusal to recognise homosexuality. The Catholic church also became an Academy sponsor, and Muslim, Sikh and Hindu organisations began to express interest. Despite revamped Codes of Admission for schools and Admission Forums in local authorities, Academies, grammar schools, foundation and voluntary-aided schools continued to control their own admissions, and nationally complaints against school admission procedures doubled.

In 2004 all government departments were required to produce a five-year strategy plan and spending review, and the DfES presented a plan for children and learners claiming that five principles would underpin advances in education and children's services. These were: greater personalisation and choice; opening up services to different providers; more freedom for headteachers and managers with more secure funding; more staff development; and more partnerships with parents, employers, local authorities and voluntary organisations. The most contentious proposal was to create 'independent specialist schools' in place of the traditional comprehensive, although by this time a majority of secondary schools claimed to specialise in one or more subjects and could notionally select 10 per cent of pupils. There was to be enhanced spending on education, rising to 5.6 per cent of GDP by 2008, which was actually a lower percentage than in the previous Conservative government and lower than many other OECD countries. Rather than build and renovate schools solely with public money, the government entered into public–private partnerships, in a Building Schools For the Future strategy, with private companies eventually set to own the land and buildings. However, there was more recognition and continued anxiety that attainment gaps between best and worst performers in schools was widening and that this was related to socio-economic position. The Five Year Plan recognised that 'we fail our most disadvantaged children' (DfES 2004a) and that a strategy for 14–19 education was lacking, allowing some young people to leave at 16 with no qualifications, and that attention to the early years was crucial. Children's Centres, Sure Start programmes, family centres and extended schools were all advocated. More attention was also given to special educational needs and disability, with claims that more integrated children's services and early intervention would reduce child poverty and educational disadvantage.

The last Education Act of the government's second term, passed in April 2005, overturned an historic funding agreement with local authorities, money would now come directly from the Secretary of State for all maintained schools. Local authorities were required to set targets for the educational performance of schools, and governors were given more powers to exclude pupils. There was to be extended competition for new schools including proposals from religious or parent groups. On re-election in June 2005 another education White Paper was prepared and published in October. This was followed by another year of Parliamentary controversy, although the House of Commons Education and Skills Committee noted that much of the content of this White Paper was a repeat of previous legislation. The contentious proposal was for schools to become 'trusts' or charitable foundations, appointing their own governors, and controlling their own admissions, staff, appointments and assets. There was immediate confusion with existing foundation and voluntary-aided religious schools, especially as the DfES produced a glossy pamphlet on 'How to become a Trust School' before Parliament had managed to debate the issue. An Education and Inspections Bill appeared in February 2006 and became law the following November.

Local authorities now needed permission from the Secretary of State to open a new community school and were also now required to provide advice to parents in expressing a preference for schools, and to provide more transport out of local areas. A duty was to be laid on schools to promote 'community cohesion', although the contradictions between urging community cohesion, in which local schools were acknowledged to play a crucial role, while encouraging movement out of local communities to supposed better schools, were obvious. The Act enlarged the Inspectorate to become an Office for Standards in Education, Children's Services and Skills and, having repudiated the proposals of Mike Tomlinson's Committee (DfES 2004b) which recommended qualifications reform leading to an overarching diploma, instead made provision for 14 vocational diplomas to be set up by 2010, thus ensuring a continuation of an academic–vocational divide in schooling. There were also to be new powers concerning the exclusion of pupils, a new duty on parents being to make sure that an excluded pupil was 'not present in a public place during normal schools hours', with parents to be fined if found to be not complying, a measure that would bear more heavily on black parents. While the Act was in passage through Parliament, Lord Baker, a former Education Secretary, proposed a legal duty on all faith schools to admit a percentage of children from other or no faiths, with 25 per cent being a suggested figure. This proposal generated much controversy among politicians and the media, was opposed by Bishops in the House of Lords, and by the Conservative opposition, the whole Act only becoming law with support from the Conservatives. Over the summer of 2007 the Conservatives appeared to change policy regarding support for grammar schools, but their leader David Cameron was forced to backtrack on this. The change of Prime Minister from Blair to Brown in June 2007 signalled yet more change, with the DfES being abolished and replaced by two new ministries, one for Children, Schools and Families, and one for Innovation, Universities and Skills. The word 'education' disappeared from the ministries but a Council for Educational Excellence was set up in July, with five members from business, five from universities, seven from schools and early years settings, and Michael Barber as advisor (whose 2007 book detailed his view of how successful all previous New Labour educational reforms had been). More legislation was immediately planned for raising the age of leaving education or training to 18, and for consolidating curriculum reforms.

Unity and diversity: ideologies and policy

Views of Britain as a disunited kingdom in which multiculturalism was the enemy were given more prominence after 2003, with many commentators suggesting that a once cohesive British society had been fractured by the presence of racial and ethnic groups, and the arrival of more migrants and refugees. The mythical nature of assumptions that a society always divided on class, wealth and gender lines was ever cohesive, and the post-imperial reluctance to recognise the contribution racial minorities had made to the kingdom, ensured that many of the contributions to the debate were unhelpful, especially to educationists struggling with the everyday reality of a multicultural society. The background to discussions of a society becoming more diverse was that of growing wealth and income inequalities between all social groups. Despite claims that New Labour policies had 'lifted' nearly a million children out of poverty[3] and the New Deal for Communities had invigorated declining areas, by 2006 the ONS recorded that the gulf between rich and poor remained the same as when Mrs Thatcher left office in 1990, and the richest fifth of UK households had incomes 16 times greater than the poorest. Research from the Rowntree Foundation published in April 2007 demonstrated again that the poorest households included a disproportionate number of Pakistani and Bangladeshi households, although a few of the richest included some Muslim and Indian (Sikh and Hindu) households, whose wealth often accrued through business developed in minority communities, and in transnational businesses.

In 2004 a debate was sparked by the editor of *Prospect* magazine attacking 'progressive liberals' for supporting diversity. He argued that diversity had become a code for ethnicity, that sharing welfare state benefits with diverse groups might increase tensions and fears, and that 'newcomers should adopt the history of their new country' (Goodhart 2004). While these appeared to be familiar right-wing arguments, two months later Trevor Phillips, then Chair of the CRE claimed that 'multiculturalism suggested separateness' and urged more focus on a common culture, he was supported by David Lammy, a young black MP, left-wing *Guardian* newspaper columnist Polly Toynbee and right-wing philosopher Roger Scruton. Political and media discussion following these assertions made no use of census or research data which showed actual patterns of residence by ethnicity. While some urban areas had increased their numbers of minorities via higher birth rates and new migrations, outer areas also had an increased minority residence.[4] Media comment also ignored a 50-year debate on unity and diversity, suggested that ethnic minority communities deliberately segregated themselves, and that uncritical acceptance of unlawful cultural practices was common. Although the Queen used her annual Christmas message to the nation at the end of 2004 to make an impassioned appeal for religious and cultural tolerance and for diversity to be recognised as a strength, Phillips continued to claim that the UK was becoming more polarised by race and faith.

In June 2005 New Labour was elected for a third time, with the then Conservative leader Michael Howard running an unpleasant losing campaign vilifying immigrants and asylum seekers. Former Birmingham MP Roy Hattersley commented that Howard 'escalated the dangers of immigration beyond Enoch Powell's wildest excesses' (Hattersley 2005). Nine black and Asian MPs were elected, although Oona King, the black MP for the predominantly Muslim area Tower Hamlets in London, was defeated by George Galloway – a man who had been an apologist for Saddam Hussein in Iraq, and who ran a campaign against King stressing that she had a Jewish mother. In July 2005 four young Muslim men, born and educated in England, became suicide bombers in London, killing 56 people and wounding 700 more, including many Muslim citizens. Two weeks later there was an attempted bombing by four more young men, originally refugees, and educated in English schools. The next two years saw more intended attacks discovered and in June 2007 there were attempted bombings of London night clubs and Glasgow airport, this time by highly educated men. These terror attacks by radicalised young men with fanatical beliefs about the Western world were promptly associated with whole Muslim communities and Phillips suggested in a speech in Manchester in September 2005 that the country was 'sleepwalking into segregation', a phrase later seized on by some politicians.[5] The reality was that the perpetrators were not the products of multiculturalism or complaining about a multicultural society. Using a variety of grievances, especially British foreign policy, they were willing to attack Western-style societies *per se*, killing any race, culture or faith, including fellow Muslims, in these attacks. Less attention was given to familiar antagonisms to any 'integration' by wide-awake white young men, illustrated at the end of July 2005, when black college student Anthony Walker was axed to death in Liverpool while with his white girlfriend. In contrast to the Stephen Lawrence murder, the police at once announced that it was a racial crime. Over the year London police recorded an average of 53 racial crimes a day in London, with anti-Semitic crime increasing, and attacks against Muslims, or indeed anyone appearing to be 'Asian', increasing after the bombings (Race Equality West Midlands 2006).

Multiculturalism continued to be blamed for what were undoubtedly serious social problems as groups endeavoured to live together in a society fractured by poverty, wealth disparity, wars abroad, terror attacks, religious bigotry from all faiths, and competition for schools and employment. In October 2005 there was rioting in Lozells, Birmingham, between black and Asian groups, in which one black man died, and over the next few years, an increase in stabbings and killings of teenagers by other young people, usually blamed on gang membership. Tony Blair angered community activists by claiming that killings were caused by 'black culture', especially absent fathers and a lack of black role models (Wintour and Dodd 2007), and there was also anger when it was disclosed that a third of all young black men were now on a police DNA database. A Violent Crime Reduction Act, passed in February 2007, did allow school staff more powers to search pupils suspected of carrying weapons, as there were indications that more young people were bringing knives into schools. In 2006 Phillips, by now designate Head of the new Commission for Equality and Human Rights

(CEHR), again attacked a social polarisation by race and faith, using yet again the James Baldwin metaphor of 'fire' on the streets due to racial and cultural tensions (Baldwin 1963). The Mayor of London Ken Livingstone rebuked Mr Phillips for using inflammatory language for the sake of 'alarmist headlines' (Muir 2006). But by August 2006, New Labour was also 'stoking public fears' as Tony Blair announced that 'terrorism and immigration were the main public concerns' (Woodward 2006). Other ministers followed with criticisms of the Muslim community's supposed failure to integrate. Dress became a flashpoint in October 2006 when former Home Secretary and Foreign Secretary Jack Straw, previously known for his support for positive race policies, criticised the wearing of the niquab, the full-face veil adopted by some Muslim women. While most schools in Britain had developed a school uniform for Muslim girls which included the headscarf (hijab), Straw was supported by many educationalists for his criticism of the niquab and a High Court case was still in progress over a pupil's right to wear the jilbad to school. A teaching assistant in Dewsbury, Aishah Azni, was suspended and then dismissed for refusing to remove her niquab while at work, a court case later supporting the local authority action, although Muslim Labour Peer Baroness Uddin predicted that more young women would adopt the niquab in defiance. The Muslim Council of Britain, representing some 400 Muslim organisations, accused the government of stigmatising Muslims in general, a situation not helped when it became known that the DfES had drawn up proposals for universities to pass information to the security services on Islamic Societies and possible 'extremism' on campuses (Dodd 2006). The University and College Lecturers Union (UCU) eventually passed a resolution rejecting the government plans (Chapman 2007).

Some religious groups, nationally and internationally, continued to claim offences against their religions. Christian groups objected to an opera depicting the life of Christ; a Sikh group in Birmingham successfully closed a play about the Sikh community; and Muslims took offence over newspaper cartoons published in Denmark and the award of a British knighthood to Salman Rushdie. On what could be described as the positive side of race relations, the British public objected when, in January 2007 Jade Goody, a contestant in a TV show 'Big Brother', made racist comments about a fellow contestant, Bollywood actress Shilpa Shetty. Channel 4 received over 40,000 complaints and Jade was 'voted out' of the programme. Politicians seized on the issue, the Culture Secretary describing the show as 'racism as entertainment', the Chancellor of the Exchequer urging the public to 'vote for tolerance' and the Education Secretary promising that revamped citizenship lessons would discuss core values of respect, fairness and 'what Britishness means' (Robinson and Hinscliff 2007). Trevor Phillips also announced that the vote to evict Jade made him 'feel good about being British'. A positive side was also demonstrated in May 2007 when some 200 Muslims were elected as local councillors around the country, Bashir Ahmed became the first

Scottish-Asian member of the devolved Scottish parliament, and Ireland's first black Mayor, Nigerian-born Rotimi Adebari, was elected in Portlaoise. At the NUT annual conference Baljeet Gale became the first Asian woman President of the National Union of Teachers, and comedian Yara-al-Sherbini became the first Muslim female to host comic quizzes in pubs! On the negative side, 56 BNP local councillors were elected in May and Margaret Hodge, then an Industry Minister, appeared to support BNP views by suggesting that immigrant families were being re-housed by her local council ahead of young white families (Hodge 2007).

Community cohesion

By the middle of the decade it was clear that ideologies of community cohesion and reconciliation of cultural differences were to be the focus of government attention, prompted by fears of 'Muslim extremism'. Local councils were given £5 million in early 2007 to work with young Muslims who might be vulnerable to extremism. Little attention was paid to structural issues, a strike for higher wages by Asian women employed at a food-supplier firm at Heathrow airport receiving no political or union support. A 'Black Manifesto', first published in 2005 by a coalition of Asian, African and Caribbean groups, including the Society of Black Lawyers, the National and the Metropolitan Black Police Associations, and the National Coalition of Black-led Organisations focused on structural inequalities in employment, education, health, housing, the criminal justice system and other areas. This also received little media attention. The manifesto suggested that in many institutional areas racial and religious discrimination was becoming worse, and that political leadership was needed. It proposed a Minister for Race in the Cabinet, and high-level civil service race champions in education, employment and criminal justice (*Black Manifesto for Equality in our Lifetime* 2005). Although after 2005 a Race Minister was appointed, the various government committees set up to examine social cohesion and community integration, managed to avoid any structural analysis, or reference to race, racism or multiculturalism in their reports. Shortly after the 2005 bombings in London the Home Secretary set up an Advisory Committee on Integration and Cohesion for British Muslims, on which all faith groups were represented. 'Moderate Muslims' were urged by Ruth Kelly, who had been transferred after a six-month period as Education Secretary to Communities Secretary, to 'take a pro-active role in tackling extremism and defending our values' (Kelly 2006), causing the Liberal Democrat Communities spokesman to object that it was no solution to demonise a whole faith because of the actions of fanatics. Keith Ajegbo, former Head of Deptford Green School in Lewisham, London, was asked to lead a curriculum review related to *Diversity and Citizenship* (Ajegbo 2007), and an Institute for Community Cohesion was set up at Coventry University, under the directorship of former MP Oona King. In September 2006 Kelly set up a Commission on Integration and Cohesion (CIC), chaired by Darra Singh, Chief Executive of Ealing Council in London, which produced a report in June 2007 (Commission on Integration and Cohesion 2007). While this Commission was at work Tony Blair asserted in a public lecture that 'the right to be in a multicultural society was always implicitly balanced by the duty to integrate and accept British values', neither defining integration nor British values (Blair 2006).

The Commission collected responses from 600 organisations and individuals, and relied heavily on the government Citizenship Survey, a household survey of 15,000 people conducted by the Communities and Local Government Department. In a distinctly bland report it identified cohesion as a process that should happen in all communities to ensure different groups get on together, and integration as the process that ensures new and existing residents adapt to each other, with a fair allocation of public services and community facilities. There was an initial reference to globalisation and global communications, 'cultural imports in terms of food and music' being singled out, and also a complaint that there was confusion in the responses they had received, many respondents apparently preferring to focus on race relations and equality rather than cohesion. The report identified five areas where cohesion was likely to be minimal; less affluent rural areas with East European workers arriving; less affluent urban areas with settled communities living 'parallel lives', as the Cantle report in 2001 had suggested; urban areas with few jobs but lower house prices attracting new migrants in competition with the locals; less affluent urban areas or coastal towns with high demand for low-skilled labour also in competition with locals; and towns or suburbs where single issues such as a terrorist act or proposed centre for asylum seekers causes tensions. The recommendations duly put the onus for cohesion on local councils with 12 key suggestions, including citizenship ceremonies, welcome packs for new migrants, myth-busting strategies to rebut misinformation, and promotion of intercultural activities. Local political parties were to improve the diversity of councillors and make voluntary agreements to conform to the Race Relations (Amendment) Act. Some local authorities were already collecting information on the 'diversity' in their areas, the Chief Executive's Office in Leicestershire producing their own report noting that 'the landscape has shifted from a multicultural focus to breaking down barriers to produce cohesive communities' (Adamson and Boek 2007). One contentious proposal from the Commission was that local councils and others should end single group funding to organisations on the basis of their 'particular identity'. Bradford-born academic Yunis Alam described this as an example of a new race logic which suggests that it is race or religious identity, rather than lack of educational and economic opportunities, that create barriers to community cohesion.

The Commission welcomed the new duty to promote community

cohesion placed on schools, with draft guidance on how to do this having been issued by the DfES in May 2007, and made a series of recommendations for schools, most of which could be found in the Education Support Grant projects that had covered 120 local authorities between 1985 and 1992. These included school twinning, extended school activities to include parents from different communities, 'buddy' schemes to help second language speakers, citizenship education, a review of the religious education curriculum, and involving local employers and voluntary groups in the 14–19 curriculum. There were also recommendations that government review the plans and allocation of resources for English for second language speakers' courses. English for Speakers of Other Languages (ESOL) funding had become part of a Skills for Life agenda from 2001, but eligibility for free classes was progressively reduced, and all courses had to work towards accreditation. Older Muslim women, refugees and asylum seekers were the main casualties of free tuition, as courses for economic migrants from the ten countries joining the EU in 2004 took precedence, and an ESOL For Work qualification was introduced. Employers, especially those who employed migrant labour, were exhorted to share the cost of ESOL training, there apparently being little memory that in the 1960s employers did recognise a responsibility to provide some English language teaching. Over the summer of 2007 the University and College Lecturers Union organised a Save ESOL campaign, noting that although some concessions had been made there was no national strategy for ESOL.

Faith segregation

By 2007 there was sufficient research to demonstrate beyond doubt what many educationalists had been pointing out for some 20 years – that 'choice' policies for an hierarchical diversity of schools, based on competitive individualism, would increase social and ethnic segregation.[6] A study by the Runnymede Trust noted the tensions between 'the overwhelmingly individualistic approach offered by the choice agenda and the broad forms of social, economic and cultural marginalisation, with the risk that only the highest achieving BME pupils will benefit, leaving the situation of the majority unchanged'. If schools are regarded as places where people from different ethnic backgrounds meet, 'choice policies can operate in precisely the opposite direction, with the result that young people from different ethnic backgrounds can be kept apart' (Weekes-Bernard 2007: 5). This research found that for the vast majority of BME parents surveyed, the schools their children were attending were not the ones they had wanted their children to attend.

The policy that continued to cause much controversy was the encouragement of more faith-based schools which controlled their own admissions, and allowed parents to choose faith-based segregation – with faith having become in some areas more or less a code for race.[7] Until the 1990s the majority of Church of England and some Catholic schools had accepted children from all faiths, particularly when a lower birth rate left empty places. The majority of young Muslim people in Bradford, when riots occurred in 2001, had been educated at primary level in the Church of England schools located in central Bradford, and minority parents, especially Muslim parents, had always preferred a school with a religious ethos. Opposition to the expansion of faith-based schools, signalled in the 2001 White Paper (see Chapter 5) was intense. Phil Willis, Liberal-Democrat education spokesman, invoked the spectre of racial and sectarian conflicts of the kind experienced between Catholics and Protestants in the Belfast Holy Cross Primary school in 2001, when the police and army had to protect children, while others pointed out that a secular education system in France had not resolved ethnic and racial conflicts.[8] However, evidence accumulated that white middle-class parents were adopting 'faith' strategies (Miles 2007) to segregate their children from minorities, and that the schools were happy to narrow their faith base, especially as examination results rose with an influx of the middle classes.

The major objections to faith school expansion and intake continued to be the contradictions between exhortations for community cohesion and religious segregation. A report by the Office of the Deputy Prime Minister in 2004 suggested that no more faith schools be approved unless they could promote a multicultural agenda, and in October 2006, the Church of England appeared to make a commitment that all new Church of England schools should have at least 25 per cent of places available to children with no requirement that they be practising Christians. The Catholic church also promised to revise its inspection frameworks to ensure the contribution of Catholic schools and colleges to social cohesion. However, by the time the issue was debated promises seemed to have disappeared and as noted, an amendment committing faith schools to take a proportion of other or no faiths was withdrawn. Research commissioned in 2007 by the organisation Comprehensive Future concluded that

> If community cohesion is to be fostered, schools with a religious character should be inclusive of all religions (or no faith). At present this is not the case. Major tensions arise in balancing policies which aim to increase the number of faith schools and promote religious inclusion . . . given that public money is used to fund schools with a religious character there is a strong case to be made for such schools to be open to the wider community in the interests of enhancing social cohesion.
>
> (Pennell *et al.* 2007, www.comprehensivefuture.org)

A subtext to the debates over faith schools was that of values. Although all schools were required to teach the basic National Curriculum, education straddles both the public and the private domain and, despite inspections, there is no guarantee that faith schools will teach universal human rights values as distinct from particular group values. A further political anxiety was concern that Imams trained overseas were entering Britain and possibly radicalising young Muslims in mosques, although a proposal that foreign-born Imams should take a 'Britishness test' was abandoned in 2005. There was concern over the extent and nature of Islamic influence in universities. In 2006 the Minister for Higher Education commissioned Ataullah Siddiqui, the Director of the Islamic Markfield Institute of Higher Education, to report on Islamic studies in British universities, in order to 'improve the quality of information about Islam available to students and staff, and ensure that students have access to material on how the teachings of Islam can be put into practice in a contemporary pluralist society' (Siddiqui 2007). This report noted that while courses in universities attracted overseas students, they did not recruit local students, 'leaving a significant gap in terms of quality of Muslim leadership within the country'.

Community antagonisms

Although reports and political rhetoric directed attention to social cohesion, and by the mid-2000s the country was 'pretty familiar with black and Asian faces on TV screens, in pop music, in football teams and in a few high profile positions in public life' (Gaine 2005: 3), it was still business as usual for old and new antagonisms. Colour, as Gaine noted, remained a critical, distorting and dangerous signifier of difference and inequality, particularly in white areas with few minorities, and while hostility was directed at EU and other economic migrants, old-style racial hostility continued to be directed mainly at black and Asian settled migrants, 'non-white' refugees and asylum seekers, and gypsies and travellers. Schools were aware that the 2000 Race Relations (Amendment) Act made it unlawful to discriminate directly or indirectly on racial grounds, that policy statements and action plans were required of schools, and that from 2004 it was unlawful to discriminate on religious grounds. But there was little evidence of a proactive movement to inform all young people, especially those in white areas, of the reality of the society they lived in. Competitive markets in school now added to the reluctance of schools to address issues of racism, with some headteachers reporting that they felt they could not give a high profile to race in case the school acquired a radical image and parents chose other schools. Cline and his colleagues, commissioned by the DfES to study the situation of minority students in mainly white schools, researched 14 schools in four areas and concluded that no school in their sample had fully developed a strategy for preparing pupils through the curriculum for life in a diverse society (Cline *et al.* 2002). Gaine (1987, 2005) continued a 20-year project researching the assertions of schools in mainly white areas that there was 'no problem here', while their pupils produced stereotyped, negative misinformation about minorities. An on-going study of young people's racial attitudes, commissioned by the Home Office and carried out at Lancaster University, reported that white children segregated from other groups had more intolerant attitudes than those who mixed with other groups, and Muslim pupils in schools studied in Blackburn, where Straw had criticised wearing the veil, were the most tolerant and wanted to know more about other religions. The researchers noted that their findings challenged ministerial pronouncements on Muslim segregation.

In multiracial schools many teachers were still unprepared to deal with the various antagonisms they encountered among their pupils, both between white and minorities and between minority groups. Pearce (2005), in a perceptive study of white teachers in multiracial classrooms, described the difficulties in recognising the overt and subtle ways in which racism works. She noted the situation many teachers still find themselves in whereby 'to be seen as a white person involved in questions of race is to risk being seen as patronising or interfering, or even being labelled racist. To remain silent is to selfishly ignore the fate of others. It's a no-win situation, and that situation is caused by the fact that white people have always placed themselves outside relations of race' (Pearce 2005: 40). Minority young people were, as always, finding ways of dealing with various racisms. A project based in Slough, set up in the late 1990s to deal with tensions between Sikh, Hindu and Muslim communities, trained teenagers to deal with racist comment and conflicts, and the project expanded later to deal with negative stereotypes, from all ethnic groups, about the new Polish community in the town (Salman 2006). Local hostility to Roma from Eastern Europe, and gypsies and travellers, gained more political recognition, with a Minister for Gypsies and Travellers being appointed in 2005, and a special funding scheme set up to expand authorised camping sites, although schools continued to report difficulties in educating the children with minimal funding.

The issue of the achievement of black African-Caribbean young people had by now become widely acknowledged, although black communities located the problem within government indifference and institutional racism, while the government continued to suggest that the causes lay within communities. A report from the London Development Agency's Education Commission concluded that black boys in particular had been betrayed by the education system for half a century and many were struggling to overcome the racism still exhibited by some teachers. In 2004 only 30 per cent of African-Caribbean boys achieved five or more GSCEs at A–C level and African-Caribbean men were least likely to have a degree (London Development Agency 2004). In 2005 practitioners and academics joined to produce a book that reprinted Bernard Coard's 1971 seminal study of *How the West Indian Child is made ESN in the British School System*, thereby bringing years of research and debate into the 21st century. The Mayor of London Ken Livingstone, pointed out in a foreword that 'the effect of years of failure to educate black children has been catastrophic for these young people and their communities' (Richardson 2005: 15) and that deprived of qualifications, black youth are consigned to low paid, low-skill jobs or unemployment. However, the emergence of a black middle class, determined that their children would succeed, had some interesting consequences. Some of the supplementary schools, for example, gained a reputation for taking 'tough' black children and were to be avoided. In 2007 the Department for Communities and Local Government commissioned yet another report on young black men, anxious about the increase in gangs and guns on inner-city estates. The Reach Group – 20 knowledgeable people selected by the department to help raise the aspirations and attainments of black boys and young men – produced a report that blamed black crime on a lack of positive role models, low aspirations, and the lure of drugs and gang culture, with young people idolising rapper musicians rather than black professionals (Reach Group 2007). Civil rights leader and possible US Presidential candidate Jesse Jackson, visiting in August, urged black business leaders to provide role models, as did Nelson Mandela, visiting England to see a statue of himself unveiled in Parliament Square. The *New Nation* newspaper compiled a list of 50 powerful black men and women in the UK, and a dinner for black leaders was held with Mandela as a guest. However, once again, the onus was put on the black community, individuals, parents and schools to deal with what were essentially structural issues concerning housing, education and employment and the negative treatment of black citizens over the decades.

Teachers unions pointed out that it was unfair to expect teachers to 'compensate for society' and noted that positive moves had been made by the Teacher Training and Development Agency (TTDA) and the General Teaching Council (GTC) to improve teacher awareness and capabilities. However, the focus of any training was less on initial teacher training for all teachers and more on continuing professional development for those in multiracial schools. The GTC set up an Archive Network in 2005, concerned with 'tackling the achievements of some black and minority pupils, preparing all pupils to live in a multiethnic and multicultural society, and recruiting and retaining black and minority teachers', the network taking the form of electronic newsletters and online forums, with occasional conferences (visit www.gtce.org.uk/achieve1 for more information) and the TTDA continued to update its multiverse website. The National Association of Head Teachers published a pamphlet on race equality and multicultural education in 2005, and the DfES attempted to explain on its Standards website the evolution of language describing racial and ethnic groups; a difficult task, as the various labels, euphemisms and changes described in the above chapters, has indicated.

Despite a rhetoric of concern, there still appeared to be a general indifference to addressing the specific situation of black young people in education and eugenic views were still being advanced, indicating that old IQ racisms were still around. In 2006 a lecturer at Leeds University, Frank Ellis, was suspended for claiming that black people were intellectually inferior to whites, writing in an article in the *Leeds Student* that 'multiculturalism is doomed to failure because it is based on the lie that all people, races and cultures are equal' and claiming that he was an 'unrepentant Powellite' (Asthana and Salter 2006). Later in the year a lecturer at the prestigious London School of Economics published a paper claiming that the causes of poverty and ill-health in African states could be traced to lower intelligence (Campbell 2006). In higher education, the assumptions were that young people on university courses would somehow be free from racist views and influences despite most having come through schools where such issues were not discussed. But while teachers in training were unlikely to have much access to courses or sessions on race issues, there was still an interest in courses in race, ethnicity, diaspora and nationalism in the social sciences generally. One study recorded 238 courses at 72 Higher Education institutions (Jacobs 2006), and classified the different types of conflicting views expressed by students. Lecturers noted that students had mostly learned liberal discourses, and anti-black racism appeared to have declined in importance compared to Islamophobic and anti-Semitic views. Discussion of issues around 'Britishness' generated conflict among students, with narrow views being expressed. Despite professed anxiety to incorporate Muslims into the wider society, research reports were still pointing to the general lower levels of qualifications gained and training offered to young people of Pakistani and Bangladeshi origin, and there appeared to be no central strategy for improvement.

Curriculum and citizenship

One major political response to a perceived lack of community cohesion was to lay on schools the duty to educate for citizenship. Citizenship education had been a virtually non-existent area in the school curriculum in Britain over the years, one pamphlet on civic education appearing in 1949, with the next one 40 years later. Although schools had attempted to approach some kind of civic understanding of a diverse, globalising society, especially during the 1980s via peace studies, world studies, multicultural, antiracist and anti-sexist education, these approaches, as documented in Chapter 3, were regarded as political indoctrination. The Thatcher government took a relatively simple view of a citizenship and national identity, encapsulated by traditional imperialistic beliefs in unproblematic 'British' values, which largely excluded the history and presence of minorities. A Parliamentary Speaker's Commission on Citizenship reported in 1990 and a National Curriculum Council pamphlet and guidelines followed. This recognised citizenship as a curriculum subject but in a cross-curricular mode, usually taken on by schools in the non-examinable PSHE (personal, social and health education) courses. Bernard Crick, who had supported citizenship education from the 1970s, was appointed to chair an advisory group, a report being produced for the Qualifications and Curriculum Authority (Crick 1998). Crick's proposed framework for 'active citizenship' was based on notions of civil, political and social rights and responsibilities but as Figueroa (2004) noted, did not develop the idea that minorities were actually an integral part of what it means to be British and should share in shaping the society's basic values and rules. From 2002 citizenship education became a compulsory area of study, and a GCSE in citizenship was developed. Political concern to create some kind of unity in a diverse society led to further activity. Keith Ajegbo was asked to produce a report on *Diversity and Citizenship* and suggested in his 2007 report that a new element be introduced into the citizenship curriculum on 'Identity and Diversity: living together in the UK', with a study of shared values and life in contemporary Britain. Courses in citizenship teaching training were encouraged via continuing professional development, and the National Foundation for Educational Research was sponsored by the DfES to carry out a long-term, nine-year study into citizenship education and its effects. A further revamp of the National Curriculum was to be put in place from September 2008, with teachers allowed more input into the design of courses, and the history curriculum was to focus less on Tudor Henry VIII and his six wives and more on recent topics, including the European Union. A study of the British Empire and slavery were also to be a compulsory part of the history curriculum and state schools were to be encouraged to teach non-European languages (Mandarin, Arabic and Urdu being suggested), although without the promise of more funding or teacher preparation for these.[9] Ofsted also reported that religious education, compulsory in the curriculum since 1944, now needed a rethink, in discussion with the local standing committees on religious education. Right-wing groups had not, however, given up on their attacks on curriculum developments, with the think-tank Civitas suggesting that 'traditional subjects have been high-jacked to promote fashionable causes such as gender awareness, the environment and anti-racism, while teachers are expected to achieve the Government's social goals instead of imparting a body of knowledge to their students' (Civitas 2007).

Refugees and asylum seekers

One group who definitely did not fall within definitions of citizen, and were persistently regarded as a burden on the economy and society, were refugees and asylum seekers. As noted in Chapter 4, refugees are people fleeing persecution, war or human rights abuse, and have been granted a status by the host country, asylum seekers are those still in the process and at risk of deportation if their asylum claim fails.[10] Although scrutiny of lurid headlines in the tabloid press in Britain gives the impression that the country was overwhelmed by refugees and illegal migrants, the majority of the world's 20 million refugees live in the developing world. In 2003 the UK ranked eighth in the European Union for the number of refugees it accepted in relation to the population size, and in contrast to headlines that the UK accepts more people than other countries, in 2000 some 85,800 people applied for asylum, only 10 per cent were granted refugee status, 24 per cent given leave to remain and 66 per cent refused asylum. Over 50 per cent of asylum seekers are children and young people, and while a majority of the children are in London schools, a policy of dispersing asylum seekers has increased the numbers of children attending schools in other local authorities around the country. The organisation Save the Children, producing a resource pack for the inclusion of refugee children in schools, noted that the negative, exclusionary and xenophobic language of some sections of the media has impacted on the safety of the children and furthered a climate of racism. The election campaign conducted by the Conservative Party in 2005 was similarly negative towards refugees. Given the political climate it was unsurprising that there had been no central government policy on refugee education, local authorities and voluntary organisations being left to deal with the issues and several authorities, notably Gloucestershire and Camden in London, producing written policies. The evidence to date is that despite additional demands placed on schools, with few resources and children arriving at different times over the year, schools have done a remarkable job in incorporating refugee children and giving confidence to children who have often experienced trauma, fear, loss and family separation (Save the Children 2004, Rutter 2006). Refugee children are also more likely than any group to suffer poverty, as well as experiencing difficulty in negotiating a bureaucratic system of entitlements to housing, food and clothing, plus fears of possible deportation. Since migrations, both voluntary and involuntary, are a permanent fixture in a globalised world, it would seem important that central government develop funded and humane policies for incorporating refugee children in schools and the society.

Summary

Chapters 5 and 6 covered the first ten years of a New Labour government with Tony Blair as Prime Minister. Younge (2007) suggested that although initially 'the potential existed for New Labour to play midwife to a confident, inclusive hybrid sense of Britishness' and there had been positive moves in the first term of office, opportunities had been squandered by continuing anti-immigration themes, playing on fears of supposedly segregated minorities and their religions, and sustaining market policies which left low-paid workers feeling threatened by asylum seekers and economic migrants. After 2003, in the wake of disastrous wars in Afghanistan and Iraq, and increased 'terror' threats from radical Islamists, the government appeared to support exaggerated claims that multiculturalism had failed, the implication being that recognition of the presence and lifestyles of minorities had disrupted a supposedly cohesive society. From 2001 the focus was to be on community cohesiveness, despite contradictory policies which encouraged individual competitiveness and separation, especially policies which encouraged a diversity of schools, and took children away from their local communities. The failure to produce policies needed to improve the educational qualifications, training and job prospects for both minorities and 'poor whites' (and the continuation of producing reports lamenting the situation and blaming communities) was not likely to encourage a cohesive society in which all groups felt they had fair shares. The continuing wealth divide and scramble for the best jobs, which put white and minority groups in further competition for scarce resources, was possibly more of a barrier to community cohesion than mode of dress. Despite this, much faith was placed in education to create good citizens for a cohesive society via citizenship education, with a familiar right wing still arguing that discussion of issues vital to all young people and their futures was somehow dangerous. The positive message from the decade was possibly that political leadership was lagging behind what was actually happening in the society, as a majority of young people were learning to live together in often extraordinarily difficult situations, and learning via global communications that around the world other multicultural societies were grappling with similar issues and conflicts.

Notes

1. Globalisation is here defined as the development and use of information and communications technology, the increased and often inequitable processes of trade and financial flows, movement and migrations of people and their labour worldwide, cultural convergences between countries and also resistance to cultural imposition, and governments becoming increasingly beholden to global markets. In 2006 two-thirds of global trade was controlled by 500 firms, in turn controlled by real individuals rather than by some 'hidden hand' of the market.
2. A considerable literature is emerging on Muslims in Britain in the context of old harassments and the newer 'war on terror'. See, for example, Rex (2002), Abbas (2005), Modood (2005), Bright (2007).
3. According to Shelter (2007) the UK still has one of the highest rates of child poverty in Europe. But the government is falling behind its target to halve child poverty by 2010. By 2005 it had lifted 700,000 children out of poverty but will need to 'lift' a further one million in the next five years to achieve its target, i.e. 200,000 a year. This is twice what it achieved in 2004–2005. Shelter estimates that a further £4 billion is required for the government to keep its promise.
4. In Birmingham, for example, suburban Perry Barr ward, next to high minority

Handsworth ward, had only 2 per cent of 'non-white' residents in 1971, by 2001 this had increased to 28 per cent.

5. In June 2007 ex-Minister Stephen Byers again used the 'sleep walking into segregation' assertion. The author pointed out (*Observer* 3 June 2007) that the long history attached to any segregation demonstrated that whatever the explanations, no-one was asleep!
6. In 1987 ten professors published a letter in *The Independent* newspaper (10 June) claiming that policies proposed by the then Conservative government would increase social inequalities. Twenty years later some of these same professors, with others, presented research studies which over the years demonstrated the extent of social and ethnic sorting and segregation (Conference on Social Selection, Social Sorting and Education, City Hall, London, 12 October 2007).
7. By 2006 faith-based primary and secondary schools, in receipt of state funding, comprised some 4,646 Church of England schools, 2,118 Catholic, 28 Methodist, 35 other Christian, 31 Jewish, 1 Seventh Day Adventist, 2 Sikh, 1 Hindu, 1 Greek Orthodox, I Humanist and 8 Muslim schools. Faith-based Academy schools were not included in these numbers.
8. The 1944 Education Act allowed Church of England, Catholic and Methodist schools to receive state funding as voluntary-aided or controlled schools. Funding for Jewish schools became available later. After 1997 Muslim and other faith schools could claim similar funding. Some 52 Muslim private schools are on a DfES approved register. The French system was based on the Republican principle of 'laicite' or secularism, although from 1989 Muslims have challenged the principle (Kastoryano 2006).
9. Private schools had always been free to teach non-European languages, with Mandarin growing in popularity. A GCSE in Urdu and Gujerati had been available in state schools since the 1980s.
10. After a 2005 Immigration, Asylum and Nationality Act, the sixth Asylum Act since the early 1990s, asylum applications had to be filed at the point of entry into the country. Applicants could eventually be granted full refugee status, or granted Humanitarian Protection or Discretionary Leave to Remain, this last replacing Exceptional Leave to Remain. An Immigration and Nationality Division of the Home Office administers money from a European Refugee Fund, which encourages social and economic integration, or funds people to return to their homeland.

chapter seven

Conclusions

The previous chapters have endeavoured to provide factual information, with some interpretation[1] of the political background of race and ethnic relations, and the education system that racial and ethnic minorities entered, over the past five decades. The chapters then documented some of the issues and conflicts that have arisen as the system has incorporated, with varying degrees of success, the descendants of children from former colonial countries, more recent economic migrants from the EU and other countries, and refugees and asylum seekers. A major premise was that the institution of education has been and continues to be a crucial element in the absorption of minority young people into the socio-economic structures in British society, but that the system is one that employs a rhetoric of meritocracy and equality of opportunity to disguise a system of increasing inequalities. While during the 1960s and 1970s there were moves towards a more equitable comprehensive system of free education from pre-school to higher education, from the 1980s and into the 2000s successive reforms have ensured that schooling has become a market commodity and the 'best' education a prize to be competitively sought, not a democratic right. Under the rubric of a 'diversity' of schools a complex hierarchy of more and less desirable schools continues to be created, leading on, for most minority pupils, either to vocational, low-level or catch-up academic courses in Further Education, to the lower end of a hierarchy of universities or to low-level employment or unemployment. It is clear that the unequal possession of economic, cultural and social capital gives different social classes and minority groups unequal chances in the competition for the best schools and universities, and thus for high-level credentials and employment. Immigrant and minority children, especially black Caribbean children, have over the years suffered more than indigenous children from the assumptions that they had 'equal chances to be unequal', but some groups, notably those from parts of India, East Africa and East Asia, have been better placed to benefit from education than others. Old and new issues have continued or arisen over the years affecting the education of minorities, and there are still major questions as to whether those perceived as racially or ethnically different will be accorded equal rights in practice, what form a multicultural society will take, and what sort of education system would best serve a democratic multicultural society. Britain is still slowly coming to terms with the end of Empire and closer links with the rest of Europe, and it was inevitable that the incorporation of those perceived as racially and culturally different would raise crucial questions concerning a shared national identity and heritage, multiculturalism and a variety of racisms. The relationship between Islam and a Christian secular West has been challenged by the assertion of a more specific Muslim identity, and wars in the Middle East have been regarded by many as attacks on Islam. Simplistic responses blaming multiculturalism, or minority segregation, for long-standing issues and for newer migrant problems have been no help to educators.

A major conclusion to this book must be that negative, defensive and contradictory central government policies directed towards racial and ethnic minorities in Britain have made it very difficult for educators to agree on the part education should play in the creation of a plural, non-racist, multicultural society. The history of the past five decades has demonstrated that while many schools, teachers, local authorities and others have attempted, sometimes naïvely, to incorporate minority children more equitably into the education system, the political climate over the years has made the task extremely problematic. A continuity throughout the book has been the contradictions between political encouragement of immigrant labour, while at the same time enacting legislation to control immigration, and allowing a discourse of antagonism to 'immigration' in general to dominate public and media discussion. There has been a distinct lack of positive political leadership over the years to address the ways migrant minorities were to be incorporated into the wider society and share political, social and economic rights. Policies have been influenced by xenophobic and racist reactions within the indigenous population, by fears of social unrest and latterly by the actions of some extreme Muslim groups and individuals. The question was seldom asked as to how the education system was expected to incorporate immigrant and minority children equitably while a vociferous anti-immigrant rhetoric and public hostility to those regarded as non-white was either supported or at least not disavowed by successive governments. By the later 1990s policies were catching up with a public mood displaying more acceptance of minorities as citizens, and confronting some of the inequalities evident within education, with the Prime Minister asserting that there was public support against racial discrimination. But in 2001 after the attacks in the USA and confrontations in England, there was a regression to blaming minorities for lack of 'community cohesion' and segregation. A further continuity running through the chapters has been the way in which from the early settlement of minorities in inner cities or towns where there was work, and where their children attended local schools, it was in fact further settlement by choice or defensive constraint, white flight, housing policies and then the disappearance of much work, which led to more segregation in areas of poverty. However, there has also been more movement of middle-class minorities to suburban areas, and in some settled minority areas people are doing well in terms of education and employment. It is clear that there has been no 'sleep walking into segregation'. The demographic separation of white and minority groups was the result of policy decisions or non-decisions, and constraints and choices over the years. The encouragement of more faith schools may well exacerbate the separation of white and some black Christian from other faiths, although there is evidence that a majority of Muslim parents and young people do not want such separation.

A third continuity has been the continued attempts to deflect attention away from the situation of racial minorities by claims that they were simply a part of the disadvantaged sector of society. This was partly true in that minorities settled in inner cities and towns among sectors of a working class where jobs were available but then disappeared, there was competition for decent housing, schools were neglected and under-resourced and not intended to educate to high levels. While subsuming minority concerns under the disadvantage label was also an attempt to avoid white xenophobic assumptions that minorities were taking extra resources, the strategy was never successful, as a white working class continued to assume minorities did have preferential treatment. Government would have been more successful in producing and defending specific policies to incorporate minorities fairly in housing, education and employment. There has been a similar lack of policy or preparation for the arrival of newer migrants, either as refugees and asylum seekers or EU economic workers. Possibly the most critical and fourth long-term continuity and policy failure has been the education and training of black young people. From the assumptions that allowed the over-placement of black children in ESN schools and the overt racism of Powellism in the 1960s, through to the subsequent demonisation of black youth as an 'alien underclass' in the 1970s and 1980s, and the exclusions from schooling and stress on black crime and violence in the 1990s and 2000s, the odds have been stacked against black children. The emergence of a black middle class, using as far as possible the strategies of the white middle class in the competitive struggle for education, may lead to the situation described by black US academic William Wilson in which 'talented and educated blacks like talented and educated whites, will continue to enjoy the advantages of their class status' while the future for black children segregated on poor housing estates and in less successful schools will not be good (Wilson 1978: 153). Attempts to close attainment gaps by urging improved black parenting, or the production of successful role models,[2] or using the 'model minority' successes of Indian, Chinese and other groups which are in fact linked to social class advantages, will not raise attainment levels overall. Attainment between black pupils may be exacerbated as via 2006 education legislation some inner-city schools will lose children who can be given 'choice advice' in the competitive schools market, and move out of their area. Over the years the attention given to teaching English as a second language and bilingualism, more positive assumptions about the capabilities of some children of Asian origin, and more structured teaching strategies, have probably assisted in the raised levels of attainment of these children as compared to black children, although levels of poverty among Pakistani and Bangladeshi working-class groups continue to contribute to their poorer attainment. The endless production of research and government reports on the lower achievements of black young people and the subsequent minimal and grudging adoption of measures to raise their attainment levels have now gone beyond blame and exhortation. It is no longer acceptable that as a group young black citizens can be allowed to fall behind all other social groups in education and employment, and be regarded as potential criminals.[3] There has never been sufficient recognition or acknowledgement of the efforts made by black families and communities over the years to obtain an equal education for their children. From the point of view of black families and young people there is nothing now to be gained from accepting what is in effect an institutionalised discrimination and human rights violation.

A fifth continuity in policy terms has been the minimal and grudging preparation of teachers to teach in a multi-ethnic society. There is much evidence that from the 1960s some teachers, local education authority advisors and others attempted, often naïvely and working within a political climate hostile to 'non whites', made positive efforts to incorporate minority children, in the often unpropitious circumstances of badly resourced inner-city schools. The improved programmes for teacher education and training the trainers over the next two decades did produce a cohort of more knowledgeable and experienced teachers, supported by their unions, but it has been possible for researchers, over the decades, to demonstrate the ignorance and racism of some teachers. From the mid-1980s a general devaluing of the teaching profession, merged with right-wing attacks on any multicultural, anti-racist or race equality courses led to a disappearance of most university, college and local authority initial or in-service work; although from the later 1990s, race relations and human rights legislation and inspection requirements did encourage schools to consider race equality issues more carefully. The lack of any national strategy to prepare and develop all teachers for a society and a world now experiencing more ethnic, racial and religious conflicts and tensions, marked by increasing migrations, global communications and a global labour market, is a serious omission.

Teachers, despite more centralised direction, continue to be the key figures in any change and development in classroom practices. A major discontinuity for teachers, however, was the absence in Britain from the 1990s of a discourse and a language concerning the preparation of all young people for a democratic multicultural society, of the kind that has continued in other countries, notably the USA, Canada and Australia (Mays 1999, Banks 2004, Banks and Banks 2004, Sleeter 2007). This was partly a result of the unhelpful antagonisms of the 1980s between varieties of multicultural and anti-racist education, and the right-wing hostility to anything with such a description, as documented in Chapter 3. A discourse attacking 'multiculturalism'[4] and urging social cohesion may be just another retreat into the idea of a nation that is homogeneous and uniform, rather than reflecting the historical reality that minority groups actually become more attached to their society when their ethnic identity is recognised, and when they can participate equally in social and economic institutions. The introduction of citizenship education, together with the legal requirement on head-teachers to develop inclusive schools, may be steps towards a more democratic education, but there is continuing reluctance to examine the structural and organisational inequalities that result in schools reproducing unequal outcomes for social and ethnic groups.

While there is no blueprint for what successful education for a democratic multicultural society might look like, it had become obvious by the early 21st century that the education systems in Britain needed to be clearer about principles, purpose and content if education was to be relevant to the kind of society that now made up 'Britain'. Education continues to reflect a society based on an hierarchical and status-based social class system, and the competitive jockeying for position in the society is encouraged by the development of a diversity of schools, higher education and employment possibilities, and by the possibility that private, business and faith incursions into schooling will create more divisions. I would advocate two principles and define a purpose. A major principle should be that education in a democratic, plural, multicultural society be shaped by a public service culture relevant to the whole society, not one that encourages private, faith, business or any particular group interest. This public culture would need to reflect agreement on common values, which would be reflected in a common curriculum, but with local dimensions. This would mean a repudiation of much of the competitiveness in the system which is currently driven by market forces and institutional and group self-interest. An equally important principle should be an acceptance that education has a duty and key role in clarifying and tackling the manifestations of inequality, racism and discrimination within its own institutions and in the wider society. Behind these principles is the assumption that politics and policies will actually be underpinned by beliefs that fairness and social and racial justice are the basis for a good society. The major purpose of education in such a society remains that of offering all young people the means to live independent and interdependent lives, economically, socially and politically, in a globalised world. Government, while exhorting schools to raise standards, and individuals to achieve and behave responsibly, does have a responsibility to ensure political and economic policies are aimed at securing a productive life for all members of the society. In this book, I have documented several times my disappointment with the negative and defensive responses of successive governments to the notion of an economically and socially successful society that manages its multicultural and migration policies for the benefit of all. My faith remains with the view documented at the end of Chapter 6, that political leadership is actually lagging behind the realities of the society. Despite continuing manifestations of xenophobia, hostility and tensions, a majority of young people in Britain are learning to live together in difficult situations. There is also more knowledge that around the world other multicultural societies are facing up to similar issues and conflicts. A small minority of white and 'non-white' in Britain may have succumbed to 'mindless violence and despair' (Rex and Tomlinson 1979: 295), but the majority have not. What is needed now is more direct political organisation and engagement to ensure that equality in terms of citizenship rights and responsibilities, and the removal of structural and institutional barriers to equal treatment, become a reality.

Notes

1. As outlined in the introduction, the author has been involved over the decades in many of the events and issues documented, and the interpretation is thus her own, and open to debate. While it is the job of a sociologist to provide, if possible, a balanced view of relations between groups in a multiracial, multi-ethnic society and the conflicts and changes that arise, it has been difficult for me, over the decades, to contemplate the political, media and public reactions to immigrant minorities in Britain with equanimity.
2. As the chapters have demonstrated, the role model solution has been around for some time; for example, from the Harambee Supplementary School in the 1970s studying successful black role models, to the Reach Report (2007). If an analogy is made with the assumptions that women from the 1950s could have improved their employment and economic position by copying role models rather than campaigning for structural and attitudinal changes, the limitations of the role model can be gauged.
3. It has to be repeated that the claims about underachieving poor white boys fall within a different sphere and cannot be used as an excuse for the absence of policy on black education. The education system has not yet come to terms with the notion of actually educating all social classes to higher levels.
4. The 'multiculturalism' under attack appears to be defined by the visibility of minorities in high minority areas in terms of skin colour, dress, languages

spoken, shops, religious observance, and claims for resources and housing, not by any claims from minorities for separation, segregation or monoculturalism. The government could have intervened in debate with the presentation of the global business and economic opportunities afforded by Commonwealth connections and current contributions by minorities. Recognising the realities of a plural multicultural society is good business in a globalised world.

Appendix
Territories of the British Empire

Name of state or colony	*Date of acquisition*	*Date of autonomy and/or leaving the Commonwealth*
Aden (South Yemen)	1839	1967
Anguilla	1650	–
Antigua	1632	–
Ascension Island	1815	–
Australia (various territories)	1788–1859	1852–1890
Bahamas	1629	1973
Bangladesh (East Pakistan)	1757–1842	1972
Barbados	1625	1966
Belize (British Honduras)	1638–1802	1982
Bermuda	1612	–
Botswana (Bechuanaland)	1884	1966
British Antarctica	1908	–
British Indian Ocean Territory	1815	–
British Somaliland	1884–1887	1960
British Virgin Islands	1672	–
Brunei	1888	1983
Burma	1826–1885	1948
Canada (various territories)	1670–1849	1847–1871
Cayman Islands	1670	–
Cyprus	1878	1960
Dominica	1763	1978
Egypt	1882–1914	1922
Falkland Islands	1765–1833	–
Fiji	1874	1970

Name of state or colony	*Date of acquisition*	*Date of autonomy and/or leaving the Commonwealth*
Florida	1763	1783
Gambia	1661–1713	1965
Ghana (Gold Coast)	1821–1901	1957
Gibraltar	1704–1713	–
Granada	1763	1974
Guyana (British Guiana)	1796–1815	1966
Heligoland	1807–1814	1890
Hong Kong	1842	1997
India	1757–1842	1947
Ionian Islands	1815	1864
Iraq	1918–1923	1932
Ireland (Irish Free State)	1169–1601	1921–1949
Jamaica	1659–1670	1962
Kenya	1887–1895	1963
Kiribati (Gilbert Islands)	1892–1918	1979
Lesotho (Basutoland)	1868	1966
Malawi (Nyasaland)	1889–1891	1964
Malaysia	1786–1882	1957–1963
Malta	1800–1814	1964
Mauritius	1815	1968
Minorca	1708–1713	1782–1783
Montserrat	1632	–
Nauru	1919	1968
New Zealand	1840	1852
Nigeria	1861–1903	1960
Pakistan (separated from India)	–	1947–1972
Palestine (Israel)	1917–1923	1948
Papua New Guinea	1884–1919	1975
Pitcairn Islands	1838–1887	–
St Christopher Nevis	1624–1628	1983
St Helena	1834	–
St Lucia	1814	1979
St Vincent, Grenadines	1627	1979
Seychelles	1814	1976
Singapore	1819–1824	1963–1965
Solomon Isles	1893–1900	1978
South Africa (various states)	1795–1902	1872–1910
South Georgia, Sandwich Islands	1908	–
South West Africa (Namibia)	1915–1919	1960
Sri Lanka (Ceylon)	1815	1948
Sudan	1898	1954
Surinam (Dutch Guiana)	1651	1668
Swaziland	1890–1902	1968

Name of state or colony	*Date of acquisition*	*Date of autonomy and/or leaving the Commonwealth*
Tanzania (Tanganyika and Zanzibar)	1870–1919	1961–1964
Tonga	1900	1970
Transjordan (Jordan)	1917–1923	1946
Trinidad and Tobago	1802–1815	1962
Tristan da Cunha	1816	–
Turks and Caicos Isles	1678	–
Tuvalu (Ellice Isles)	1892–1918	1978
Uganda	1888–1895	1962
United Kingdom (England,Wales, Scotland, Ireland)	1707–1801	–
United States of America (13 colonies)	1636–1732	1776
Vanatu (New Hebrides)	1887–1906	1980
Western Samoa	1919	1961–1970
Zambia (Northern Rhodesia)	1889–1900	1964
Zimbabwe (Southern Rhodesia)	1888–1893	1980

Source: Adapted from Lloyd, T.O. (1984) *The British Empire 1558–1983*. Oxford, Oxford University Press, pp. 405–11 and Foreign & Commonwealth Office 'Overseas Territories Country Profiles'.

Bibliography

Abbas, T. (2004) *The Education of British South Asians*. London: Palgrave-Macmillan

Abbas, T. (ed.) (2005) *Muslim Britain*. London: Zed Books

ACE (1991) Editorial 'A Shameful Affair' *Advisory Centre for Education* 4(1) May/June

Adamson, J. and Boek, T. (2007) *Cohesive Communities in Leicestershire*. Leicestershire County Council.

Ajegbo, K. (2007) *Diversity and Citizenship: the impact of schools*. London: DfES

Apple, M. (1999) 'The absent presence of race in educational reform' *Race Ethnicity and Education* 2(1): 9–16

Archbishop of Canterbury (1985) *Faith in the City*. Report of the Archbishop of Canterbury's Commission, London: Church House Publishing

Archer, L. and Francis, B. (2007) *Understanding Minority Ethnic Achievement*. London: Routledge

Armstrong, K. (1991) *Muhammad*. London: Victor Gollanz (2nd edn 2001 Phoenix Press)

Asthana, A. and Salter, J. (2006) 'Campus storm over racist don' *Observer* 5 March

Avon NUT (1980) *After the Fire: a Report on Education in St Paul's, Bristol* Bristol: Avon National Union of Teachers

Bagley, C. (1968) 'The Educational Performance of Immigrant Children' *Race* 10/1

Bagley, C.A. (1992) *Back to the Future: Section 11 of the Local Government Act 1966*. Slough: National Foundation for Educational Research

Baldwin, J. (1963) *The Fire Next Time*. London: Michael Joseph

Ball, S.J. (1990) *Politics and Policy-Making in Education*. London: Routledge

Ballard, R. and Ballard, C. (1977) 'The Sikhs: The development of South Asian Settlements in Britain' in J. Watson (ed.) *Between Two Cultures*. Oxford: Blackwell

Banks, J. (2004) *Diversity and Citizenship Education*. San Francisco: Jossey-Bass

Banks, J. and Banks, C.A.M. (2004) *Handbook of Research on Multicultural Education*. San Francisco: Jossey-Bass

Banks, J. and Lynch, J. (1986) *Multicultural Education in Western Societies*. London: Holt, Rhinehart and Winston
Barker, M. (1981) *The New Racism*. London: Junction Books
Barber, M. (2007) *Instruction to Deliver*. London: Politics Publishing
Barry, B. (2001) *Culture and Equality*. Cambridge: Polity Press
Beckett, F. (2007) *The Great City Academy Fraud*. London: Continuum
Benn, C. and Chitty, C. (1996) *Thirty Years On*. London: David Fulton
Bernstein, B. (1973) *Class, Codes and Control*. London: Routledge and Kegan Paul
Bhatnager, J. (1981) *Educating Immigrants*. London: Croom-Helm
Bhavani, R., Mirza, H.S. and Meetoo, V. (2005) *Tackling the Roots of Racism*. Bristol: Policy Press
Birley High School (1980) *Multicultural Education in the 1980s*. Manchester: Birley High School
Black Manifesto for Equality in our Lifetime (2005) London: The 1990 Trust
Black Parents Fight Back (1985) *Special Issue number 1*. London: Camberwell Publications
Black to Black (1993) 'Racist attacks and harassment: the epidemic of the 1990s?' Issue no 1 July. London: The 1990 Trust
Blair, M. (2001) *Why Pick On Me: school exclusion and black youth*. Stoke-on-Trent: Trentham Books
Blair, M. and Bourne, J. (1998) *Making the Difference: teaching and learning strategies in successful multiethnic schools*. Research report 59. London: DfES
Blair, T. (1998) *The Third Way: new politics for a new century*. London: The Fabian Society (pamphlet 588)
Blair, T. (1999a) Speech to Labour Party Conference, Bournemouth 8 October
Blair, T. (1999b) Prime Minister's Millennium Message. Speech at Trimdon Community Centre, County Durham, December
Blair, T. (2006) Public Lecture. London: Runnymede Trust. www.runnymedetrust.org
Blair, T. (2007) Speech to Trimdon Labour Club, County Durham
Bleich, E. (2003) *Race and Politics in Britain and France: Ideas and Policy-making since the 1960s*. Cambridge: Cambridge University Press
Blunkett, D. (2000) 'Influence or irrelevance: can social science improve government?' *Research Intelligence* 71: 12–21
Bolton, E. (1979) 'Education in a Multiracial Society' *Trends in Education* No. 4: 3–7
Bourne, J., Bridges, L. and Searly, C. (1994) *Outcast England: How Schools exclude Black Children*. London: Institute of Race Relations
Brandt, G.L. (1986) *The Realization of Anti-Racist Teaching*. London: Falmer Press
Bright, M. (2007) *When Progressives Treat with Reactionaries*. London: Policy Exchange
Brown, C. (1984) *Black and White Britain: The Third PSI Survey*. London: Policy Studies Institute
Brown, C. (1988) 'The White Highlands: Anti-racism' *Multicultural Teaching* 6(2): 38–9
Brown, J. (1977) *Shades of Grey: Police–West Indian Relations in Handsworth*. Cranfield: Cranfield Police Studies
Bullock, Lord A. (1975) *A Language for Life*. London: HMSO
Burgess, S. and Wilson, D. (2003) *Ethnic Segregation in England's Schools*. CMPO Discussion paper 3/86. Bristol: Centre for Management and Policy Organisation

Burgin, T. and Edson, P. (1967) *Spring Grove: The Education of Immigrant Children*. Oxford: Oxford University Press, for the Institute of Race Relations

Burroughs, E. (1919) *Tarzan the Untamed*. London: Methuen

Campaign for Real Education (1989) *What is the CRE?* York: Campaign for Real Education

Campbell, A. with Stott, R. (2007) *The Blair Years*. London: Hutchinson

Campbell, D. (2006) 'Low IQs are Africa's curse, says lecturer' *Observer* 5 November

Cantle Report (2001) *Community Cohesion: The Report of the Independent Review Team*. London: The Home Office

Chapman, H. (2007) 'Lecturers unanimously refuse to spy on Muslim students' *The Muslim News* 29 June

Chevannes, M. (1979) 'Supplementary Education: the Black Arrow Night School Project' *The Social Science Teacher* 8(4)

Chitty, C. (2004) *Educational Policy in Britain*. London: Palgrave-Macmillan

Civitas (2007) *The Corruption of the Curriculum*. London: Civitas.

Clark, N. (1982) 'Dachwyng Saturday School' in A. Ohri, B. Mannin and P. Curno (eds) *Community Work and Racism*. London: Routledge and Kegan Paul

Cline, T., de Abreu, G. *et al.* (2002) *Minority Ethnic Pupils in Mainly White Schools*. London: DfES

Coard, B. (1971) *How the West Indian Child is made ESN in the British School System*. London: New Beacon Books

Commission on Integration and Cohesion (2007) *Our Shared Future*. London: Department for Communities and Local Government

Commission for Racial Equality (1978) *Schools and Ethnic Minorities*. London: CRE

Commission for Racial Equality (1980) *Youth in Multi-Racial Society: The Fire Next Time*. London: CRE

Commission for Racial Equality (1988) *Learning in Terror: A Survey of Racial Harassment in Schools and Colleges*. London: CRE

Commission for Racial Equality (1992) *Set to Fail*. London: CRE

Commonwealth Immigrants Advisory Council (CIAC) (1964) Second Report. Cmnd 2266. London: HMSO

Constantine, Lord Learie (1954) *Colour Bar*. London: Stanley Paul and Co

Cork, L. (2005) *Supporting Black Pupils and Parents*. London: Routledge

Cox, C. (1986) 'From Auschwitz – Yesterday's Racism – to GCHQ' in F. Palmer (ed.) *Anti-Racism: an Assault on Education and Values*. London: The Sherwood Press

Cox, C.B. (1995) *The Battle for the English Curriculum*. London: Hodder and Stoughton

Cox, C.B. and Boyson, R. (1977) *Black Paper 1977*. London: Temple-Smith

Craft, A. and Bardell, G. (1984) *Curriculum Opportunities in a Multicultural Society*. London: Harper & Row

Craft, A. and Klein, G. (1986) *Agenda for Multicultural Teaching*. London: Schools Council Development Committee

Craft, M. (ed.) (1981) *Teaching in a Multicultural Society: The Task for Teacher Education*. Lewes: The Falmer Press

Craft, M. (1986) *Teacher Education in a Multicultural Society*. Nottingham: National Programme for Training the Trainers

Craft, M. (ed.) (1996) *Teacher Education in Plural Societies*. London: The Falmer Press
Craig, G. (2007) *Sure Start and Black and Minority Ethnic Populations*. Nottingham: DfES Publications
Crick, B. (1998) *Education for citizenship and the teaching of democracy in schools*. Report of an advisory group on citizenship. London: DfES
Crossman, R. (1975) *Diaries of a Cabinet Minister 1964–70 Vol. 1*. London: Hamish Hamilton and Cape
Daily Mail (2004) Editorial Comment, 6 May
Davies, N. (1999) 'Political coup bred educational disaster' *Guardian* 6 September
Dearing, R. (1993) *The National Curriculum and its Assessment*. London: SCAA
Dearing, R. (1996) *Review of Qualifications for 16–19-year-olds*. London: SCAA
De Haviland, J. (1988) *Take Care Mr Baker*. London: Fourth Estate
Department for the Environment (1977) *A Policy for the Inner Cities*. London: HMSO
Derbyshire, H. (1994) *Not in Norfolk: Tackling the Invisibility of Racism*. Norwich: Norfolk and Norwich Racial Equality Council
Derrick, J. (1967) *English for the Children of Immigrants*. London: Schools Council
DES (1965) *The Education Of Immigrants*. Circular 7/65. London: Department of Education and Science
DES (1971a) *Potential and Progress in a Second Culture*. London: HMSO
DES (1971b) *The Education of Immigrants*. Education Survey 13. London: HMSO
DES (1971c) *The Continuing Needs of Immigrants*. London: HMSO
DES (1974) *Educational Disadvantage and the Needs of Immigrants*. Cmnd 5720. London: HMSO
DES (1977) *Education in Schools: A Consultative Document*. London: Department for Education and Science
DES (1978) *Special Educational Needs: Report of the Enquiry into the Education of Handicapped Children and Young People*. (The Warnock Report) Cmnd 7212. London: HMSO
DES (1981a) *West Indian Children in Our Schools: A Report from the Committee of Enquiry into the Education of Children from Ethnic Minorities*. (The Rampton Report). London: HMSO
DES (1981b) *The School Curriculum*. London: HMSO
DES (1985a) *Education for All: Report of the Committee of Enquiry into the Education of Children from Minority Groups*. (The Swann Report). London: HMSO
DES (1985b) *Better Schools*. Cmnd 9469. London: HMSO
DES (1987) *Education Support Grants*. Circular 1/87. London: Department for Education and Science
DES (1991) *HMI Criticise Ethnic Teacher Training Courses*. London: Department for Education and Science
DfE (1992a) *Choice and Diversity: A new framework for schools*. London: Department for Education
DfE (1992b) *Exclusions from School*. London: Department for Education
DfEE (1996) *Learning to Compete: Education and Training for 14–19 Year Olds*. Cmnd 3486. London: HMSO
DfEE (1997) *Excellence in Schools*. Cmnd 3681. London: The Stationery Office

DfES (2001) *Schools: Achieving Success*. Cmd 5230. London: The Stationery Office
DfES (2003a) *Transforming London Secondary Schools*. London: DfES.
DfES (2003b) *Aiming High: Raising the Achievement of Minority Ethnic Groups*. London: DfES
DfES (2004a) *Five-year Strategy for Children and Learners*. Cmd 6272. London: The Stationery Office
DfES (2004b) *14–19 Curriculum and Qualifications Reform* (Tomlinson Report). Nottingham: DfES
DfES (2005) *Youth Cohort Study. The activities and experiences of 16-year-olds*. SFR/04/2005. London: DfES
Dhondy, F. (1974) 'The Black Explosion in Schools' *Race Today* 2: 43–8
Dodd, V. (2006) 'Universities urged to spy on Muslims' *Guardian* 16 October
Donegan, L. (1995) 'Muslim leaders warn of other cities on verge of violence as police give up' *Guardian* 12 June
Dorn, A. and Hibbert, P. (1987) 'A Comedy of errors: section 11 funding and education' in B. Troyna (ed.) *Racial Inequality in Education*. London: Tavistock
Drew, D. and Gray, J. (1990) 'The Fifth Year Examination Achievements of Black Young People' *Educational Research* 32(2): 107–17
Driver, G. (1980) 'How West Indians do Better at School: Especially the Girls' *New Society* 17 January
Durkheim, E. (1933) *The Division of Labour in Society*. Chicago: The Free Press
Edwards, T., Fitz, J. and Whitty, G. (1989) *The State and Private Education*. London: Falmer
EEC (1977) *Council Directive on the Education of the Children of Migrant Workers*. (77/486/EEC). Brussels: European Economic Community
Elton, Lord R. (1965) *The Unarmed Invasion*. London: Geoffrey Bless
Etzioni, A. (1988) *The Moral Dimension*. New York: The Free Press
Eysenck, H.J. (1971) *Race, Intelligence and Education*. London: Temple-Smith
Figueroa, P. (1992) 'Assessment and achievement of ethnic minority pupils' in J. Lynch, C. Modgil and S. Modgil (eds) *Education for Cultural Diversity: Convergence and Divergence*. London: The Falmer Press
Figueroa, P. (2004) 'Diversity and Citizenship Education in England' in J.A. Banks (ed.) *Diversity and Citizenship Education*. San Francisco: Jossey-Bass
Fitzpatrick, B. and Rees, O.A. (1980) 'Mother Tongue and English Teaching Project' *Disadvantage in Education* 3(1): 7–8
Floud, J., Halsey, A.H. and Martin, F.M. (1956) *Social Class and Educational Opportunity*. London: Routledge and Kegan Paul
Foster, P. (1990) *Policy and Practice in Multicultural and Anti-Racist Education*. London: Routledge
Fryer, P. (1984) *Staying Power: The History of Black People in Britain*. London: Pluto Press
Fuller, M. (1980) 'Black Girls in a London Comprehensive School' in R. Deem (ed.) *Schooling for Women's Work*. London: Routledge and Kegan Paul
Gaine, C. (1987) *No Problem Here: A Practical Approach to Education and Race in White Schools*. London: Hutchinson
Gaine, C. (2005) *We're All White, Thanks*. Stoke-on-Trent: Trentham Books
Gaine, C. and George, R. (1999) *Gender, Race and Class in Schooling*. London: Falmer

Gamble, A. (1988) *The Free Economy and the Strong State*. London: Macmillan
Gardiner, J. (1997) 'Blunkett to continue shaming' *Times Educational Supplement* 14 November
Gerwirtz, S., Ball, S.J. and Bowe, R. (1995) *Markets, Choice and Equity in Education*. Buckingham: Open University Press
Giddens, A. (1998) *The Third Way: The Renewal of Social Democracy*. Cambridge: Polity Press
Giddens, A. (2002) 'The Third Way can beat the far right' *Guardian* 3 May
Gill, D. (1982) 'Geography and Multi-Cultural Education: a Critical Review of Some Materials' *Multiracial Education* 10(3): 13–26
Gillborn, D. (1990) *'Race' Ethnicity and Education*. London: Unwin Hyman
Gillborn, D. (1995) 'Racism and Exclusion from School' European Conference on Educational Research. Bath: University of Bath. September
Gillborn, D. (1998) 'Policy and research in race and education in the UK: symbiosis or mutual abuse'. Paper presented to the 14th World Congress of Sociology. Montreal, Canada, July
Gillborn, D. (2001) 'Racism, policy and the (mis)education of black children' in R. Majors (ed.) *Educating Our Black Children*. London: Routledge Falmer
Gillborn, D. (2008) *Racism and Education: Coincidence or Conspiracy*. London: Routledge Falmer
Gillborn, D. and Gipps, C. (1996) *Recent Research into the Achievements of Ethnic Minority Pupils*. London: Office for Standards in Education
Gillborn, D. and Mirza, H.S. (2000) *Educational Inequality: Mapping Race, Class and Gender*. London: Ofsted
Gillborn, D. and Youdell, D. (2000) *Rationing Education*. London: Routledge
Gillborn, D. and Youdell, D. (2001) 'The new IQism: Intelligence, "Ability" and the Rationing of Education' in J. Demaine (ed.) *Sociology of Education Today*. London: Palgrave
Gilroy, P. (1982) 'Steppin' out of Babylon – race, class and autonomy' in Centre for Contemporary Cultural Studies *The Empire Strikes Back*. London: Hutchinson
Gilroy, P. (1987) *There Ain't No Black in the Union Jack*. London: Hutchinson
Goldman, R.J. and Taylor, F. (1966) 'Coloured Immigrant Children: A Survey of Their Educational Problems and Potential in Britain' *Educational Research* 8(3)
Goodhart, D. (2004) 'Discomfort of strangers' *Guardian* 24 February
Goring, B. (2004) *The Perspectives of Caribbean Parents on Schooling and Education: Continuities and Change*. PhD study. London: University of the South Bank
Graham, D. (1993) *A Lesson For Us All: The Making of the English National Curriculum*. London: Routledge
Gray, J. (1998) *False Dawn: The Delusions of Global Capitalism*. London: Granta Books
Hall, S. (1991) 'Old and new identities: Old and new Ethnicities' in A. King (ed.) *Culture, Globalisation and the World System*. London: Macmillan
Halstead, M. (1988) *Education, Justice and Cultural Diversity: an Examination of the Honeyford Affair 1984–85*. London: Falmer Press
Hansard 685 (1963) London: House of Commons
Hansard 1336 (1966) London: House of Commons
Hansard 965 (1976) London: House of Commons

Hansard (1992) cols 149–202. London: House of Commons
Hargreaves, D. (1984) *Improving Secondary Schools*. London: ILEA
Hargreaves, D. (1993) Preface in A.S. King and M.J. Reiss (eds) *The Multicultural Dimension of the National Curriculum*. London: Falmer Press
Hastie, T. (1981) 'Encouraging Tunnel Vision' *Times Educational Supplement* 6 March: 20–1
Hastie, T. (1986) 'History, Race and Propaganda' in F. Palmer (ed.) *Anti-Racism: an Assault on Education and Values*. London: The Sherwood Press
Hastings, M. (2007) 'Premiership of Tony Blair tainted by mendacity' *Guardian* 12 April
Hattersley, R. (2005) 'Even Enoch did not stoke fears like this' *Guardian* 25 April
Heath, E. (1970) Letter to Bexley Community Relations Council, Bexley, Kent, June
Heath, A. and McMahon, D. (1997) 'Educational and occupational attainments: the impact of ethnic origins' in A.H. Halsey, H. Lauder, P. Brown and A.S. Wells (eds) *Education Culture Economy and Society*. Oxford: Oxford University Press
Hebdige, D. (1976) 'Reggae, Rastas and Rudies' in S. Hall and T. Jefferson (eds) *Resistance through Rituals*. London: Hutchinson
Heim, A. (1954) *The Appraisal of Intelligence*. London: Tavistock
Hemming, R. (1984) 'Mathematics' in A. Craft and G. Bardell (eds) *Curriculum Opportunities in a Multicultural Society*. London: Harper
Herrnstein, R.J. and Murray, C. (1994) *The Bell Curve*. New York: The Free Press
Hewitt, I. (1988) 'At odds with Islam' *Times Educational Supplement* 25 November
Hicks, D. (1987) *World Studies 8–13*. Lancaster: St Martins College
Higher Education Funding Council for England (1995) *Special initiative to encourage widening participation of students from ethnic minorities in teacher training*. Bristol: HEFCE
Hillgate Group (1989) *Learning to Teach*. London: The Claridge Press
HM Treasury (2003) *Every Child Matters*. Cm 5860. London: The Treasury
Hodge, M. (2007) 'A message to my fellow immigrants' *Observer* 20 May
Home Affairs Committee. Fifth Report (1981) *Racial Disadvantage* (4 vols). Cmnd 6234. London: HMSO
Home Office (1965) *Immigration From the Commonwealth*. Cmnd 2739. London: HMSO
Home Office (1975) *Racial Discrimination*. Cmnd 6234. London: HMSO
Home Office (1978) *Proposals for Replacing Section 11 of the 1966 Local Government Act: a consultative document*. London: The Home Office
Home Office (1988) *A Scrutiny of Grants under Section 11 of the Local Authority Act 1966*. London: The Home Office
Home Office (2002) *Secure Borders: Safe Haven: Integration with Diversity*. Cmnd 5387. London: The Stationery Office
Home Office (2007) *Report of the Commission on Integration and Community Cohesion*. London: The Stationery Office
Honeyford, R. (1982) 'Multiracial myths' *Times Educational Supplement* 19 November
Honeyford, R. (1984) 'Education and Race – an Alternative View' *Salisbury Review* Winter 1984: 30–2
Honeyford, R. (1988) *Integration or Disintegration*. London: The Claridge Press

Honeyford, R. (1990) 'The National Curriculum and its official distortion' *Salisbury Review* 8(4): 6–9
House of Commons Education Committee (1995) *Performance in City Schools*. Third Report. London: HMSO
House of Commons Education and Skills Committee (2003) *Secondary Education: Pupil Achievements*. Seventh report session 2002–03. London: The Stationery Office
Hughill, B. (1987) 'Dramatic steps that will carry Britain forward' *Times Educational Supplement* 16 October
Hughill, B. (1989) 'After ILEA: new wave of officers sweep in' *Times Educational Supplement* 27 January
Hughill, B. (1991) 'Parents take on schools over "racist" expulsions' *Times Educational Supplement* 16 December
Humphries, S. (1981) *Hooligans or Rebels*. Oxford: Oxford University Press
Hunt, Lord J. (1967) *Immigrants and the Youth Service*. Report for the Youth Service Development Council. London: HMSO
Husain, E. (2007) *The Islamist*. London: Penguin
ILEA (1968) *The Education of Immigrant Pupils in Special Schools*. London: Inner London Education Authority Paper no. 657.
ILEA (1977) *Multi-Ethnic Education: Joint Report of the Schools Subcommittee and the Further and Higher Education Subcommittee*. London: Inner London Education Authority
ILEA (1981) *Education in a Multiethnic Society: an Aide-memoire for the Inspectorate*. London: Inner London Education Authority
Institute of Race Relations (1983) *How Racism Came to Britain*. London: IRR
Islamia (1991) 'Resources Review' *Islamia* 16(8)
Jacobs, S. (2006) 'Interactional issues in the teaching of race and ethnicity in UK higher education' *Race Ethnicity and Education* 9(4): 341–60
James, A. and Jeffcoate, R. (eds) (1981) *The School in the Multicultural Society*. London: Harper and Row
Jeffcoate, R. (1979) *Positive Image: Towards a Multicultural Curriculum*. London: Harper and Row
Jenkins, R. (1966) *Address by the Home Secretary to a Meeting of Voluntary Liaison Committees* 23 May. London: National Council for Commonwealth Immigration
Jensen, A. (1969) 'How much can we boost IQ and scholastic ability?' *Harvard Education Review* vol. 39: 1–23
Joseph, K. (1974) 'Sir Keith calls for remoralization and reassertion of civilized values' *The Times* 21 October
Joseph, K. (1986) 'Without prejudice: education for an ethnically mixed society' *New Community* 13(2): 200–3
Kaletsky, A. (2000) 'Who do these worthy idiots think they are?' *The Times* 12 October
Karakasoglu, Y. and Luchtenberg, S. (2006) 'Islamophobia in Germany' *Lifelong Learning in Europe* 3: 195–201
Kastoryano, R. (2006) 'French secularism and Islam' in T.T. Modood, A. Riandafyllidou and R. Zapata-Barrero (eds) *Multiculturalism, Muslims and Citizenship*. London: Routledge

Kelso, P. (2000) 'Prisoner killed in race hate attack' *Guardian* 25 October
Kennedy, H. (1997) *Learning Works: Widening Participation in Further Education*. Coventry: Further Education Funding Council
Kelly, R. (2006) Open letter to the Muslim Council of Great Britain. London: Department for Communities and Local Government, House of Commons.
Kenny, M. (1984) 'Race Madness' *Daily Mail* 13 September
Kerner Report (1968) *Report of the National Advisory Committee on Civil Disorders*. New York: Bantam Books
Khan, V.S. (1978) *Bilingualism and Minority Languages in Britain*. London: The Runnymede Trust
Killian, L.M. (1979) 'School bussing in Britain – policies and perceptions' *Harvard Educational Review* 49(2)
Kirp, D.L. (1979) *Doing Good by Doing Little*. Berkeley: University of California Press
Kitwood, T. and Borrill, C. (1980) 'The Significance of Schooling for an Ethnic Minority' *Oxford Review of Education* 6(3): 241–52
Klein, G. (1985) *Reading into Racism: Bias in Children's Literature and Learning Materials*. London: Routledge
Kogan, M. (1975) 'Dispersal in the Ealing School System' Report to the Race Relations Board, July. London: RRB
Kymlicka, W. (2004) 'Foreword' in J.A. Banks (ed.) *Diversity and Citizenship Education*. San Francisco: Jossey-Bass
Labour Party (1989) *Multi-Cultural Education: Labour's Policy for Schools*. London: The Labour Party
Labour Party (1996) *Learn As You Earn: Labour's Plans for a Skills Revolution*. London: The Labour Party
Labov, W. (1972) *Languages in the Inner City*. Pennsylvania: University of Pennsylvania Press
Lawlor, S. (1990) *Teachers Mistaught*. London: The Claridge Press
Lawrence, D. (2006) *And Still I Rise: a Mother's Search for Justice*. London: Faber and Faber
Lawton, D. (1994) *The Tory Mind on Education*. London: Falmer
Lawton, D. (2005) *Education and Labour Party Ideologies*. London: Routledge-Falmer
Lewis, P. (1994) *Islamic Britain*. London: I.B. Tauris Publishers
Lewis, R. (1988) *Anti-Racism: A Mania Exposed*. London: Quartet Books
Linguistic Minorities Project (1983) *Linguistic Minorities in England*. London: Routledge and Kegan Paul
Little, A. (1975) 'The Performance of Children from Ethnic Minority Backgrounds in Primary Schools' *Oxford Review of Education*
Little, A., Mabey, C. and Whitaker, G. (1968) 'The Education of immigrant pupils in inner London primary schools' *Race* 9(4)
Little, A. and Willey, R. (1981) *Multi-ethnic Education – the Way Forward*. London: Schools Council Working Paper No. 18. London: The Schools Council
Lloyd, T.O. (1984) *The British Empire 1558–1983*. Oxford: Oxford University Press
London Development Agency (2004) *Rampton Revisited: The Educational Experiences and Achievements of Black Boys in London*. London: London Development Agency

MacCrae, S., Maguire, M. and Ball, S.J. (1997) 'Competition, Choice and Hierarchy in a Post-16 Market' in S. Tomlinson (ed.) *Education 14–19: Critical Perspectives*. London: Athlone Press

MacDonald, I., Bhavani, T., Khan, L. and John, G. (1989) *Murder in the Playground: The Report of the MacDonald Enquiry into Racism and Racial Violence in Manchester Schools*. London: Longsight Press

MacKenzie, J.M. (1986) *Imperialism and Popular Culture*. Manchester: Manchester University Press

MacIntyre, D. (1991) 'Baker seeks extra police after riots' *The Independent* 15 September

Macpherson, Sir W. (1999) *The Stephen Lawrence Inquiry*. Cmnd 4262. London: The Stationery Office

Majors, R. (2001) *Educating Our Black Children*. London: Routledge/Falmer

Majors, R. and Billson, J. (1992) *Cool Pose: The Dilemmas of Black Manhood in America*. New York: Lexington Books

Marshall, T.H. (1950) *Citizenship and Social Class*. Cambridge: Cambridge University Press

Martinson, J. (1994) 'Racial attacks drive pupils out' *Times Educational Supplement* 25 February

Mays, J. (1962) *Education and the Urban Child*. Liverpool: Liverpool University Press

Mays, S. (ed.) (1999) *Critical Multiculturalism*. London: Falmer

McClelland, A. and Varma, V. (1989) *Advances in Teacher Education*. London: Routledge

McLaughlin, E. and Neal, S. (2004) 'Misrepresenting the multicultural nation: the policy-making process, news media management and the Parekh report' *Policy Studies* 25(3): 155–74

McNeal, J. and Rogers, M. (1971) *The Multiracial School*. Harmondsworth: Penguin Books

Midwinter, E. (1972) *Projections*. London: Ward Lock Educational

Miles, A. (2007) 'Sneaky, unfair, divisive: welcome to church schools' *The Times* 23 May

Milner, D. (1983) *Children and Race: Ten Years On*. London: Ward Lock Educational

Ministerial Working Group on Public Order and Community Cohesion (2001) *Report to the Home Secretary* (December). London: The Home Office.

Mirza, H.S. (1992) *Young, Female and Black*. London: Routledge

Mirza, H.S. (ed.) (1997a) *Black British Feminism*. London: Routledge

Mirza, H.S. (1997b) 'Black women in education: a collective movement for social change' in H.S. Mirza (ed.) *Black British Feminism*. London: Routledge

Mirza, H.S. (1998) 'Race, gender and IQ: the social consequences of a pseudo-scientific discourse' *Race Ethnicity and Education* 1(1): 111–28

Modood, T. (1992) *Not Easy Being British: Colour, Culture and Citizenship*. Stoke-on-Trent: Trentham Books and Runnymede Trust

Modood, T. (1993) 'The number of ethnic minority students in British Higher Education: some grounds for optimism' *British Journal of Sociology of Education* 19: 167–78

Modood, T. (2005) *Multicultural Politics: Racism, Ethnicity and Muslims in Britain*. Edinburgh: Edinburgh University Press

Modood, T., Berthood, R. *et al.* (1997) *Ethnic Minorities in Britain: Diversity and Disadvantage* (fourth national survey of ethnic minorities). London: Policy Studies Institute
Moodley, K. (1983) 'Canadian Multiculturalism as Ideology' *Ethnic and Racial Studies* 6(3): 320–31
Morrell, F. (1989) *Children of the Future*. London: The Hogarth Press
Moynihan, P. (1965) *The Negro Family: The Case for National Action*. Washington: United States Department of Labor
Muir, H. (2006) 'Mayor's new onslaught on "alarmist" race watchdog' *Guardian* 17 November
Mullard, C. (1973) *Black Britain*. London: Allen and Unwin
Mullard, C. (1982) 'Multi-racial Education in Britain: from Assimilation to Cultural Pluralism' in J. Tierney (ed.) *Race, Migration and Schooling*. Eastbourne: Holt, Rinehart and Winston
Mullard, C. (1984) *Anti Racist Education: The Three O's*. London: NAME Publications
Murray, C. (1994) 'Underclass: the crisis deepens' *The Sunday Times* 22 May
Myrdal, G. (1969) *The American Dilemma: The Negro Problem and Modern Democracy*. New York: Harper and Row (3rd edn)
Nandy, D. (1971) Foreword in J. McNeal and M. Rogers (eds) *The Multiracial School*. Harmondsworth: Penguin Books
National Union of Teachers (1967) *The NUT view on the education of immigrants*. London: NUT
National Union of Teachers (1979) *In Black and White: Guidelines for Teachers on Racial Stereotyping in Textbooks and Learning Materials*. London: NUT
National Union of Teachers (1981) *Mother Tongue Teaching*. London: NUT
National Union of Teachers (1992) *Anti-Racist Curriculum Guidelines*. London: NUT
Naylor, F. (1988) 'Political Lessons of Dewsbury' *The Independent* 22 December
Naylor, F. (1992) 'A whiff of centralism' *Times Educational Supplement* 26 June
New Society (1978) 'Race and Teachers: The Schools Council Study' *New Society* 16 February
Newsom Report (1963) *Half Our Future: A Report of the Central Advisory Committee on Education*. London: HMSO
Noden, P., West, A., David, M. and Edge, A. (1998) 'Choices and destinations in transfer to secondary schools in London' *Journal of Education Policy* 13: 221–36
Nuffield Report (2006) *The Education of 14–19 year olds*. Third report. 2005–06. Oxford: University of Oxford
Observer (2007) Comment 3 June
O'Connor, M., Hales, E., Davies, J. and Tomlinson, S. (1999) *Hackney Downs: The School That Dared to Fight*. London: Cassell
OECD (1994) *Schools: A Matter of Choice*. Paris: OECD
Ofsted (1993) *Access and Achievement in Urban Education: a Report from HMI*. London: Ofsted
Ofsted (1995) *The Framework for the Inspection of Schools*. London: Ofsted
Ofsted (1999) *Raising the Attainment of Minority Ethnic Pupils: School and LEA Responses*. London: Ofsted

Ofsted (2002) *Achievement of Black Caribbean Pupils: Good Practice in Secondary Schools*. HMI/448. London: Ofsted

Osler, A. (1997) *The Education and Careers of Black Teachers*. Buckingham: Open University Press

Osler, A. and Morrison, M. (2000) *Inspecting Schools for Race Equality*. Stoke-on-Trent: Trentham Books

Osler, A. and Starkey, H. (2005) *Changing Citizenship: Democracy and Inclusion in Education*. Berkshire: Open University Press/McGraw-Hill

Osler, A. and Vincent, K. (2003) *Girls and Exclusion*. London: Routledge/Falmer

Palmer, F. (1986) *Anti-Racism: an Assault on Education and Value*. London: The Sherwood Press

Parekh, B. (2000) *The Future of Multi-Ethnic Britain*. Report of the Commission on the Future of Multi-Ethnic Britain. London: Profile Books for the Runnymede Trust

Parker, D. and Song, M. (2006) 'New ethnicities online: reflexive rationalities and the internet' *The Sociological Review* 54(3): 575–94

Patterson, S. (1963) *Dark Strangers: A Study of West Indians in London*. Harmondsworth: Penguin

Payne, J. (ed.) (1974) *Educational Priority. EPA Surveys and Statistics*. London: HMSO

Peach, C. (1968) *West Indian Migration to Britain*. Oxford: Oxford University Press

Pearce, Sarah (2005) *You Wouldn't Understand: White Teachers in Multiethnic Classrooms*. Stoke-on-Trent: Trentham Books

Pearce, Simon (1986) 'Swann and the Spirit of the Age' in F. Palmer (ed.) *Anti-Racism – an Assault on Education and Values*. London: The Sherwood Press

Pennell, H., West, A. and Hinds, A. (2007) *Religious Composition and Admission Processes in Faith Secondary Schools in London*. London: Comprehensive Future and the Joseph Rowntree Reform Trust

Phillips, M. and Phillips, T. (1999) *Windrush: The Irresistible Rise of Multiracial Britain*. London: HarperCollins

Phillips-Bell, M. (1981) 'Multicultural Education: What is it?' *Multiracial Education* 10(1): 21–6

Pilkington, A. (2003) *Racial Disadvantage and Ethnic Diversity in Britain*. London: Palgrave-Macmillan

Plowden Report (1967) *Children and their Primary Schools: A report of the Central Advisory Committee on Education (England)*. London: HMSO

Pyke, N. (1995) 'Ethnic monitoring scaled down' *Times Educational Supplement* 24 March

QCA/DfEE (1999) *The Review of the National Curriculum: the Secretary of State's Proposals*. London: Qualifications and Curriculum Authority

Race Equality West Midlands (2006) *British Urban Ethnic Group Conflict and Violence*. Working Paper no. 1. Birmingham: Race Equality West Midlands

Race on the Agenda (ROTA) and 1990 Trust (1999) *The Ethnic Minority Achievement Grant*. London: ROTA

Race Today (1975) 'Whose Afraid of Ghetto Schools?' No.1 January

Rafferty, F. (1992) 'Stratford warning ignored' *Times Educational Supplement* 28 February

Ramesh, R. (2003) *The War We Could Not Stop*. London: Faber and Faber

Reach Group (2007) *The Reach Report*. London: Department for Communities and Local Government
Redbridge (1978) *Cause for Concern: West Indian Pupils in Redbridge*. Black Parents Progressive Association and Redbridge Community Relations Council. London: Redbridge
Rex, J. (1972) 'Nature versus nurture: The significance of the revived debate' in K. Richardson, D. Spears and M. Richards (eds) *Race, Culture and Intelligence*. Harmondsworth: Penguin
Rex, J. (1986) *Race and Ethnicity*. Milton Keynes: Open University Press
Rex, J. (1996) *Ethnic Minorities in the Modern Nation State*. London: Macmillan
Rex, J. (2002) 'Islam in the United Kingdom' in S. Hunter (ed.) *Islam: Europe's Second Religion*. Washington: Centre for Strategic and International Studies
Rex, J. and Moore, R. (1967) *Race Community and Conflict*. London: Oxford University Press
Rex, J. and Tomlinson, S. (1979) *Colonial Immigrants in a British City: A Class Analysis*. London: Routledge and Kegan Paul
Rich, P.S. (1986) *Race and Empire in British Politics*. Cambridge: Cambridge University Press
Richardson, B. (ed.) (2005) *Tell It Like It Is: How our Schools Fail Black Children*. London: Bookmark Publications/Trentham Books
Richardson, R. and Wood, A. (1999) *Inclusive Schools, Inclusive Society*. Stoke-on-Trent: Trentham Books
Robbins, Lord A. (1963) *Higher Education*. Report of the Prime Minister's Committee. Cmnd 2154. London: HMSO
Robinson, J. and Hinscliff, G. (2007) 'C4 boss faces Big Brother backlash' *Observer* 21 January
Rose, E.J.B. and Associates (1969) *Colour and Citizenship: A Report on British Race Relations*. Oxford: Oxford University Press
Rosenthal, R. and Jacobson, L. (1968) *Pygmalion in the Classroom*. New York: Holt Reinhart and Wishart
Rushdie, S. (1982) 'The New Empire Within Britain' *New Society* 9 December
Rushdie, S. (1988) *The Satanic Verses*. London: Viking Books
Rutter, J. (2003) *Supporting Refugee Children in 21st Century Britain*. Stoke-on Trent : Trentham Books
Rutter, J. (2006) *Refugee Children in the UK*. Berkshire: Open University Press
Rutter, M. and Madge, N. (1976) *Cycles of Disadvantage*. London: Heinemann
Rutter, M., Maughan, B., Mortimore, P. and Ouston, J. (1979) *Fifteen Thousand Hours*. London: Open Books
Salman, S. (2006) 'Victory over violence' *Guardian (Society)* 4 October
Save the Children (2004) *Home From Home: a resource pack for the welcome and inclusion of refugee children in school*. London: Salusbury World and Save the Children
Scarman Report (1982) *The Brixton Disorders 10–12 April 1981*. Report of an inquiry by Lord Scarman. London: Penguin Books
Sarup, M. (1986) *The Politics of Multi-Racial Education*. London: Routledge and Kegan Paul
Sawar, G. (1983) *Educational Problems of Muslims in the UK*. London: The Muslim Educational Trust

Scruton, R. (1986) 'The Myth of Cultural Relativism' in F. Palmer (ed.) *Anti-Racism – An Assault on Education and Value*. London: The Sherwood Press
Select Committee on Race Relations and Immigration (1969) *The Problems of Coloured School-Leavers*. London: HMSO
Select Committee on Race Relations and Immigration (1973) *Education* (3 vols). London: HMSO
Select Committee on Race Relations and Immigration (1977) *The West Indian Community* (3 vols). London: HMSO
Sen, A. (2006) *Identity and Violence*. London: Allen Lane
Sewell, T. (1997) *Black Masculinities and Schooling*. Stoke-on-Trent: Trentham Books
Shaw, C. (1994) *Changing Lives 3*. London: Policy Studies Institute
Shelter (2007) *Poverty Target Will Be Missed*. London: Shelter
Sherman, A. (1978) 'Why Britain can't be wished away' *Daily Telegraph* 8 September
Shiner, M. (1997) *Entry into the Legal Profession*. London: The Law Society
Shotte, G. (2002) 'Education, migration and identities: relocated Montserratian children in London schools' PhD thesis. London: Institute of Education, London University
Siddiqui, A. (2007) *Islam at Universities in England*. London: DfES
Sikes, P. and Rizvi, F. (1997) *Researching Race and Social Justice in Education: Essays in Honour of Barry Troyna*. Stoke-on-Trent: Trentham Books
Sivanandan, A. (1982) *A Different Hunger*. London: Pluto Press
Sklair, L. (1995) *Sociology of the Global System*. Oxford: Blackwell
Sleeter, C.E. (2007) *Facing Accountability in Education*. New York: Teachers College Press, Columbia University
Smith, D.J. (1977) *Racial Disadvantage in Britain*. Harmondsworth: Penguin
Smith, D.J. and Tomlinson, S. (1989) *The School Effect: A Study of Multiracial Comprehensives*. London: Policy Studies Institute
Social Trends (2003) No. 33. London: The Stationery Office
Social Trends (2005) No. 35. London: The Stationery Office
Spencer, D. (1990) 'Muslim girls await scarf ruling' *Times Educational Supplement* 19 January
Steiner, J. (1991) 'An accent on religion marks the advent of equality' *The Independent* 2 May
Stembridge, J. (1956) *The World: A General Regional Geography*. Oxford: Oxford University Press (2nd edn)
Stone, M. (1981) *The Education of the Black Child in Britain*. London: Fontana
Sunday Telegraph (1975) Editorial 15 June
Sutcliffe, D. (1982) *Black British English*. Oxford: Blackwell
Sutcliffe, D. and Wong, A. (1986) *The Language of the Black Experience*. Oxford: Blackwell
Taylor, A. (1994) *Opening Doors to a Learning Society*. London: The Labour Party
Taylor, M. (1981) *Caught Between: a Review of the Education of Pupils of West Indian Origin*. Berkshire: NFER-Nelson
Taylor, M. (1988) *World's Apart?* Berkshire: NFER-Nelson
Taylor, M. (1992) *Multicultural Antiracist Education After ERA*. Slough: NFER
Taylor, M. with Hegarty, S. (1985) *The Best of Both Worlds: a Review of Research into the Education of Pupils of South Asian Origin*. Berkshire: NFER-Nelson

Taylor, C., Fitz, J. and Gorard, S. (2005) 'Diversity, specialisation and equity in education' *Oxford Review of Education* 31(1): 47–70

The Independent (1987) Letters page 10 June

Thatcher, M. (1978) Interview, Granada Television, 30 January

Thatcher, M. (1993) *The Downing Street Years*. London: Harper-Collins

Thornton, K. (1998) 'Blacks 15 times more likely to be excluded from school' *Times Educational Supplement* 11 November

Tickley, L., Osler, A. and Hill, J. (2005) 'The ethnic minority achievement grant: a critical analysis' *Journal of Education Policy* 20(3): 283–312

The Times (1981) Editorial: 'Educational Achievement' 18 June

The Times (1990) Editorial: 'Tebbitt Defend Comments on Asians' 21 April

Times Educational Supplement (1987) Editorial: 'Waiting for the Bill' 10 November

Times Educational Supplement (1990) Editorial 23 June

Tomlinson, S. (1977) 'Race and Education in Britain 1960–1977: an overview of the literature' *Sage Race Relations Abstracts* 2(4): 3–33

Tomlinson, S. (1980) 'The educational performance of ethnic minority children' *New Community* 8(3): 213–34

Tomlinson, S. (1981) *Educational Subnormality: a Study in Decision Making*. London: Routledge and Kegan Paul

Tomlinson, S. (1983a) *Ethnic Minorities in British Schools*. London: Heinemann

Tomlinson, S. (1983b) 'Black women in higher education – case studies of university women in Britain' in L. Barton and S. Walker (eds) *Race, Class and Education*. London: Croom-Helm

Tomlinson, S. (1984) *Home and School in Multicultural Britain*. London: Batsford

Tomlinson, S. (1986) 'Political Dilemmas in Multi-Racial Education' in Z. Layton-Henry and P.B. Rich (eds) *Race, Government and Politics in Britain*. London: Macmillan

Tomlinson, S. (1987) 'Curriculum Option Choices in Multi-ethnic Schools' in B. Troyna (ed.) *Racial Inequality in Education*. London: Tavistock

Tomlinson, S. (1988) 'Education and training' *New Community* 15(1): 103–9

Tomlinson, S. (1989) 'The origins of the ethnocentric curriculum' in G.K. Verma (ed.) *Education for All: A Landmark in Pluralism*. London: Falmer

Tomlinson, S. (1990) *Multicultural Education in White Schools*. London: Batsford

Tomlinson, S. (1992) 'Disadvantaging the Disadvantaged: Bangladeshis and Education in Tower Hamlets' *British Journal of Sociology of Education* 13(2): 337–46

Tomlinson, S. (1993) 'The Group That Never Was' in A.S. King and M.J. Reiss (eds) *The Multicultural Dimension of the National Curriculum*. London: Falmer

Tomlinson, S. (1997) 'Sociological Perspectives on Failing Schools' *International Studies in Sociology of Education* 7(1): 81–98

Tomlinson, S. (2005a) *Education in a Post-Welfare Society*. Berkshire: Open University Press/McGraw-Hill Educational (2nd edn)

Tomlinson, S. (2005b) 'Race, ethnicity and Education under New Labour' *Oxford Review of Education*. 31(1): 153–72

Tomlinson, S. (2008) 'Gifted, talented and high ability: selection for education in a one-dimensional society' *Oxford Review of Education* 34(1) February.

Tomlinson, S. and Craft, M. (eds) (1995) *Ethnic Relations and Schooling*. London: Athlone Press

Townsend, H.E.R. (1971) *Immigrant Pupils in England: The LEA Response*. Slough: National Foundation for Educational Research

Townsend, H.E.R. and Brittan, E.M. (1972) *Organization in Multiracial Schools*. Slough: National Foundation for Educational Research

Townsend, H.E.R. and Brittan, E.M. (1973) *Multiracial Education: Need and Innovation*. London: Evans-Methuen

Travis, A. (2007) 'Britain competes to attract migrants' *Guardian* 19 June

Troyna, B. (1984) 'Fact or Artefact: The Educational Under-Achievement of Black Pupils' *British Journal of Sociology of Education* 5(2): 153–66

Troyna, B. (1986) 'Swann's song: the origins, ideology, and implications of education for all' *Journal of Education Policy* 7(2): 1–11

Troyna, B. (1987) *Racial inequality in Education*. London: Tavistock

Troyna, B. (1993) *Racism and Education: Research Perspectives*. Buckingham: Open University Press

Troyna, B. and Smith, D.I. (1982) *Racism, School and the Labour Market*. Leicester: National Youth Bureau

TTA (2000) *Raising the Attainment of Minority Ethnic Pupils: Guidance and Resource Materials*. London: Teacher Training Agency

Turner, G. (1977) 'Is it counter-revolution or consensus?' *Daily Telegraph* 10 January

Turner, G. (1999) 'g Whizz' *Right Now*. Issue 22 January–March: 4–5

Twitchen, J. (1988) *The Black and White Media Show*. Stoke-on-Trent: Trentham Books

Venning, P. (1983) 'Menacing Warning to Haringey Heads over exams' *Times Educational Supplement* 11 February

Verkaik, R. (2001) 'McPherson's fury at right-wing vendetta' *The Independent* 28 April

Verma, G. K. and Bagley, C. (1979) *Race, Culture and Identity*. London: Macmillan

Vernon, P. (1968) 'What is potential ability' Fifth C.S. Myers lecture. London: Institute of Education

Weber, M. (1968) Economy and Society. 3 vols. New York: Bedminster Press

Weekes-Bernard, D. (2007) *School Choice and Ethnic Segregation*. London: The Runnymede Trust

West, A. and Hinds, A. (2003) *Secondary School Admissions in England: Exploring the Extent of Overt and Covert Selection*. London: Centre for Research and Information on State Education, LSE

Widlake, P. and Bloom, D. (1979) 'Which Culture to Teach Immigrant Pupils?' *Education* 14 December

Wilby, P. (1988) 'Anti-racist teachers to be removed from school' *The Independent* 9 December

Williams, S. (1988) Foreword in G.K. Verma (ed.) *Education for All – A Landmark in Pluralism*. London: Falmer Press

Willis, P. (1977) *Learning to Labour: How Working Class Lads Get Working Class Jobs*. Farnborough: Saxon House

Wilson, W.J. (1978) *The Declining Significance of Race*. Chicago: The University of Chicago Press

Winder, R. (2004) *Bloody Foreigners: The Story of Immigration to Britain*. London: Abacus

Wintour, P. and Dodd, V. (2007) 'Blair blames spate of murders on black culture' *Guardian* 12 April

Woodward, W. (2006) 'Blair sees migration and terror as key issues' *Guardian* 26 August
Worsthorne, P. (1982) Editorial *Sunday Telegraph* 23 May
Working Party on Catholic Education (1984) *Learning from Diversity*. London: Catholic Media Office
Wright, C. (1986) 'School Processes: an ethnographic study' in J. Eggleston, D. Dunn and M. Anjali (eds) *Education for Some*. Stoke-on-Trent: Trentham Books
Yorkshire Post (1996) Editorial: Bottom of the Underclass 6 September
Younge, G. (2007) 'A Decade of Blair has left society more segregated, fearful and divided' *Guardian* 28 May

Index